GULF OF

LAURENCE

ATLANTIC

NEW

FOUND

LAND

A New Chart of the
Coast of
NEW ENGLAND, NOVA SCOTIA,
NEW FRANCE or CANADA,
with the Islands of
NEWFOUNDL.D CAPE BRETON
S.T JOHN's &c.
Done from the Original Publish'd in 1744.
at Paris,
BY MONS.R N. BELLIN.
Enginier to the Marine Office.
This Chart is most humbly
Dedicated to the BRIT.SH MERCH.TS
trading to NORTH AMERICA
by the Editor.

HISTORICAL SEA CHARTS

Visions and Voyages Through the Ages

WHITE STAR PUBLISHERS

HISTORICAL SEA CHARTS

Visions and Voyages Through the Ages

Katherine Parker

Barry Lawrence Ruderman

Contents

Meerwunder und Seltzame Thier/Wie Die in Den Mitnacßtigen Landern Gefunden Werden—Sebastian Münster (1570)

Introduction

As with many historical objects, nautical charts are admired today for their charm and aesthetic appeal. They are windows into how a past world saw the oceans and seas, rivers and ports. However attractive they appear to the modern viewer, it is important to keep in mind that beauty was only sometimes a criterion for past viewers. More important was the ability of a chart to orient a ship while sailing. Charts are a visual tool to convey a plethora of information quickly. They help a navigator to find their bearing, indicate possible dangers and obstructions, and, in many cases, estimate distance. To achieve this, charts employ a specific set of symbols and features distinct from terrestrial maps and born of centuries of development. How these styles and structures have shifted over time is the work of this book.

While many of the conventions of charts come from innovations at sea, many of the charts that survive today were made with terrestrial audiences and aesthetics in mind. Due to the harsh conditions of life at sea, many of the charts that were brought on board ships were ravaged by wind, water, sun, and heavy use. Thus, many charts that actually saw service on ships were destroyed or damaged and discarded. Particularly after the advent of print and the widespread adoption of paper rather than the more durable vellum or parchment, charts were seen as ephemeral and replaceable; indeed, periodically obtaining updated charts was routine for mariners by the nineteenth century. Many surviving charts, therefore, including many of those in this book, were created as presentation items for patrons and institutions or were items made for a land-bound audience eager to understand more about the watery edges of empire and commerce. They were meant to convey the power and wealth of a company or state, and they suggest the centrality of seafaring trade and travel to human history.

While maritime mobility may be a common trait of cultures around the world, the use of charts is not necessarily so universal. Indeed, charts have a relatively short and regionally specific history, especially when compared to the longer history of human migration via water. Charts are only necessary when one is out of sight of the shoreline or sailing in unknown waters. Furthermore, they are only one of a variety of navigational tools and tactics that sailors can use to orient themselves. In the European context, which is the main focus of this book, navigation shifted from a practice based on experience and intuition to one dominated by mathematics and instrumentation over the course of nearly a millennium. Currently, it is undergoing another shift, from mathematics and instrumentation to electronics and data analysis.

Other cultures have very different navigational practices. In Oceania, for example, skilled navigators led the ancestors of Polynesians to populate practically every habitable island in the South Pacific by ca. 1200 CE. They sailed intentionally and masterfully, based on a mixture of techniques that read the swells, currents, clouds, animal and plant life, and the stars. This method of sailing was learned from masters who shared mass amounts of memorized information, as well as through training and quotidian voyages. While navigators sometimes used mnemonic and teaching devices like the

*Dessein Du Compas Tournant, ou Instrument aux Estoilles Du ques Cy Dessus Est Faict Mention—**Lucas Janszoon Waghenaer** (1583)*

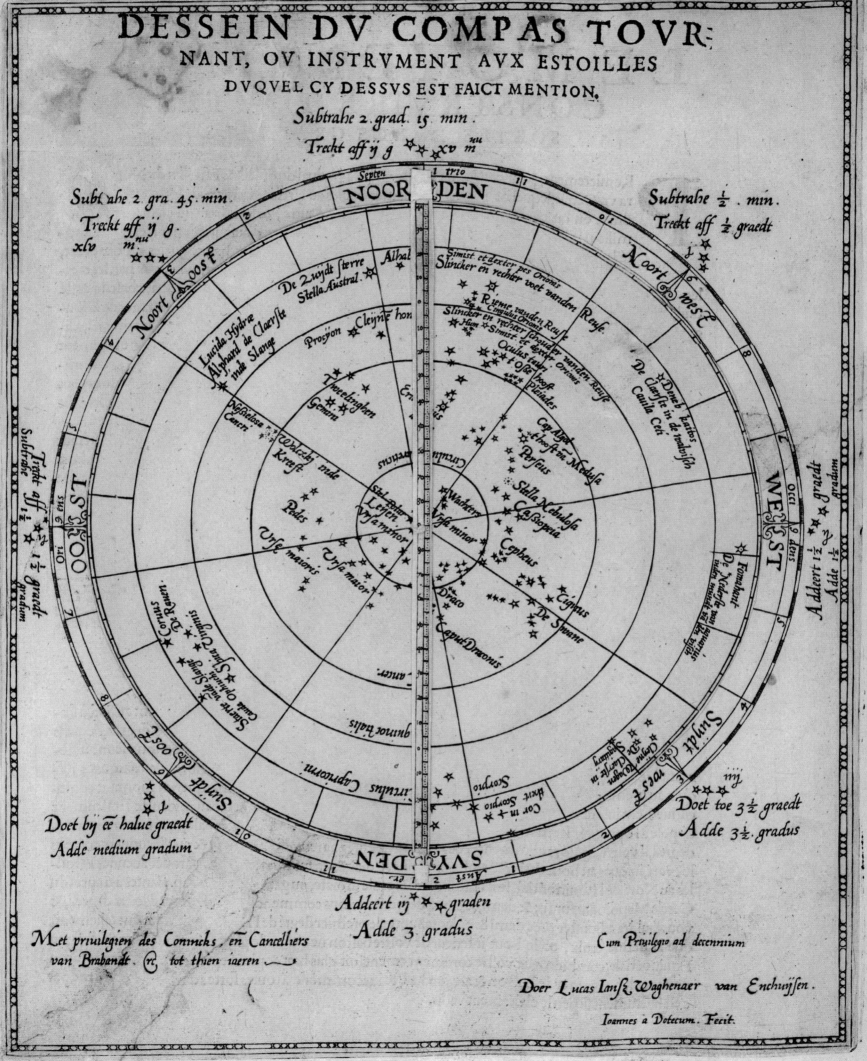

DESSEIN DV COMPAS TOVR:
NANT, OV INSTRVMENT AVX ESTOILLES
DVQVEL CY DESSVS EST FAICT MENTION.

Subtrahe 2. grad. 15. min.

Treckt aff ij g ☆ ☆ xv m

Cum Priuilegio ad decennium

Met priuilegien des Conincks, en Cancelliers
van Brabandt (r) tot thien iaeren

Doer Lucas Iansz. Waghenaer van Enchuijsen.

Ioannes à Dotecum. Fecit.

C 3   LE MOYEN

famed stick "charts" to learn relationships between islands and navigational features, they sailed from memory using an embodied and experiential knowledge that grew over generations. It is a method still practiced today, thanks to a renaissance of interest in Polynesian sailing that connected with the few remaining master navigators in the 1970s.

In the Indian Ocean, navigation was a hybrid process influenced by overlapping traditions provided by the many cultures who sailed there, including the Egyptians, Romans, Chinese, Indians, and Arabs. These techniques centered around the lived reality of the monsoons, which dictated the schedule of sailing in the region. Compare this overlap of cultures and encounters of technology and tradition with the Mediterranean, where navigation developed as a result of adoption and adaptation, conflict and displacement in a closed sea. It is this Mediterranean navigational culture that this book discusses, as it is in the Mediterranean initially, and later in Europe more widely, that charts began to be commonly used as navigational instruments.

This is not to imply that charts are simply a European invention. Scholars know of Chinese river charts that date to the sixth century CE, while Arabic charts date from at least the tenth century CE. The modern charts in use today, however, find their lineage in the portolan charts of the Mediterranean from the late Medieval period. The earliest known list of ports and coastal features, a periplus, was used by the Greeks, with an example surviving from the fourth century CE. These textual sailing directions are known to have existed alongside visual aids in the Mediterranean from at least the thirteenth century CE, the date from which the earliest surviving portolan dates (ca. 1290 CE).

Portolan charts, with their distinctive style and features, are the subject of chapter one. Portolan charts lack a projection. However, as European ships sailed longer and longer distances, they found that they needed charts that could reflect distance and bearing over a curved surface. While many mathematicians and geographers focused on this problem, the first to create a chart that allowed navigators to chart their courses with straight lines was Gerard Mercator. His world map of 1569 was the first to adopt the graduated distance between lines of latitude as they approached the poles. However, as with many developments in navigation and charting featured in this book, the use of the Mercator projection took decades, even centuries, to be widely adopted by mariners.

There are often centers of production and innovation in chartmaking. Portolan charts were made in several sites across the centuries, including Genoa, Mallorca, and Sicily. In the seventeenth century, the most important city for chart production was Amsterdam, seat of the Dutch East India Company (VOC) in Europe. Charts made during the Dutch Golden Age feature in chapter two. In chapter three, two other centers, London and Paris, are highlighted, as they were important for chartmaking in the eighteenth century, when chartmaking acumen spread more widely across Europe. These cities also feature prominently in chapter four, which discusses the rise of state-sponsored hydrographic bodies, a trend that reached its zenith in the early to mid-nineteenth century. Chapter five discusses another source of chart production, private companies, which both complemented and competed with state-sanctioned charting offices. Finally, chapter six highlights the continuing manuscript tradition in charting to emphasize that no technological development was adopted singularly and with finality.

Today, charts are regulated by international bodies like the International Hydrographic Organization (IHO). The goal of charts today is to ensure consistency and accuracy across national boundaries and regions, although *local variations might still exist. Ships now are mandated to carry updated charts when at sea, a requirement laid down in the International Convention for the Safety of Life at Sea (SOLAS), the first version of which was adopted in 1914 in the wake of the Titanic disaster.*

These requirements reflect modern priorities brought on by globalization and ship technology that allow ships to carry more people and cargo than ever before. As this book stresses, these priorities were not always the same in previous centuries, and it is not fair to think of charts as progressing in a linear fashion from vague and erroneous to correct and precise. The definition of words like "correct" and "precise" are culturally determined and are historical constructs in and of themselves, constructs that can be analyzed through objects like charts.

Before embarking on the history of European charting from the fifteenth to the nineteenth centuries, the period covered in this work, a few important caveats need to be explained. First, there are several examples in this book that are more strictly maps, not charts; that is, they are cartographic objects not intended for marine navigation but for other purposes. These include propaganda, to share current events, and to reflect interest in scientific experiments. These are also part of the history of hydrography, thus their inclusion here.

The examples shown here and the stories told are overwhelmingly Eurocentric in origin and content. This is not to imply that European charting is superior or more successful than other navigational traditions. Charts are a tool, not an inevitability. Indeed, while the form and function of the modern chart came from the European tradition, the compass originated in East Asia and the Indian Ocean, spreading from China to Europeans, likely via Arab intermediaries and practitioners.

The collection from which this book draws examples—the Barry Lawrence Ruderman Collection, an archive of digital map images—is predominantly formed of European-origin maps and charts. It would be disingenuous to try to discuss all charting practices across the world in all periods to 1900 in one book, especially when the base collection does not support examples across this spectrum of dates and places. Additionally, the proficiencies of the authors lie in European charting practices; they would not presume to project an aura of expertise where they have none.

Finally, the makers and individuals identified with the production and use of these charts are overwhelmingly white and male. They are the ones that history has traditionally linked with navigation and charting, even though many women and people of color are implicated in the practices of exploration, surveying, drawing, printing, and use of charts across the chronological period covered in this book. Charts are widely understood to be straightforward representations of marine space; historians of cartography, however, understand maps and charts to be partial representations that can hide as much as they reveal. They are not transparent windows into the past, but distorted, if important, lenses through which a viewer can glimpse certain aspects of historical practices and actors.

In an age when many are losing the ability to read maps and charts, preserving the history of hydrography and chartmaking is important. Similarly, the standardization of charts in the international twenty-first century means that many local charting traditions are being obscured or erased. There are many stories hidden in the details of a nautical chart; this book tells a few of those stories in an attempt to share part of this significant and fascinating history.

Isolarios, Portolans, and the Charting of the Early Modern Mediterranean World

The development of the chart was not a foregone conclusion. Charts are first recorded at the conjunction of several world historical trends, including the expansion of trade over wider maritime networks, and at the conjunction of several navigational technologies, including the written sailing direction, or rutter, and the use of the magnetic compass, originally invented in China.

Charts are a tool for open-water navigation. If one is near a coastline, one can use a book or list of sailing directions—the aforementioned rutter, derrotero, *or* roteiro—*and a lead and line. The latter is a conical weight daubed with tallow and connected to a rope that is thrown overboard to take the depth of the water surrounding a boat, as well as a sample of the sea floor which could indicate both anchorages and possible obstructions nearby. This sort of navigating is known as pilotage and was often performed from memory after years of training in local waters.*

Beyond local waters, however, other objects might be needed to aid navigation. In the early fifteenth century, the renowned Chinese navigator Zheng He led his famous treasure fleets using a scroll that recorded information such as sounding depths, coastal features, distances, and altitudes. The development of a chart as an instrument of navigation—that is, as a tool that could help to plot and follow a course, not simply act as a consulting aid—seems to be a Mediterranean development dateable to the mid- to late Medieval period (1100–1400).

The first known charts, portolans, emerged in a region renowned for its seafaring cultures. The ancient Minoans, Mycenaeans, and Phoenicians all sailed by observing the stars and winds, without the use of a chart. These older ways of navigating were never abandoned, just adapted to be used in tandem with new instruments such as cross staffs, magnetic compasses, astrolabes, and, of course, charts.

Another older sailing technology—written, and later printed, sailing directions—was still popular in the Medieval period. One famous example is Lo Compasso de Navigare *(1296), which survives in manuscript. One permutation of the long-used sailing direction was the popular* isolario, *or book of islands, which paired geographic descriptions of the world's islands and ports with maps showing each in detail. A forerunner to the maritime atlas, the isolario genre developed in Italy in the mid-fifteenth century. This chapter contains an example from Benedetto Bordone's* Isolario, *showing islands in the Americas, which Europeans had only recently encountered when Bordone's work appeared.*

The word portolan *developed from the Italian word for sailing directions,* portolano *or* portulano, *again underlining the close connection between different types of navigational tools. The first surviving portolan chart dates to ca. 1290. The* Carte Pisane, *probably made in Genoa and held at the Bibliotheque Nationale in Paris, depicts the Mediterranean Sea, as do many portolan charts. While the earliest example of a navigational chart to exist, it is certainly not the first of its type, as its striking accuracy and defined features attest. Historians must rely on the surviving record for their interpretations and the development of the portolan chart before the* Carte Pisane—*that is, before we have reliable sources. This is still a hotly contested academic debate. Portolan charts typically consist of ink on vellum, made of calfskin, or parchment, usually goatskin. Vellum and parchment are durable, an important attribute for objects that were to be used in the trying conditions of a ship at sea. Additionally, vellum and parchment can be corrected by scraping off a layer of ink and replacing it with new words or images, which was useful for correcting changeable navigational information. While many portolans were made to be used at sea, those that survive are usually those that were intended for an easier life on land, as luxurious presentation items, decorations, or instructional aids. Those that saw service at sea seldom survived the ordeal to enter the historical record, but other sources mention their use aboard ships.*

Portolan charts share a set of conventions that would become standard for later nautical charts. They usually include a scale bar, although the unit of measure differed depending on its place of production. Important port names were written in red, while others were listed in black. These were written at right angles to the shore, and were written inland, so as not to obscure the coastline. Black dots or a cross were used to indicate rocks, while red dots indicated sandy shallows or a sandbar. Inland areas were usually devoid of geographic content, but could be filled with decoration and imagery indicating the ruler and religion prevalent in each place, not to mention local animals, plants, and other details.

Many surviving portolans show the Mediterranean coastline, but others also depict the Black Sea, the Atlantic Coast of Europe and West Africa, the Indian Ocean, and other maritime spaces. Their zenith was in the fourteenth and fifteenth centuries, but they continued to be made up to roughly 1700, as the examples in this chapter show. The main centers of production were Genoa, Venice, and Catalonia, with important hubs in Mallorca and Sicily. Additionally, this was not uniquely a European phenomenon, as seen in this chapter with the beautiful Pîrî Reis maps.

Another defining feature of portolan charts are the rhumb lines, or loxodromes, that crisscross their surfaces. Rhumb lines are lines of consistent bearing. Originally, they were based on wind roses of 16 or 32 directions. The main winds would be indicated in black (or sometimes red), half winds in green, and quarter winds in red. Scholars have shown that this matrix of lines was often laid down first, followed by the coasts and names, indicating that these charts were intended as instruments to find direction and bearing, not just as representations of space. Later portolan charts have the rhumb lines joined at compass roses, which use cardinal and ordinal directions.

As indicated by the shift from wind to compass roses, portolan charts were made and used across a transitional time in chartmaking. While portolan charts are plane charts that do not account for the curvature of the earth, other chartmakers like Gerard Mercator were attempting to solve just this problem for mariners who were setting out on ever-longer voyages and needed to plot courses over entire oceans. This time of transition is represented in this chapter by the world chart of Giacomo Gastaldi and discussed at greater length in the next chapter.

Map of Scandinavia and Map of North America

Known simply as the *Isolario* in later editions, Bordone's book of islands (*Libro di Benedetto Bordone nel qual si ragiona de tutte l'isole del mondo*) was intended as a guide for mariners. As such, it includes textual descriptions of islands, along with maps showing their terrain and surrounding waters. First published in 1528 in Venice by Nicolò Zappino, these maps are from the 1547 edition of the work, which was popular in the sixteenth century. Bordone's book was the second book of islands to be printed, and it helped to promote the genre, the production of which centered on Venice. Many of the maps in his book were some of the first cartographic depictions of the islands to appear in print. Additionally, Bordone's book was the first to have a global scale, including chapters on the recently encountered Americas.

Above is a map of Scandinavia, specifically Norbegia (Norway), Gottia (Gothenburg), Livonia, Datia (Denmark), and Engronelant (Greenland). It suggests that Greenland was connected to Scandinavia, a common cartographic hypothesis in the sixteenth century. To the north is the *mare congelato*, or frozen sea.

Below is a map of the New World, including Labrador, or Lavoratore, which most likely got its name from the voyages of the Portuguese navigator, João Fernandes Lavrador, in 1500. A strait separates North and South America. North of the very real Azores are the mythical islands of Brasil and Asmaide. Early modern maps and charts often included features that would prove to be chimerical. Geography was not a subject set in stone, but rather an emerging field of study that was updated by practically every ship that returned to Europe from overseas. Brasil, or Hy Brasil, a supposed paradise, wandered around on maps from Ireland to the Azores from the fourteenth to the nineteenth centuries. Asmaide, or Mayda, was another wayward island that may refer to a stretch of sunken land in the North Atlantic.

Chartmaker Biography

Benedetto Bordone (1460–1531) was a talented man of letters; he was an astrologer and a miniaturist in addition to his work as an engraver and mapmaker. He worked for the elite of Venice, engraving illustrations and maps.

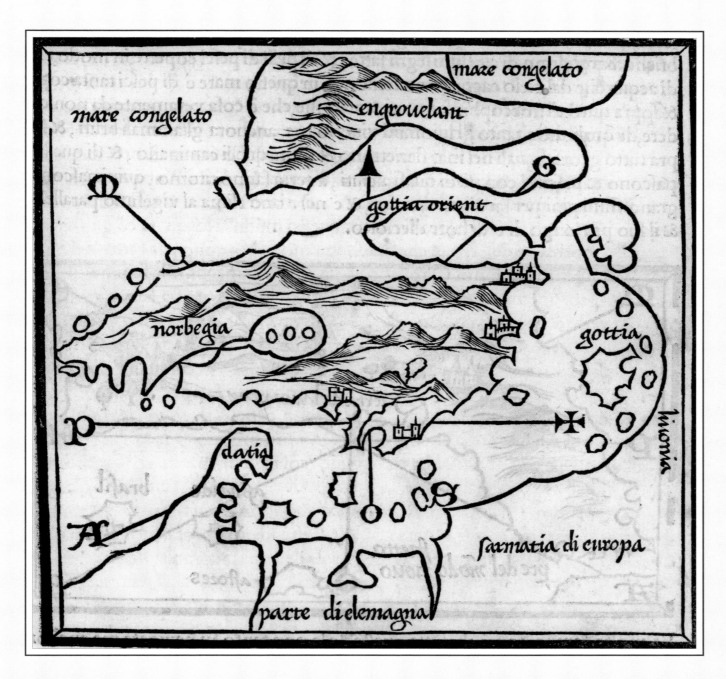

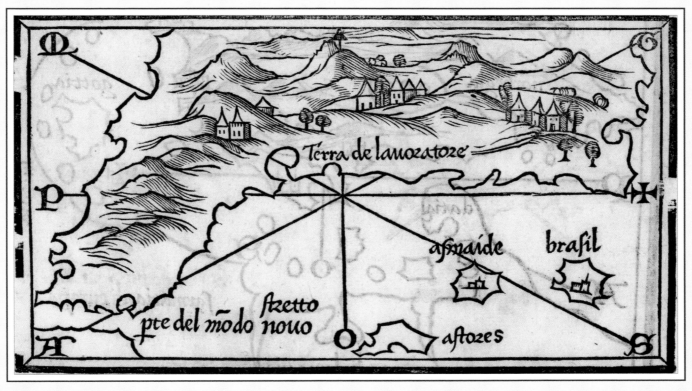

Pîrî Reis,
Kitāb-i baḥriye
Charts of the Adriatic coast from Budva to Dubrovnik: Methana (Mutūn fortress)

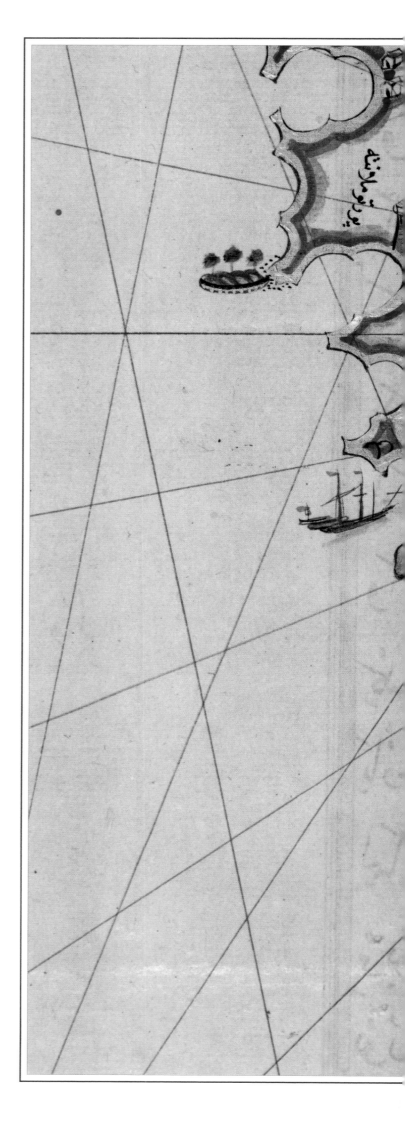

The *Kitab-i baḥriye*, or book of navigation, was compiled by Pîrî Reis as he sailed around the Mediterranean as a member of the Ottoman Navy. The 1521 original was composed of Pîrî's notes and charts, which he then revised and presented to Sultan Suleiman the Magnificent (r. 1520–1566) in 1526. An illustrated maritime manual, similar to an *isolario*, the work included detailed and beautiful charts. One of the most complete portolan atlases, the 1521 *Kitāb-i baḥriye* contains 131 charts, while the 1526 edition has 219 charts. While no extant copies are in Pîrî Reis's hand, roughly two dozen sixteenth-century manuscript copies survive, with others dating to the seventeenth century.

These charts are part of a late-seventeenth century expanded manuscript copy held by the Walters Art Museum, which contains 240 stunning charts. They are in the portolan style, with practical red and green rhumb lines—differentiated so as to allow a navigator to plot a course—but also with beautiful decorations, including elaborate compass roses, bright colors, and gilt-gold embellishments.

The first image, on this page and on page 16 (f. 150a), is a chart of the Adriatic coast, from Budva in Montenegro (east) to fortified Dubrovnik in Croatia (west). The coastline has exaggerated indents and bays so that a navigator could recognize them from their shape and appearance of the cities and hills included on this chart—verisimilitude was not the goal of portolan charts, the rationale was recognizability of features and inclusion of information that would be of interest to a navigator.

The second image, on page 17 (f. 130b), shows Methana (Mutūn) fortress on the Bay of Saronikos (Aiyina Bay). While this chart has more detail inland than a typical portolan chart, it still contains information important to sailors, such as the "x" marking a rock obstruction near the fortress, and the dotted line indicating a sandy beach in the bay.

Chartmaker Biography

Pîrî Reis (ca. 1465–d. 1554) was an Ottoman admiral who sailed widely as part of his uncle's crew and as an officer in the Ottoman Navy. In addition to the Kitāb-i baḥriye, *Pîrî Reis made two world maps (1513 and 1528). After seven decades at sea, he was beheaded for hesitating to attack the enemy.*

15

16

قلعه متون

طلویر قلاطه

17

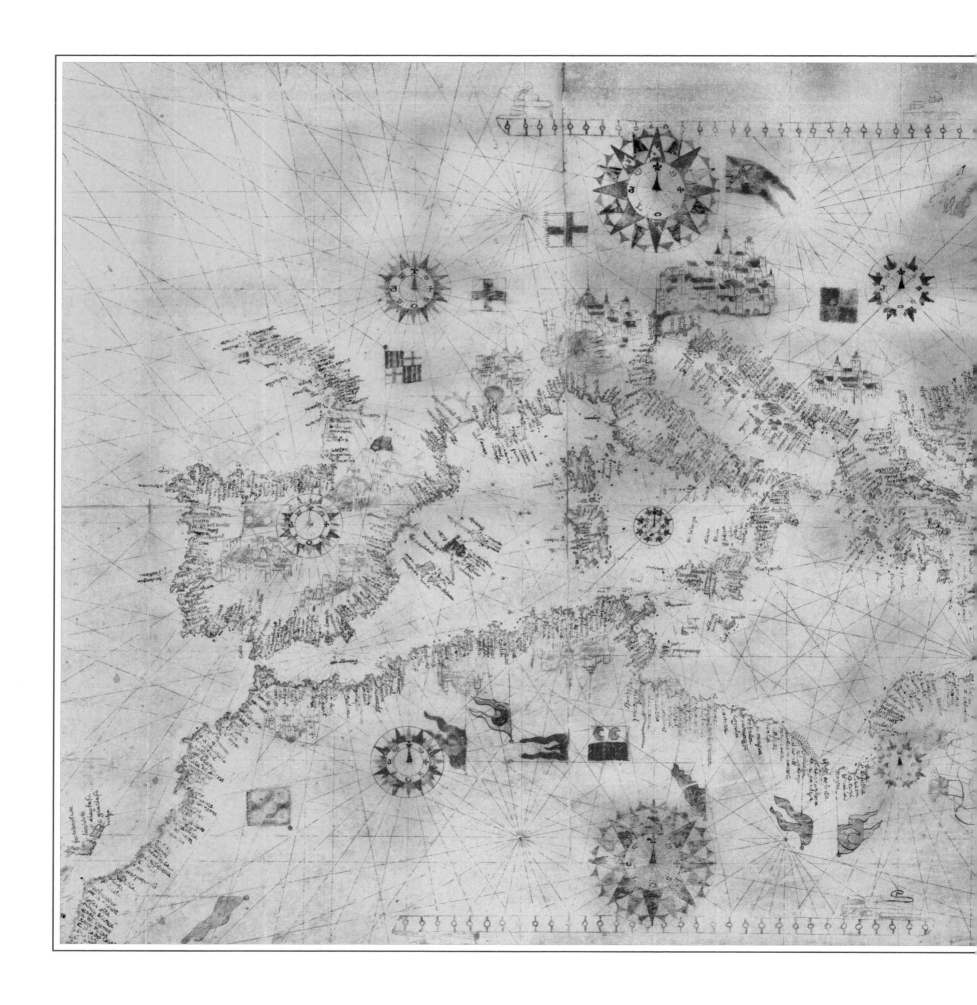

Manuscript Portolan Chart of Europe

This is a fine example of a portolan chart showing the entirety of Europe. Portolan atlases often showed a mariner a close-up view of one section of coastline. However, some portolan charts, and reference charts that began portolan atlases, usually showed a larger area, most commonly the Mediterranean, in order for longer journeys to be plotted or to allow a navigator to relate places to each other more easily.

Here there is the characteristic labeling of ports in red and black, the decorative compass roses at intervals around the chart, and rhumb lines radiating through the seas, allowing for course plotting. Additionally, there are large rippling flags placed inland to indicate the religion and ruler of certain polities; for example, those in Northern Africa include the crescent moon, a reference to Islam. This style of flag, and the decorative style in general, is typical of portolan charts made in Mallorca. The chart was originally made in 1563 by Mateo Prunes and is now held in the Museo Naval in Madrid.

What makes this example particularly interesting is that it is a nineteenth-century copy of the sixteenth-century original chart. It is on vellum, just as the original would have been. Paleographic evidence on the verso indicates it was made pre-1850 in Spain. It is likely that this portolan was copied as part of a concerted effort on the part of the Spanish government to make reproductions of the rare and important charts in their repositories. At the time, European governments and individual scholars were increasingly concerned with the quality and longevity of their archives, and it was thought that extra copies could allow for more and closer study, and an increased likelihood of the survival of the materials.

Chartmaker Biography

Mateo Prunes (1532–1594) was one of the patriarchs of a Catalan family of portolan chartmakers based in Palma, Mallorca. The Prunes family was active from the mid-sixteenth century to 1651. Mateo has at least thirteen nautical charts attributed to him.

20

Portolan Chart of the Mediterranean

Joan Riczo Oliva's portolan chart of the Mediterranean (Naples, 1586) shows the region in remarkable detail from Cape Finisterre to the Holy Land. The decorative nature of this chart is evident; it was never intended to go to sea, but instead to grace a drawing-room table, a study desk, or a dining-room wall.

The Red Sea is painted its namesake color, a common convention on Medieval and early modern maps and charts. Numerous compass roses dot the chart, the point of origin for rhumb lines to criss-cross the waters. Detailed city-views are topped with flags of the local rulers, with the black crescent moon on a red background representing the Ottoman Empire. Camels, elephants, lions, and monkeys smile, prance, and roar from the inland of Northern Africa.

Perhaps the most interesting decorative elements are in the Holy Land and at the top of the chart. In this example, it is possible to see the shape of the animal that forms the writing surface, with its narrow neck toward the top, or west. In the top center is Jesus crucified on the cross. Decorating the neck of the vellum became common in the sixteenth century, and different images could be associated with different families or ports of production. The crucifixion scene was quite commonly used by several members of the Oliva family. At the bottom of the chart is the hill of Calvary, with three crosses, meant to symbolize Jerusalem. The religious symbolism could be attributed to the faith of the chartmaker and the general religiosity of much of sixteenth-century Mediterranean life, but it could also be added, or downplayed, at the request of the patron.

Chartmaker Biography

*The **Olives-Oliva-Ollive family** was one of the most prolific families of portolan chartmakers, a practice that often was passed down from generation to generation. This chart was by Joan Riczo Oliva, who worked in Naples from 1580 to 1588 and in Messina from 1590 to 1594.*

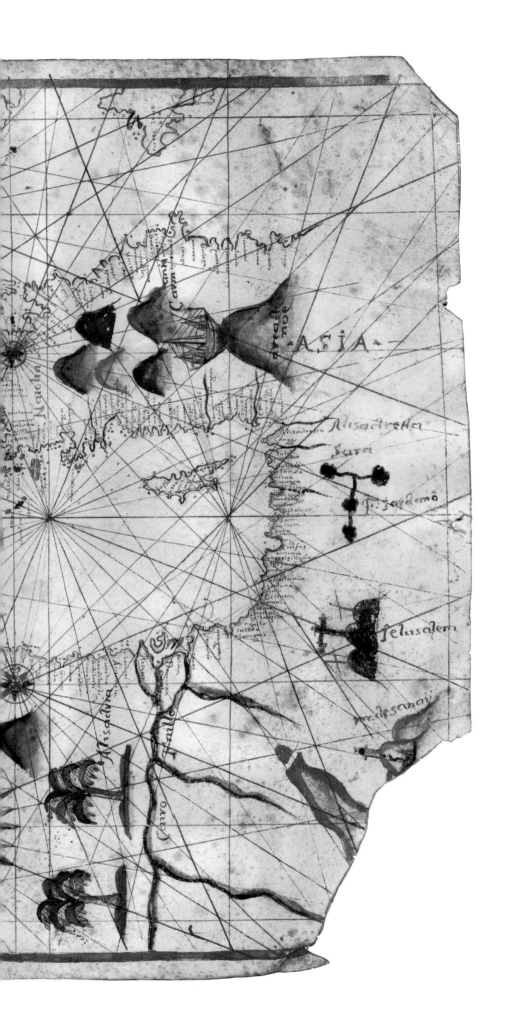

Portolan Chart of the Mediterranean

Placido Caloiro et Oliva's portolan chart fragment of the Mediterranean (Messina, ca. 1650) is again highly decorative and heightened in gold leaf. The brightness of the hills is matched by the vibrancy of the compass roses. The scale bar is encased within a scrollwork cartouche, a convention that was increasingly common on seventeenth-century cartographic objects.

Religious imagery again plays a large role in this portolan chart. In the east, three specific places are represented: Mount Sinai, Mount Calvary with three crosses, and the Jordan River. On Mount Sinai is a small building, which may be a reference to St. Catherine's Monastery, built in the sixth century CE. Today, it operates the oldest continuously operating library in the world and is one of the oldest working monasteries extant. Mount Calvary, outside Jerusalem, is where Jesus was crucified. The Jordan River is the river in which Jesus was baptized and over which the Israelites entered the Promised Land. The most unusual representation is located in Anatolia, in the eastern part of Asia Minor. Atop a sharp brown peak is a precariously balanced vessel. It is Noah's Ark at the top of Mount Ararat. The famed ship is shown here with rigging and masts.

The distinctive ark is not the only detail that makes this particular example interesting for the scholar and collector. For centuries prior to the production of this chart, most nautical charts showed a rotation of about 9° counterclockwise relative to the magnetic declination in the Mediterranean. Although in the mid-seventeenth century some cartographers identified the shift and indicated the true geographical orientation, the author of this chart chose to follow the more traditional pattern of rotation.

Chartmaker Biography

Placido Caloiro et Oliva worked in Messina from 1617 to 1657. Charts by Oliva family members were made in Mallorca, Malta, Venice, Naples, Marseilles, Leghorn, and, especially, Messina.

Portolan Atlas of the Mediterranean

Some of the most densely and extravagantly decorated portolan charts extant, these images are included in a portolan atlas (1658) by François Ollive, who worked in Marseilles. While the waters remain empty, underlining the purpose of these depictions as nautical charts no matter how fancy or embellished they are, this atlas was clearly intended as a prestige object to be prized. It contains six double-page and four single-page charts, each in full color and dotted with gold leaf.

One of three charts that together form a complete view of the Mediterranean, the first image is packed with symbolic and dedicatory imagery. The compass roses double as title cartouches to name the continents. The scale bars are contained within vase and feather-topped motifs. The compass roses contain north arrows of varying design, including large fleur-de-lis. As we have seen before, the flags of various rulers represent political loyalty and power, while the three crosses of Calvary mark the Holy Land.

The second image from this atlas shows the tiny, yet important, island of Malta. Very few portolan charts were produced in Malta. Instead, the Knights of St. John, who ruled Malta from 1522 to 1798, preferred to purchase their charts from other centers of production like Messina and Venice, a nod to their cosmopolitan lives and the location of Malta at the crossroads of the Mediterranean. Unusually for a portolan chart, this image reveals much inland. The road network is marked, as is the old capital of Mdina, or the *"Cita Vechia,"* coastal fortifications, and the salt pans. The many buildings of Valletta and the Three Cities in the Grand Harbor are also evident.

On the facing page are the Balearic Islands of Mallorca, Minorca, and Ibiza. Both pages continue with the ornate decoration of the chart of the Eastern Mediterranean, with a shell-themed scale bar on the Malta chart and a floral scale on the Balearics.

Chartmaker Biography

François Ollive worked in Marseilles from 1650 to 1664. The first known work by a member of the Oliva dynasty was in 1538 by Bartomeu Olives in Palma, Mallorca.

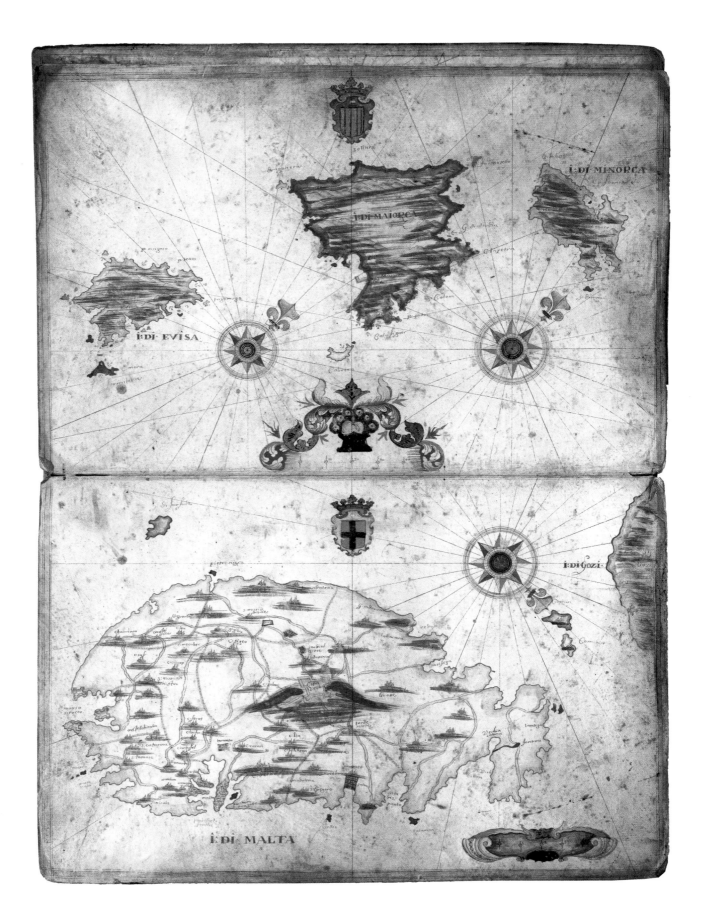

Carta Marina
Nova Tabula

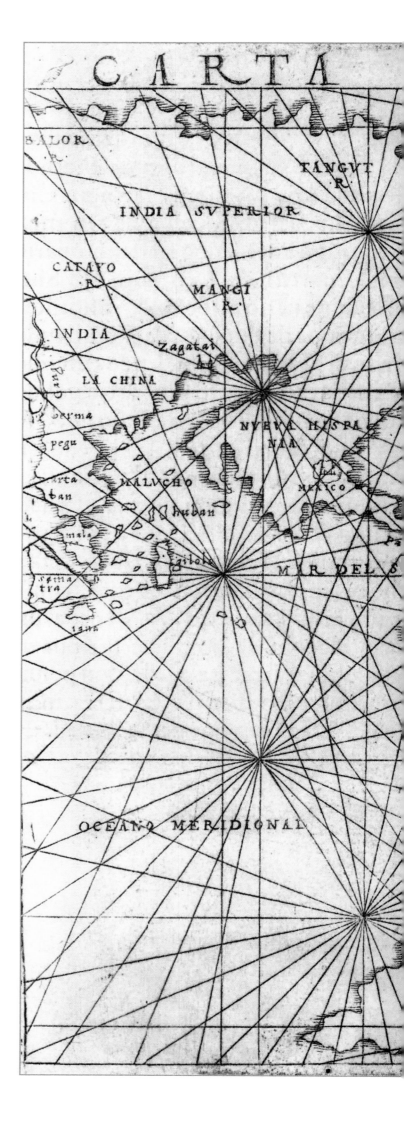

Gastaldi's chart was one of the first printed sea charts of the world. It was included in Gastaldi's edition of *Geographia*, published in Venice in 1548, the first pocket-sized edition of the book to appear on the market. Gastaldi's edition of Ptolemy, with 26 Ptolemaic maps (no Ptolemaic world map) and 34 modern maps printed on interlocking copper plates, took Gastaldi six years to complete. Its success cemented Gastaldi's reputation as one of Italy's, and Europe's, premier geographers.

The chart includes an unusual configuration of North America. The continent merges with Asia to the west. Gastaldi also connects Europe and North America via a long land bridge, suggesting a massive, interconnected northern landmass. The only landmass not connected to the other continents is Tierra del Fuego, in the south. This island represents European cartographic conjecture about the region at the time. Magellan had sailed through the Strait of Magellan, marked here, a quarter of a century before this chart was made. However, the Dutch traders Schouten and Le Maire would not round Cape Horn until the early seventeenth century, leaving many to think that Tierra del Fuego was a part of a large southern continent.

While the presence of rhumb lines and a lack of inland detail marks this as a nautical chart in style, it would not be overly useful for any mariner sailing across an ocean. To do that, more detailed charts and maps had to be used in conjunction with instruments and experience to sail successfully to the Americas, or around the world. However, this chart does point to the fact that, by the mid-sixteenth century, Europeans were sailing in every ocean around the world. The charting of these new (to Europeans) waters will be the subject of the following chapters.

Chartmaker Biography

Giacomo Gastaldi (1500–1566) hailed from Piedmont, but he established himself in Venice in 1539. He was originally an engineer, but shifted to cartography and publishing in the 1540s. Close to the halls of power, Gastaldi was named cosmographer to the Republic of Venice and is perhaps most famous today for the maps included in Navigationi et Viaggi, *by Ramusio.*

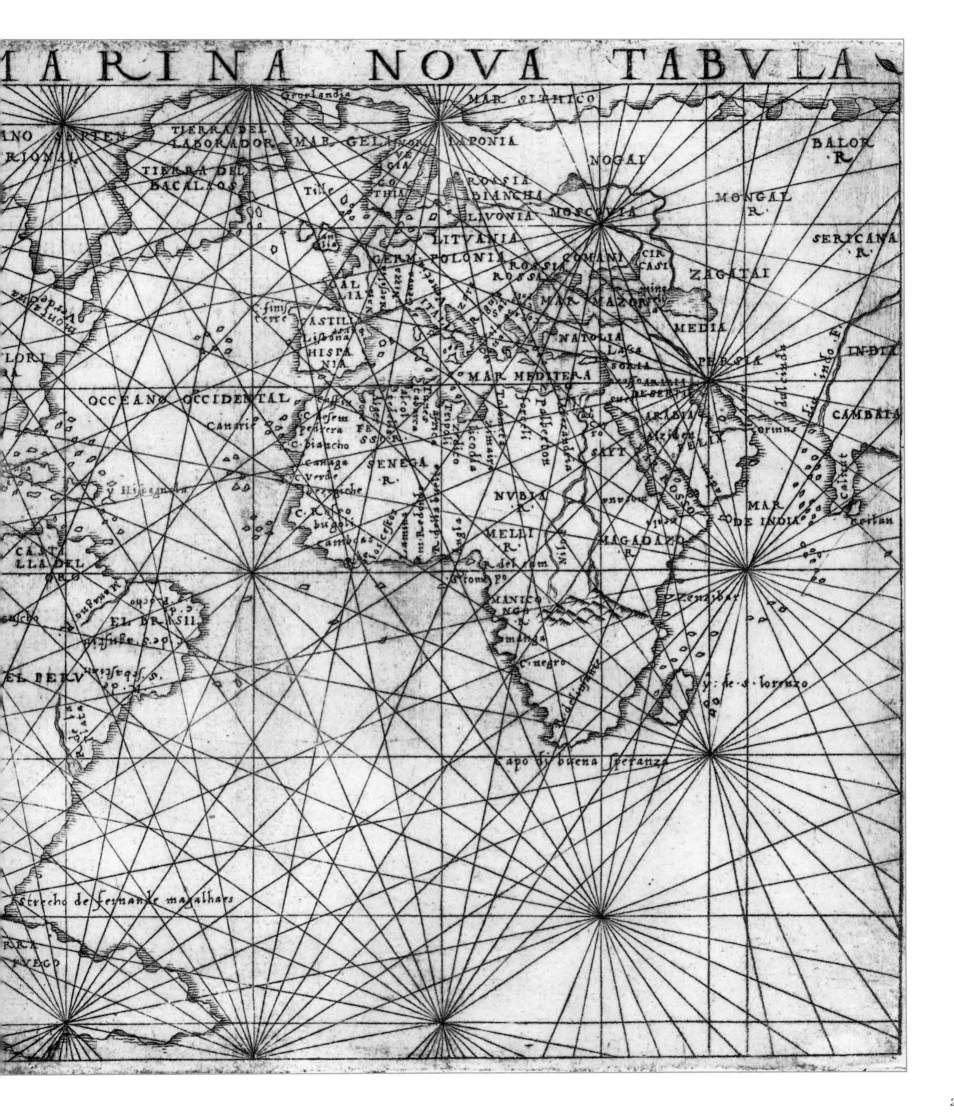

27

Dutch Hydrography in the Golden Age (1600-1700)

The center of portolan production was undoubtedly the Mediterranean, with most charts produced in or near ports on this busy maritime highway. However, as European empires expanded overseas in the fifteenth and sixteenth centuries, chart production expanded. First, it migrated west, to the Iberian Peninsula, as the Spanish and Portuguese encountered new lands and peoples in the Americas, Africa, and Asia. However, the Portuguese and Spanish tightly controlled their chart production, keeping geographic materials under centralized control in repositories in Lisbon and Seville.

No prison is impregnable; similarly, no archive is without leaks. Spanish and Portuguese geographic knowledge did spread, to a certain extent, beyond their ships and ports, often thanks to the information shared by pilots and by foreigners in the employ of the Iberian empires. By the 1580s, another European entity was beginning to exercise major influence in trade, navigation, and hydrography: the Low Countries.

With global navigation came a need for a new type of chart. Previously, charts did not correct for the curvature of the earth, which meant that charts that covered large geographic areas were inaccurate in terms of distance and bearing. Adriaen Veen, a Dutch chartmaker, attempted to address this problem with spherical charts that featured curved loxodromes; this system was complicated to calculate, and no spherical charts are known to survive today.

Gerard Mercator, a Flemish geographer, invented a new projection, shown most famously in his world map of 1569, that corrected for the earth's curvature. The projection, now named for Mercator, extended the space between far northern and southern latitudes, allowing for loxodromes to be drawn as straight lines. While Mercator's innovation would eventually dominate chartmaking, its was slow to be adopted by mariners. The first Mercator-projection charts appeared in the Low Countries in the 1590s, and they continued to be experimented upon throughout the seventeenth century.

Detailed sailing directions were lacking for northern waters, where a greater tidal range and dangerous shoals made sailing especially difficult. There were rutters for northern waters, which the Dutch called leeskaart, literally "a book to be read as a chart." These sometimes contained coastal profiles, but the genre was revolutionized with the work of Lucas Janszoon Waghenaer, a pilot and chartmaker. Waghenaer published the first set of sailing directions accompanied by detailed charts– a sea atlas. These comprehensive pilot guides became known as waggoners and led to a change in the way hydrographic works were produced across the continent. Three of his charts feature in this chapter.

After Waghenaer published Spieghel der zeevaert (Leiden: Christoffel Plantijn, 1584), the first of his three pilot guides, Amsterdam became the epicenter of hydrographic printing in Europe. Initially, chartmaking had clustered in the northern Low Countries, especially Edam, but it shifted to Amsterdam as that city became a trading juggernaut and a cosmopolitan hub. Interestingly, print largely preceded manuscript chartmaking in the Low Countries, thanks to a demand for sailing directions that were cheaper; printed paper was less expensive than time-consuming manuscripts made on vellum or parchment.

The seventeenth century is often referred to as the Dutch Golden Age, when the Dutch led Europe in art and intellectual pursuits.

Luminaries like Rembrandt, Vermeer, Huygens, Spinoza, and Descartes all lived and worked in the Netherlands in the seventeenth century. Locke took refuge there, and Hobbes published his books there.

The Dutch also had the largest merchant fleet in Europe at this time. They perfected the corporation and corporate finance, and their two biggest overseas ventures, the Dutch East India Company (VOC) and the West India Company (WIC), spread Dutch power, wealth, culture, and people around the world. The VOC was founded in 1602 and was granted a trading monopoly over all trade east of the Cape of Good Hope and west of the Strait of Magellan. The WIC, chartered in 1621, controlled Dutch trading in West Africa and the American littoral.

Chartmaking also experienced a Golden Age, with some of the most beautiful and sought-after charts produced in Amsterdam and the Low Countries during this period. Indeed, the demand for maps, charts, atlases, globes, and other cartographic objects was so high that publishers engaged in price wars to produce the most lavish, up-to-date works for discerning customers.

The likes of Cornelis Claesz, the Hondius family, and the Blaeus operated out of shops "on the water," today the Damrak, near the lavish Town Hall which was the architectural embodiment of the Dutch Golden Age. One of the building's major features is a pair of terrestrial hemispheres, along with a northern celestial hemisphere, embedded in the floor of the Central Hall. The hemispheres, based on a world map by Joan Blaeu of 1648, showed the global reach of the Low Countries' companies and ships.

Blaeu also served as the official hydrographer of the VOC, a position previously held by his father, Willem Blaeu, and before that by his father's former assistant, Hessel Gerritsz. In the 1620s, Gerritsz was simultaneously the hydrographer to the VOC and the WIC, providing charts to navigators who set off for Dutch colonies and factories from the Caribbean to Japan. The companies maintained their headquarters in Amsterdam, but they also had chartmaking workshops in Brazil and Batavia, which updated official company charts which were issued to navigators who were expected to return them upon completion of their voyages. However, company hydrographers were also private entrepreneurs who sold their charts to the wider public.

The Dutch in the seventeenth century were some of the most cartographically literate people to have lived to that point in history, and they sought maps and charts to decorate their homes and businesses, as did wealthy Europeans far from Amsterdam. Between ten and sixty maps and charts adorned each office of the VOC and WIC, while Vermeer's paintings frequently feature cartographic objects in the homes of burghers. The brightly colored and lavishly decorated charts made for land-side consumption are largely those that survive and which are featured in this chapter. The plainer, more utilitarian charts used at sea survive in far fewer numbers, if at all, but related sources tell us that they were used in large numbers.

Finally, as shown with Dudley's chart produced in Florence which finishes this chapter, Amsterdam and the Low Countries may have been the main center of European chartmaking in the seventeenth century, but they were far from the only places where charts were published. While Dutch-made charts are today considered some of the most engaging and striking from this period, charts continued to be made from England to France to Croatia and beyond.

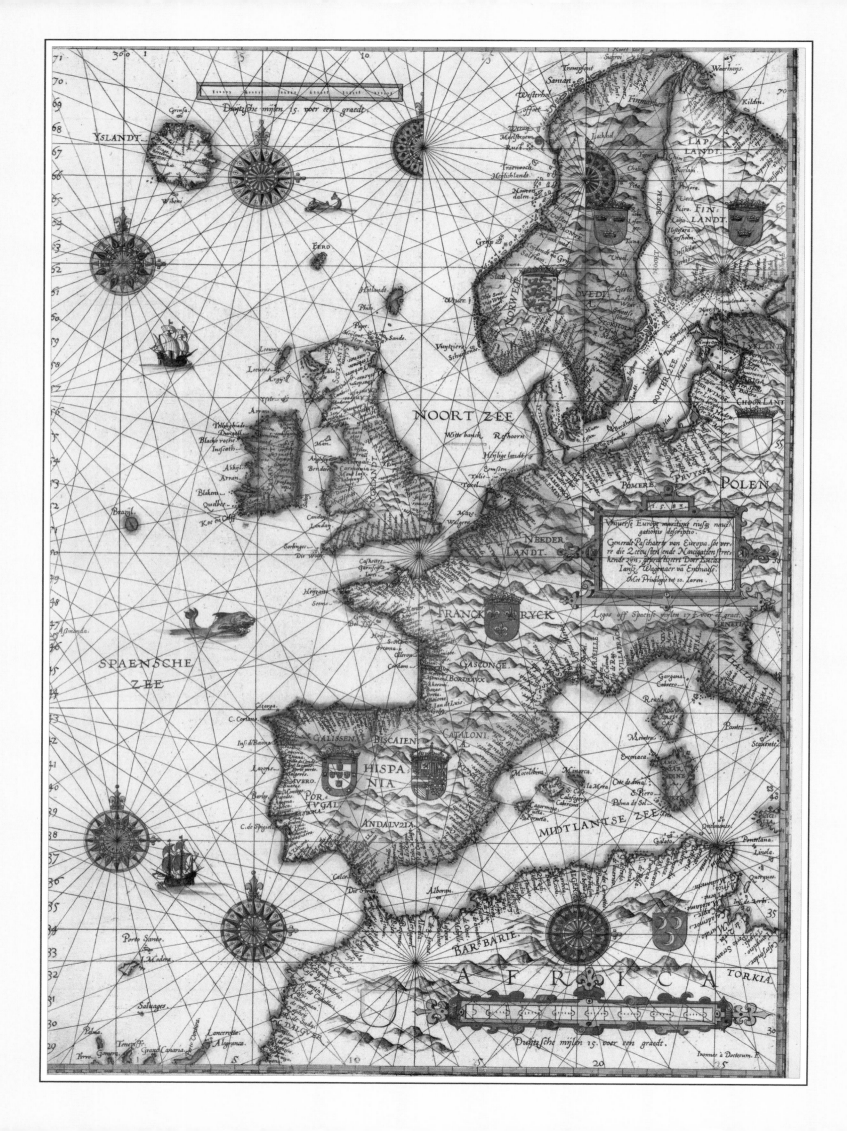

30

Universe Europe maritime eiusque navigationis descriptio...

Lucas Janszoon Waghenaer was one of the most influential chartmakers in the history of cartography, thanks to his *Spieghel der zeevaerdt*, or the "Mariner's Mirror." This sea atlas was the first to publish sailing directions alongside corresponding charts, many of which were based on Waghenaer's own experiences sailing from Norway to Cádiz. The first part, published in 1584, featured this map, while the second part followed in 1585. The second part detailed a voyage north and east of the Low Countries.

The first part of *Spieghel der zeevaerdt* features charts detailing a voyage west and south of the Low Countries. The contents describe and show the coastline from Texel to Cádiz. This stunning map was the overview or reference map that preceded the more detailed charts, which are set at a uniform scale of 1:400,000 (except for the entrances to ports and rivers, which were at higher resolution).

The map features all of Western Europe and much of Northwest Africa as well. The coastline is outlined from Finland to the British Isles to the Iberian Peninsula to Italy, with Iceland in the northwest and the Canary Islands peeking out of the southwest corner. Compass roses of varying designs and details serve as the source of rhumb lines that criss-cross the chart. Mountains line the interior of many countries, while ships and a lone sea monster patrol the waters. The coats of arms of various leaders also help to orient the reader.

This map featured in the first part of the *Spieghel*, but it was also issued separately when first made in 1583, as indicated by the date in the cartouche in the interior of Europe. Several of Waghenaer's charts were sold separately, as well as being included in his sea atlases.

Chartmaker Biography

Lucas Janszoon Waghenaer (ca. 1533–1606) was a Dutch marine cartographer and navigator. He grew up in the important port of Enkhuizen. From 1550 to 1579, he served at sea, increasing his practical knowledge of sailing and charting. His most important contribution to hydrography was the publication of the first book of sailing directions to include charts, Spieghel der zeevaerdt.

Die Caerte vande Zeekusten van biscaien

Also included in the first part of *Spieghel der zeevaerdt*, first published in Leiden in 1584, this chart details the Spanish coast from the Rio de Sella to Aviles, in the Bay of Biscay. The scale bar and title cartouche contain the intricate strapwork design that was characteristic of the charts in the *Spieghel*, while two large whales spout water from their blowholes. The whales dwarf the sailing vessel between them, while two more sea creatures look on near the bottom border. The finely-crafted compass rose reveals this chart to be south-oriented.

The shoreline shows both a plan view of the coastline, as from above, and a profile view of the shore and the mountains behind. This would provide a navigator with important information about the area, while also proving quite aesthetically pleasing. Further aids to mariners are sounding depths in the coves and bays, as well as small anchors that indicate safe places for ships to drop anchor. Conventions such as these were standardized through widely-read sea atlases like Waghenaer's.

The *Spieghel* was published in several editions and translated into various European languages. It proved so popular because of the high quality of the production and the efficiency and ease of its design. Waghenaer made the atlas a set of units, with four pages for each unit. Each unit included a description and sailing instructions, a two-page chart, and a blank fourth page. The charts were engraved by the skilled Joannes van Doetecum and first published by Christoffel Plantijn, one of the most respected publishers of the period.

Chartmaker Biography

Lucas Janszoon Waghenaer (ca. 1533–1606) was a Dutch marine cartographer and navigator. He grew up in the important port of Enkhuizen. From 1550 to 1579, he served at sea, increasing his practical knowledge of sailing and charting. His most important contribution to hydrography was the publication of the first book of sailing directions to include charts, Spieghel der zeevaerdt.

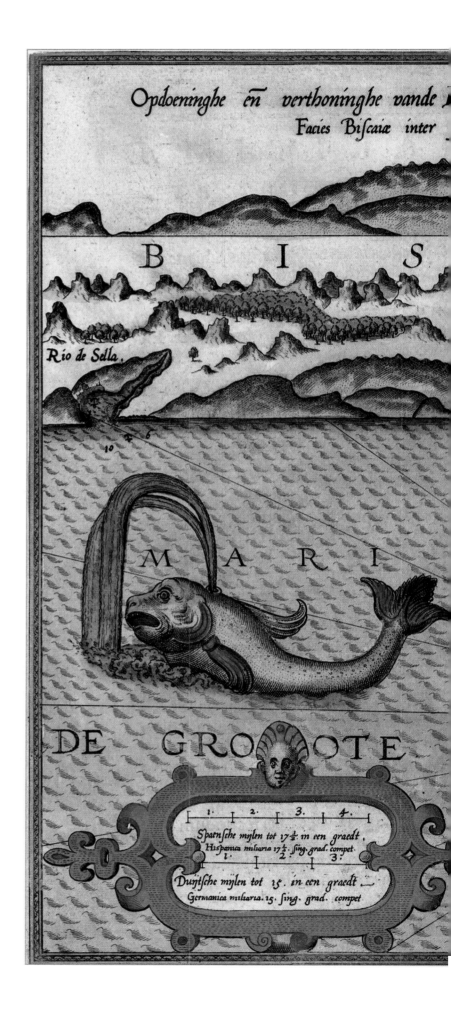

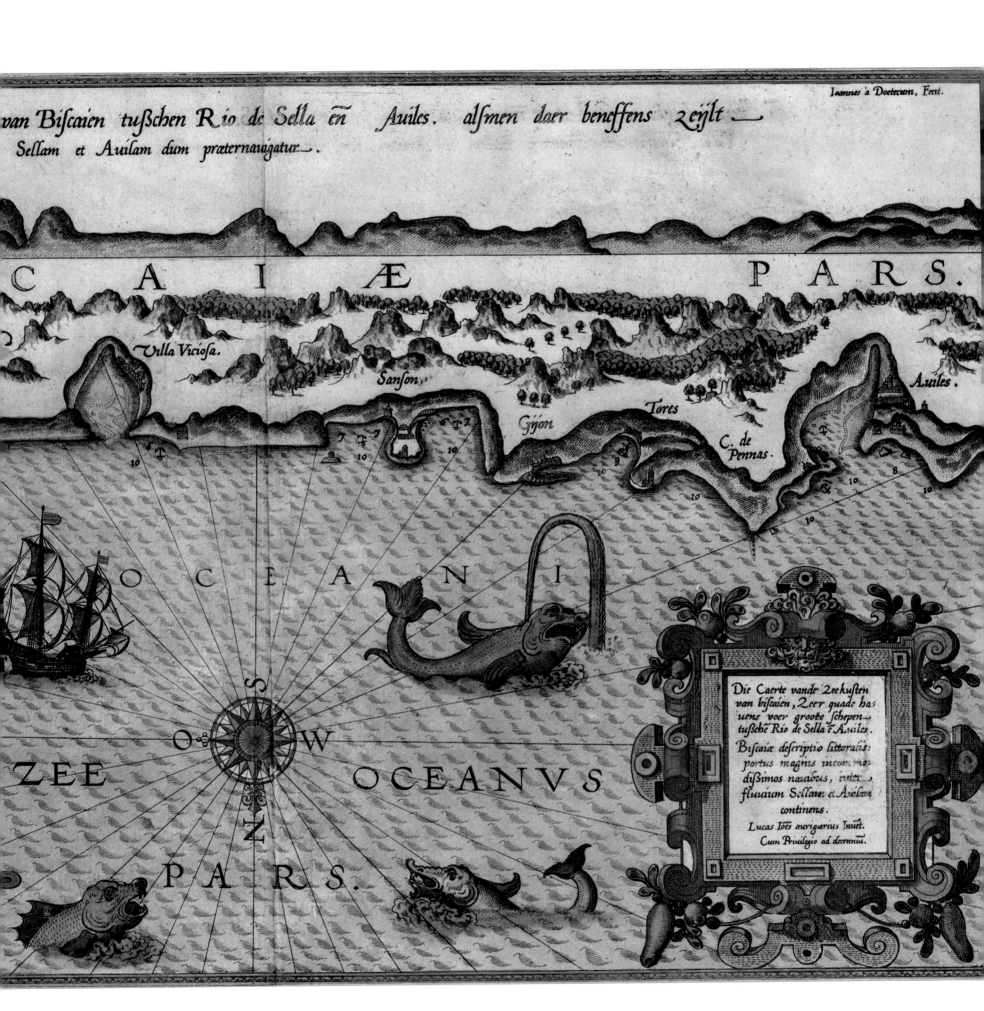

van Biscaien tuſſchen Rio de Sella ēn Auiles. alſmen daer beneffens zeijlt

Sellam et Auilam dum præternauigatur.

Ioannes à Doetecum, Fecit.

CAIÆ PARS.

Villa Viciosa.

Sanſon

Gijon

Tores

C. de Pennas.

Auiles.

OCEANI

ZEE

OCEANVS

PARS.

Die Caerte vande zee kuſten van biſcaien, zeer quade ha uens voer groote ſchepen tuſſche Rio de Sella ē Auiles.

Biſcaiæ deſcriptio littoralis: portus magnis incommo diſſimos nauibus, inter fluuium Sellæ et Auilam continens.

Lucas Iōīs aurigarius Inuet.
Cum Priuilegio ad decenniū.

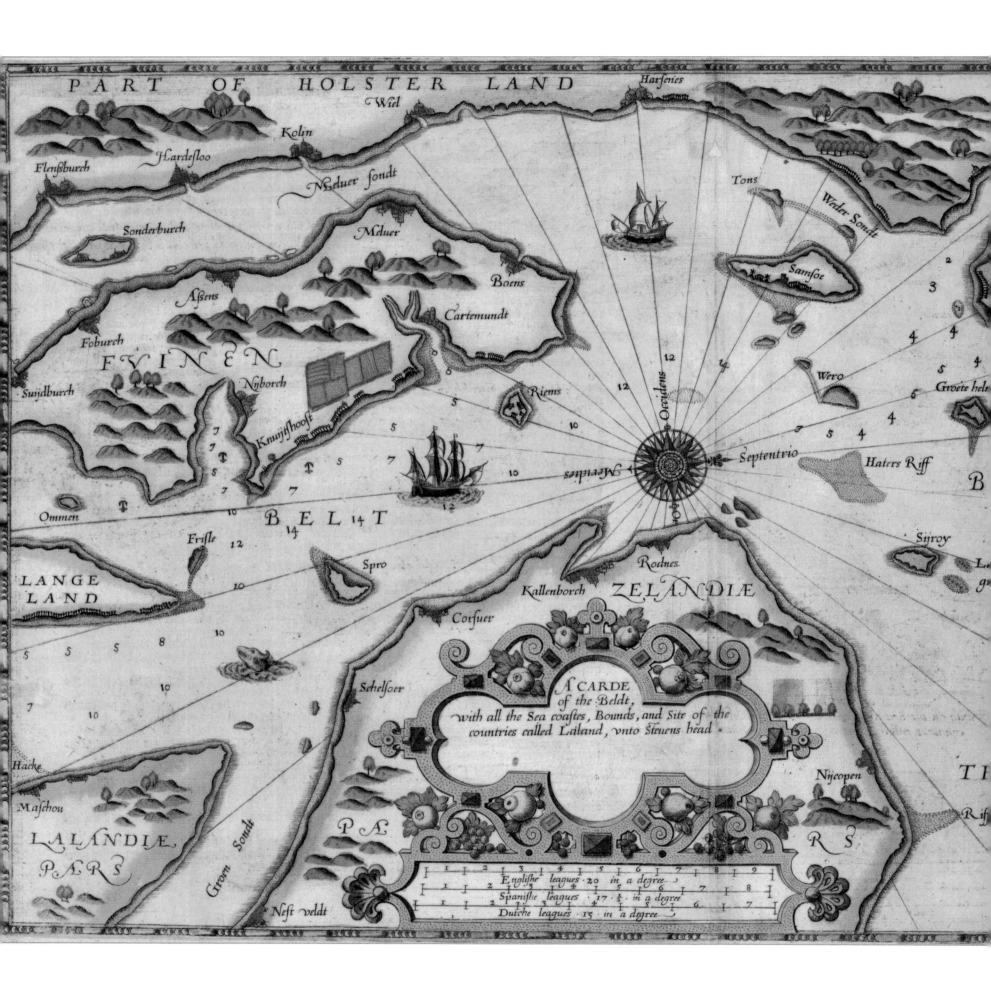

PART OF HOLSTER LAND

Harsenes

Wiel

Kolin

Flensburch   Hardesloo

N.eluer sondt   Tons   Weder Sondt

Sonderburch   Meluer

Assens   Boens   Samsoe

Foburch   FVINEN   Cartemundt   Wero   Groete heln

Sundburch   Nyborch   Occidens   12

Knuijshooft   Riems   Septentrio   Haters Riff

Ommen   Meridies

BELT   Siiroy

Frisle   Spro

LANGE   Rodnes.   ZELANDIÆ

LAND   Kallenborch

Corsuer

Schelsoer

A CARDE
of the Beldt,
with all the Sea coastes, Bounds, and Site of the
countries called Laland, vnto Steuens head.

Hacke   Nyeopen

Maschou

LALANDIÆ   PÆRS   Groen Sondt   PÆRS

PÆRS   Nest veldt

Englishe leagues 20 in a degree
Spanishe leagues 17½ in a degree
Dutche leagues 15 in a degree

34

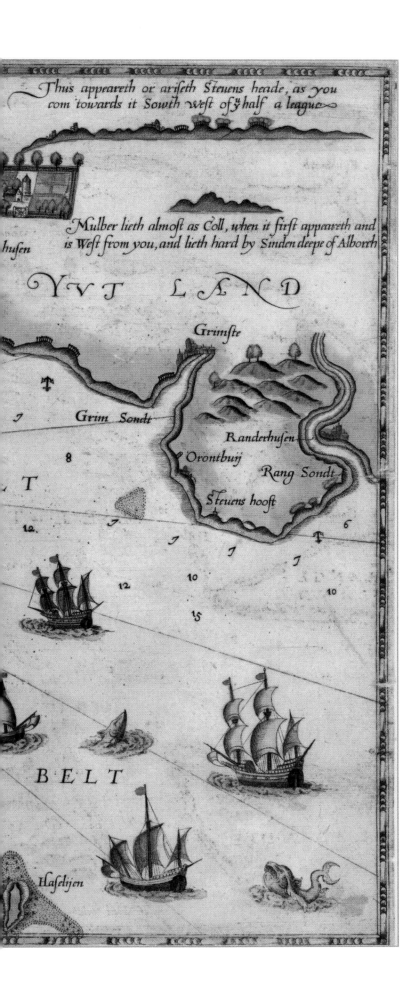

Thus appeareth or ariseth Steuens heade, as you com towards it Sowth west of y^e half a league

Mulber lieth almost as Coll, when it first appeareth and is West from you, and lieth hard by Sinden deepe of Alborch

...husen

YVT LAND

Grimste

Grim Sondt

8

T

Randerhusen

Oronthuij

Rang Sondt

Steuens hooft

9

12.

7

7

6

7

10

7

12

10

15

10

BELT

Hasetijen

A Carde of the Beldt with all the Sea coastes, Bounds, and Site of the countries called Laland, unto Stevens head

This is also a Waghenaer chart, but one that has been translated into English. The chart shows a part of the Danish Straits called the Great Belt, which passes between the islands of Zealand and Funen. The chart is oriented with west at the top and includes sounding depths, anchorage locations, and sandbars to aid a sailor in making the passage.

Waghenaer's work proved important not just for Dutch sailors, but for seamen across Europe, including England. In 1588, a skilled team of engravers reproduced the charts from *Spieghel* in London, the first sea charts printed in England. The engravers included Augustine Ryther, Jan Rutlinger, Theodor de Bry, and Jodocus Hondius. The latter two had fled from religious persecution in the Low Countries. All except Ryther were initially trained on the Continent before coming to work in London. The text was translated by Anthony Ashley, Clerk of the Privy Council and a favorite of Queen Elizabeth I.

The English edition closely followed the Dutch original, with a few corrections to the charts of the English coastline. The majority of charts for the English market came from Dutch publishers throughout the late sixteenth and seventeenth centuries, showing the power of the Dutch chart producers and the relative weakness of the English. Many English publishers would acquire Dutch plates and rub out the Dutch names, re-engraving them with English words.

Chartmaker Biography

Lucas Janszoon Waghenaer (ca. 1533–1606) was a Dutch marine cartographer and navigator. He grew up in the important port of Enkhuizen. From 1550 to 1579, he served at sea, increasing his practical knowledge of sailing and charting. His most important contribution to hydrography was the publication of the first book of sailing directions to include charts, Spieghel der zeevaerdt.

Delineatio Orarum maritimarum, Terrae vulgo indigetatae Terra de Natal...

This map appeared in Jan Huygen van Linschoten's famous *Itinerario* (Amsterdam: Claesz, 1595–1596), which was a hybrid text. The work, including its maps, would have a powerful influence on the early Dutch voyages to the East Indies. Upon returning from Goa, in India, Linschoten sought to record his experiences. Encouraged by successful geographic publisher Cornelis Claesz, Linschoten sought collaborators to help him add to the text. These included Bernardus Paludanus, a savant who wrote the sections on Africa and America, and many navigators who provided information on the sailing route between the Low Countries and Indonesia. These sailing directions were published first and travelled with Cornelis Houtman and Gerrit van Beuningen on the first Dutch fleet to the East Indies in 1595.

Claesz also thought it fitting to add maps to the collection, for which he sought the help of Arnoldus and Henricus Van Langren. The Van Langrens were an established family of map and chartmakers. The maps in the work consisted of a world map, by Petrus Plancius, and five detail maps, by the Van Langrens. This is one of the detail maps, showing the maritime passage from southern Africa to the Maldives.

The map is heavily decorated with large compass roses. Both scale bar and title cartouche groan under the weight of strapwork embellishment that includes flora and fauna. Africa and Madagascar contain many details inland, while the islands that fill the Indian Ocean are surrounded by sandbanks, shoals, and other obstacles. Most spectacularly, a ship faces off against a sea monster south of Madagascar, while farther north two vessels fire broadsides at each other. This map was made just as the Dutch were eclipsing the Portuguese in terms of maritime power and trade, and it trumpets this ascendency.

Chartmaker Biography

Jan Huygen van Linschoten (1562–1611) grew up in Enkhuizen, like Waghenaer. He traveled abroad and ended up in the company of João Vicente da Fonseca, Archbishop of Goa. He spent five years in Goa, then was shipwrecked and returned to Enkhuizen in 1592. He later sailed on two voyages to find the Northeast Passage and published several works, including the famous Itinerario, *a travel collection and geography.*

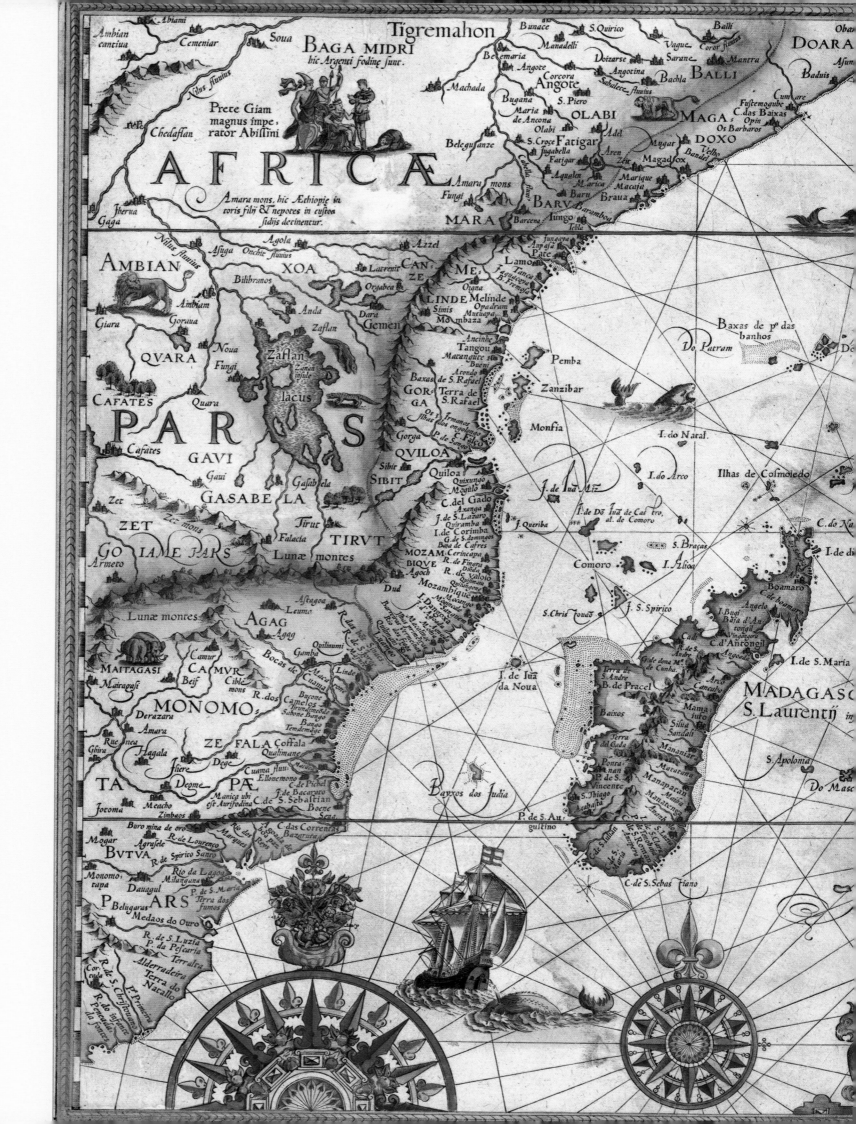

AEQVINOCTIALIS

TROPICVS CAPRICORNI

Macanaj
De Pᵒ dos ban
Quelua
Timor
Pruaca
Candical
Candaluz
Ganfar
Maldiua
Pᵒ de Galle
ceylon

Canal

I. de Cedu

Ilhas de
Diego Roiz

Ruo Moluço
J. do Gamo

Baixos dás Chagos

Adu
Candu

do Mazcarenhas
As Sete Irmanas
Os tres Irmanos

J. da Poluara

Abrolho
J. de Roque Piz
De Pᵒ dos banhos
J. de Diego Graciofa

anto
de S. Francisco

Da Galega
Baixos de S. Miguel
J. de Roque Piz

Saya de Malha

Do Garaiao

S. Brandaon

azare

J. de Diego Roiz

Lixboa

Dos Romeyros
dos Caſtelhanos

Delineatio Orarum
maritimarum, Terræ vulgo
indigetatæ Terra de Natal, item
Sofalæ, Mozambicæ & Melindæ,
Insulæ, Sancti Laurentij, Insularum
Malduicarum, Seylon insulæ, & Promon-
torij Comorini, ad Indiam siti unà cum
insulis, Scopulis, Puluris, Vadis, veris
Ventorum tractibus & genuino sin-
gulorum locorum situ, ad exac tis-
simas Ichnographicas India-
rum tabulas retognita atq́
emendita.

Affbeeldinghe der custen des landts genaempt Terra do
Natal, item van alle de custen van Coffala, Mozambique,
Melinde, ende t'eylandt van S. Lorenzo: met alle haere eylanden, clippen, droochten, ende ondiepten, item d'eylanden van Maldiua tot het eylandt Çeylon, ende den hoeck
van Comori toe, aende custen van Jndien liggende, met de
wuerachtighe streckinghe ende gheleghentheyt der zeluer, alles
seer correct telnick naer d'allerbeste Jndiaensche Pas ende
Lees-caerten, ouersien ende verbeetert.

Arnoldus
F. à Lan-
gren. deli-
neauit &
sculpsit.

Miliaria Germanica, quorum 15. uni gradui respondent.
10 20 30 40 50 60 70 80 90 100 10 20 30 40 50
Lispanicæ leucæ 17½. uni gradui competentia.
10 20 30 40 50 60 70 80 90 100 110 120 130 140 150 160 170 180

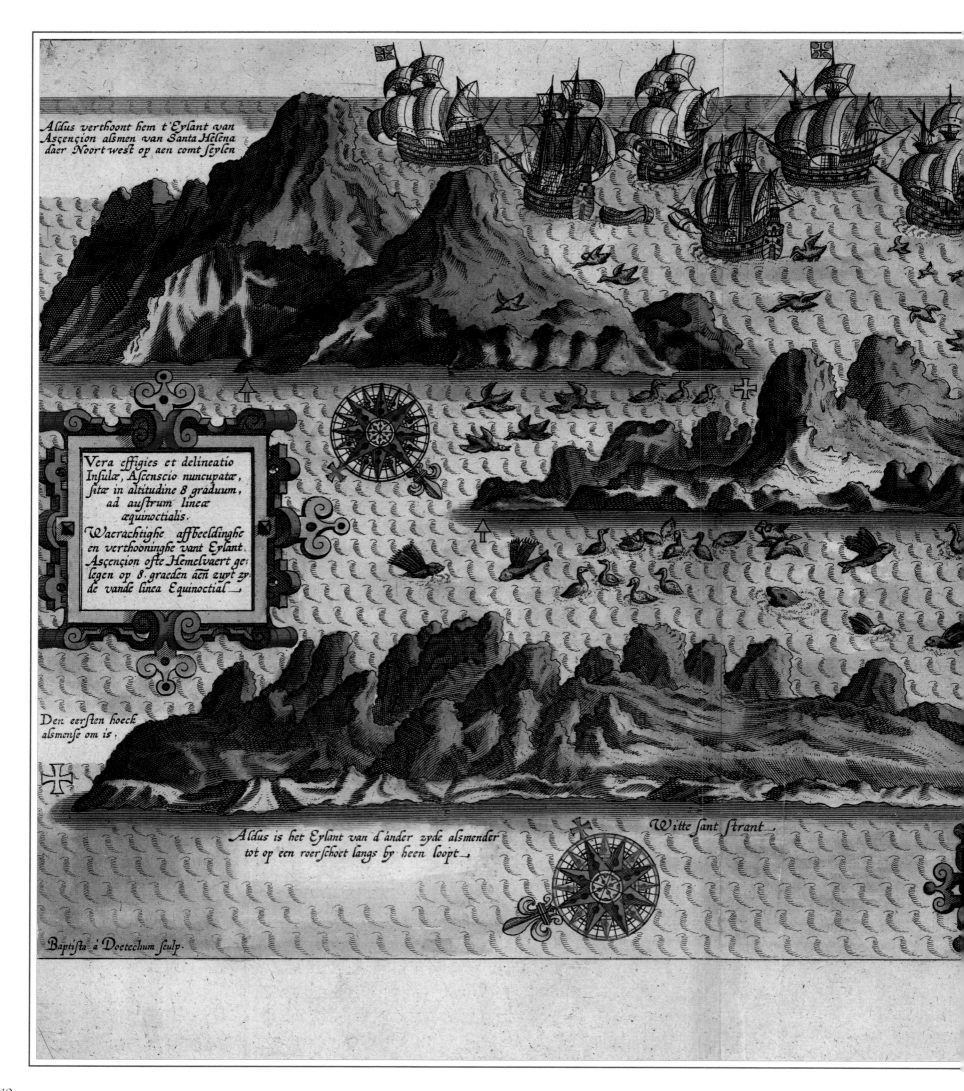

Aldus verthoont hem t'Eylant van
Ascencion alsmen van Santa Helena
daer Noort west op aen comt seylen

Vera effigies et delineatio
Insulæ, Ascenscio nuncupatæ,
sitæ in altitudine 8 graduum,
ad austrum lineæ
æquinoctialis.
Waerachtighe affbeeldinghe
en verthooninghe vant Eylant
Ascencion ofte Hemelvaert ge:
legen op 8. graeden aen zuyt zy=
de vande linea Equinoctial

Den eersten hoeck
alsmense om is.

Aldus is het Eylant van d'ander zyde alsmender
tot op een roerschoet langs by heen loopt

Witte sant strant

Baptista à Doetechum sculp.

Den eerften hoeck
die wy om liepen.

Aldus verthoont hem tfelffde Eylant alsmender een
roer fchoet van aff by heen loopt van dit merck ✠ aff
naert ✠ toe.

DOCTISSIMO DÑO BERNALDO PALLVDANO ENCHV:
SANÆ REIPVB. MEDICO PERITISSIMO,DÑO ET AMI:
CO SVO SINGVLARI IOĀNES HVGONIS A LINSCHOTEN D.D.

Nullius mihi terra ferax atque indiga potus
Piscatu dives littus et aucupio :
Tota rubore fatur medijs atollor in Vndis,
Qua videt auftrinum torrida zona polum .
Hooger:

142 en 14

Vera effigies et delineatio Insulae, Ascenscio nuncupatae...

Another image from Linschoten's important *Itinerario*, this view shows three profiles of the island of Asunción, or Ascension, a remote island in the middle of the Atlantic Ocean. The island was first sighted by the Portuguese in 1501, who populated it with goats for passing ships. It was also known for its abundance of fish and waterfowl, which are illustrated on this chart, as is a hungry seal. There is also an anchoring spot in the northwest of the island, which is shown in the top of the three profiles where several ships are passing.

The island is shown from different angles, as indicated by the two compass roses and the notes around the profiles, so that mariners could recognize it no matter what direction they come from. This sort of information was especially helpful to mariners, as Ascension was at the crossroads of the Atlantic for ships traveling between South America, the Caribbean, Africa, the Indies, and Europe.

There are three strapwork cartouches containing the title (left), a quote about geography (lower right corner), and a dedication (upper right corner). The latter is the most ornate, with birds, fruit, and jewels surrounding a coat of arms. These arms represent the lineage of Bernardus Paludanus, or Berent ten Broecke, a resident of Enkhuizen, Linschoten's home town. Paludanus was a doctor and natural philosopher who had collected many objects and books about the European voyages overseas. He wrote the parts of the *Itinerario* that had to do with Africa and America. The dedication on this view shows how grateful Linschoten was to his colleague for his help.

Chartmaker Biography

Jan Huygen van Linschoten (1562–1611) grew up in Enkhuizen, like Waghenaer. He traveled abroad and ended up in the company of João Vicente da Fonseca, Archbishop of Goa. He spent five years on the island, then was shipwrecked, and returned to Enkhuizen in 1592. He later sailed on two voyages to find the Northeast Passage and published several works, including the famous Itinerario, *a travel collection and geography.*

Caerte vande gehele voiage des Experiments vanden Regel des Gesichts des Grooten Zee-vaerts...

This chart, previously unrecorded, was intended to illustrate a possible solution to the longitude problem. It was engraved by Nicolas van Geilkercken and published in 1618. Although the calculation of latitude at sea was relatively straightforward, methods to find longitude either proved inaccurate or required more sophisticated astronomical measurements than were then in use. Most ships relied on dead reckoning: the calculation of location based on the estimation of speed and time from an initial, fixed position and, thereafter, from the ship's estimated position at sea day after day.

This chart shows a voyage intended to test a solution suggested by Jan Hendrick Jarichs van der Ley (1565–1639) in pursuit of a prize offered by the States General for a solution to this navigational issue. His solution was an improvement on dead reckoning by using trigonometric calculations. Whereas the use of trigonometry to calculate longitude may seem obvious to people today, in the early seventeenth century it was only just being applied to navigation. Jarichs was one of the earliest adopters in this sense.

Jarichs was also pioneering in the charts he used to show his method; he was one of the first to develop his own version of a stereographic projection, of which this chart is an example. Jarichs presented the States General with his innovative charts showing curved parallels, meridians, and loxodromes, perhaps a nod to Adriaen Veen's now-lost spherical charts. The curved chart, along with his improved calculations, was supposed to more accurately capture a ship's location.

An expert panel found Jarichs's method lacking, but a trial voyage was planned to the North Atlantic in 1618. The ship, the *Bruyn-Visch*, sailed north from the Netherlands to Scotland, Iceland, Greenland, and the Azores. Its track is shown on this chart. This chart was most likely prepared for the States General as part of Jarichs's continuing application for the prize, which he received in part when he was awarded an annuity.

Chartmaker Biography

Nicolaes Geilkerck, or Nicolas van Geilkercken (ca. 1585–1656), was a Dutch engraver. In addition to engraving, Nicolas was also a publisher, cartographer, and surveyor who lived in Amsterdam and Friesland (1614–1616), Leiden (1616–1628), and Arnhem. He engraved works for Joannes Janssonius, Joris van Silbergen, and others.

GROENLANDT.

DAVIS.

OCEANUS SEPTE

TRIONALIS.

Ingelis fiort

Lagenes

Bern fiort

Bredevic

YSLANDT.

S. Oosthoeck

Londrap

Hetmsfior

sui Zuyst Oosthoeck

Snellhoost

Westkant

Sorandt

Aqua

FRYS
LAND

S.W.Hoeck

FIN:
LANDT.

LAPLANDT.

Hoffoet

Higholant

Dronten

SWE-
DEN.

LYFLAND.

Hillandt

Anslow

Stockholm

Oesel

Riga

Gotlandt

Bergen

Vleckr.

Der Nues

PRUSSEN.

Dinant

S. Magni

DE
MERCK

Emden

Pomeren.

Mekelenburg.

Dar Vorno

Litnus

Catnes

Bokenes

Scot
landt.

Edenburg

Tinmuts

Texel

Amsterdam.

DUYTS-

NEDERLANT.

Middelburg

LANDT.

W

Dara

S. Gregori

IRLANDT

Nie Casti

Isul

Iarmuth
Londen

d'Mao

Antwpen

FRANCKRYCK.

Savona

Dover

Colis

Walesfoort

Bristi

Penbroeck

Plemuiten

Bristi

Roan

Garuth

C. Argo

Buly

Rechelle

C. Clara

Sorlings

Brest

Bordeaux

Baia

Brazil

I.Ussant

Baiona

Momplers

Corsica

Sardinia

OCEANUS OCCIDENTALIS.

Andero

S. Sebastian

Narbona

I. das Maidas

Ortgal

Rubadeos

Barcelona

Ortigal
Acarona

HISPA-

C. Finisterræ

Bajona

Toresa

Majorca et Menora

I. Verde.

Ho

Pora à port

Valencia

NIEN.

Avero

Cartagena

Portugal

MARE

Lixbona

Setubal

Almeria

Roxent

S. Lucas

Onne

Bagarca

Tercera

C. Vincent

Gibraltar

Floris

S. Michguel

De stract

Tangera

BARBARIEN

Ho

S. Gevigi

Faijael

ATLANTICUM.

43

INSVLÆ AMERICANÆ
IN OCEANO SEPTENTRIONALI,
cum Terris adiacentibus.

VIRGI-
NIA.

MAR

FLO RIDA.

NOVÆ HISPANIÆ PARS.

GORFO DE MEXICO.

CVBA.

ESPA

YUCATAN.

HONDVRAS.

NICARAGVA.

Ampl^{ma} Prud^{ma} Doct^{maq} Viro
D. ALBERTO CONRADI VANDER BVRCH,
I. C. Reip. Amsterdamensis Senatori, Collegii
Scabinorum Præsidi, Societatis Indicæ, quæ
ad Occidentem militat, aßeßori, et nuper
ad Magnum Moscoviæ Ducem Legato,
Tabulam hanc inscribit Guilielmus Blaeu.

MAR DEL ZVR.

CAR-TAGENA. S. MARTHA

Milliaria Germanica
Milliaria Hispanica.

44

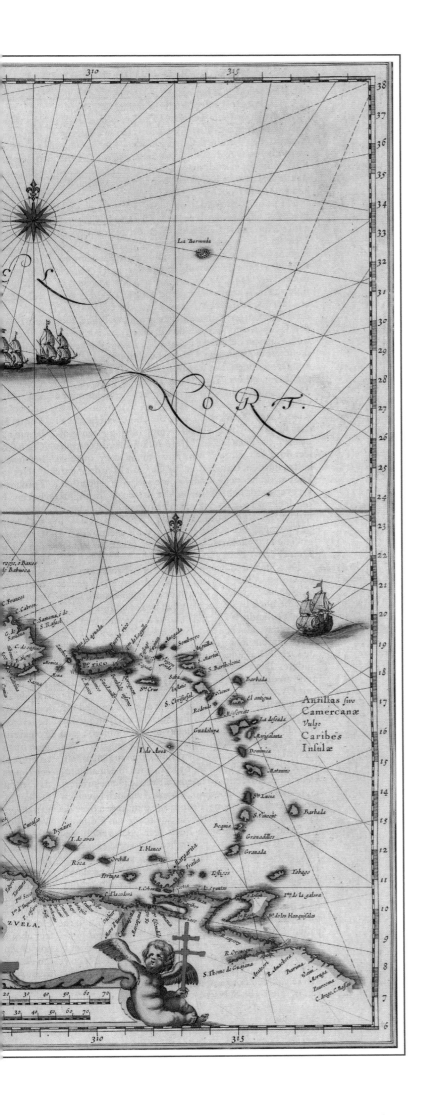

Insulae Americanae in Oceano Septentrionali cum Terris adiacentibus

This luxurious chart (Amsterdam, ca. 1635) in full original color is the work of one of the most-revered chartmakers of the Dutch Golden Age, Willem Blaeu. It is based on a section of Blaeu's famous *West Indische Paskaert* (ca. 1630) and Hessel Gerritsz' rare chart of 1631. The chart was considered excellent when produced and was used throughout the seventeenth century.

The chart covers practically the same area as the Gerritsz chart, but adds the west coast of Central America and the South Sea (*Mare del Zur*). A delicate scrolling script and rhumb lines fill the seas, as do five ships in full sail. The ships underline the region's importance to Europeans; it was a major center for trade and resources, and a site for enslaved and forced labor.

The cartouches underline the novelty of the region to Europeans. The title cartouche at the top is guarded by two putti. They hold aloft a long ribbon which serves as a tether for the seemingly exotic animals of the Americas: iguanas, snakes, bats, and turtles. In the lower left corner is another cartouche, this one holding a dedication to Albert Conrad van der Burch, an Amsterdam politician and military officer. It is flanked by a putti reading a book, and a woman—perhaps meant to represent America—with a snake and instrument. Two more putti adorn the scale bar in the lower right, holding a cross-staff and dividers, tools of the navigator's trade.

Chartmaker Biography

Willem Janszoon Blaeu *(1571–1638) was a prominent Dutch geographer and publisher. He studied with the famous Danish astronomer Tycho Brahe and then set up shop in Amsterdam, where he sold instruments and globes, published maps, and edited the works of intellectuals like Descartes and Hugo Grotius. In 1635, he released his atlas,* Theatrum Orbis Terrarum, sive, Atlas novus.

MAR DI ÆTHIOPIA Vulgo OCEANUS ÆTHIOPICUS.

OCEA

ÆT

PI

Circulus Æquinoctialis

Tropicus Capricorni

AMERICA

PERU

XARAYES

BRASILIA

Paraguaes
Pto de la Candellaria
Bascherepos

MERIDIO:

TUCUMAN

GUARANIS

Terra
dos
Patos

CHILIS

Rio de la plata

Straet van Magallanes

Jncet le Maire

de G. Brouwers passage

Terra
del fuego

C. Hoorn

TERRA AUSTRALIS

Mill. Germanica Communia.

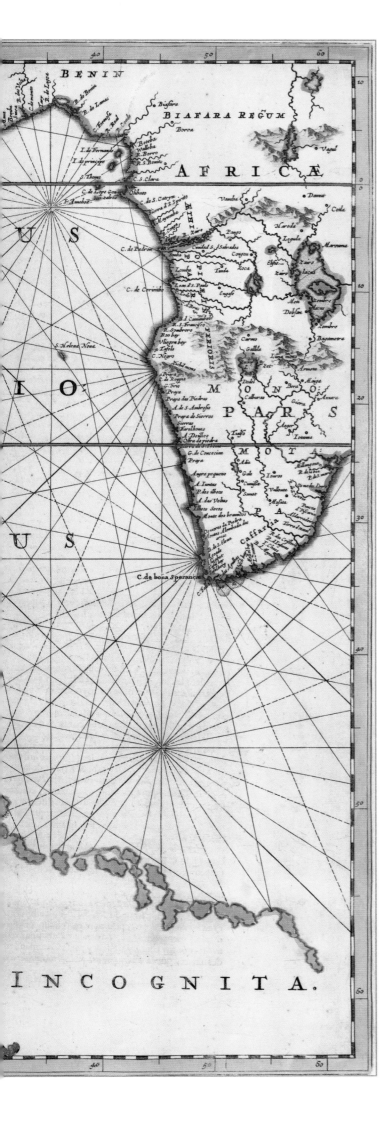

Mar Di Aethiopia Vulgo Oceanus Aethiopicus

Jansson's fine chart of the South Atlantic (Amsterdam, 1650) emphasizes the trade that flowed between Africa and South America in the early modern period. Practically the entirety of South America is shown, while sub-Saharan Africa is to the east. Both continents have lakes and rivers marked out, although European trade and colonization, especially in Africa, focused more on the coastal regions.

The cartouche in the upper left corner divulges what a large part of that trade consisted of: the traffic of enslaved peoples from Africa to the Americas. A turbaned man, most likely a reference to an Arab trader, is at the left, while a black man in a loincloth is to the right. Between them are more animals that would have been novel to Europeans, parrots and iguana-like lizards, a trope also seen in the Blaeu chart. Another embellished cartouche houses the scale bar in the lower left; this is surrounded by a clothed, white surveyor being helped, or perhaps hindered, by winged putti.

The most striking geographical feature on this chart is the large *Terra Australis Incognita* that fills the far south. To the east, the coastline is made up of a string of islands; to the west, the relationship between Tierra del Fuego and the southern continent is left undefined. The 1615–1617 circumnavigation by Dutch navigators Le Maire and Schouten had shown that Tierra del Fuego was an archipelago unconnected to a continent, but precisely what sort of landmass lay at the south pole, if any, was still a matter of debate amongst geographers.

Chartmaker Biography

*Born in Arnhem, **Jan Janssonius (also known as Johann or Jan Jansson or Janszoon)** (1588–1664) was the son of a bookseller and publisher. In 1612, Jan married the daughter of Jodocus Hondius, who was also a prominent mapmaker and seller. Jonssonius's first maps date from 1616. In the 1630s, Janssonius worked with his brother-in-law, Henricus Hondius. Their most successful venture was to reissue the Mercator-Hondius atlas.*

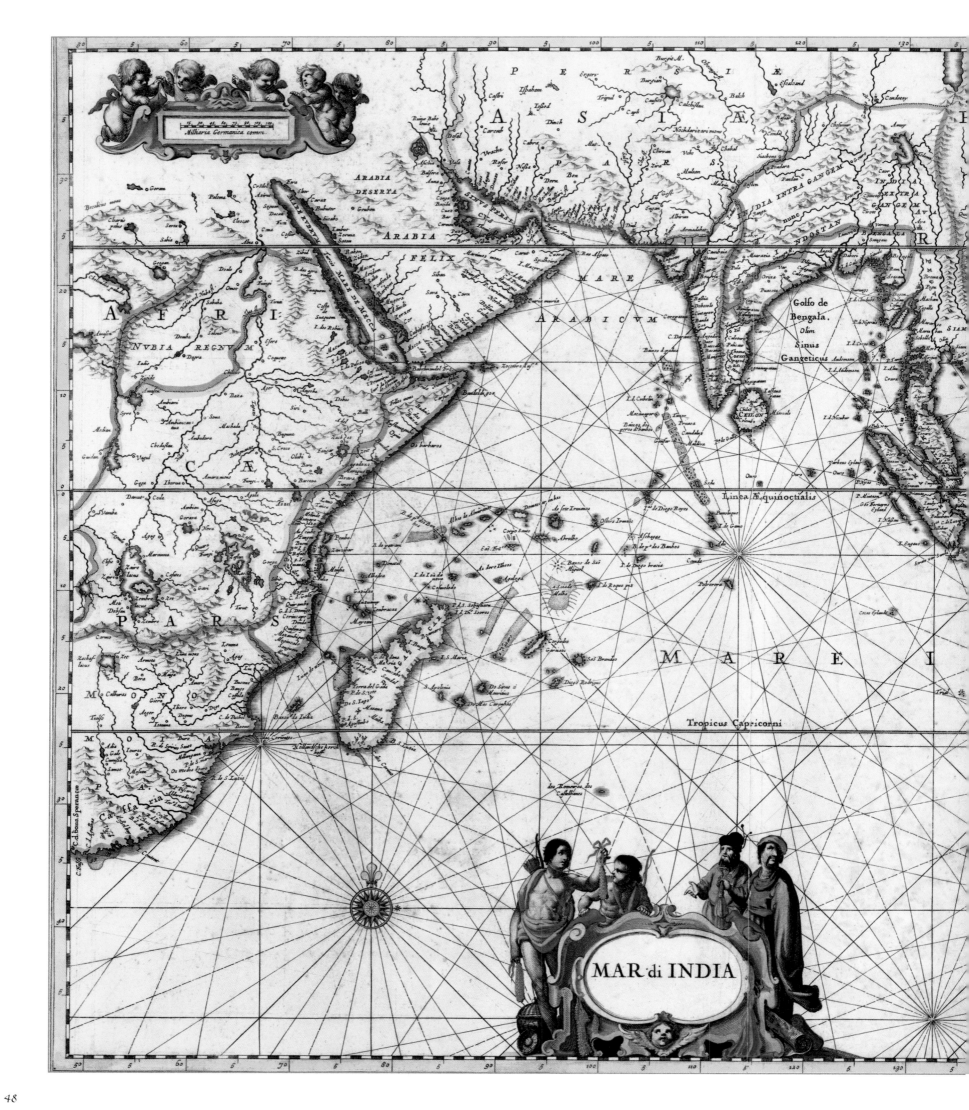

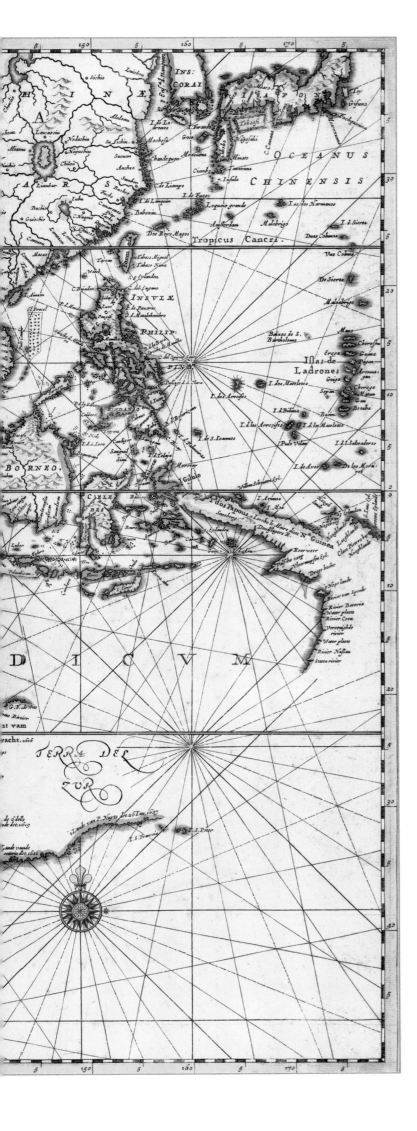

Mar di India

This chart, also by Jan Jansson and featured in his *Atlas Maritimus* of 1650, extends from Cape of Good Hope to a nascent outline of what is now Australia. From south to north, it stretches from the empty ocean at 50°south latitude to Japan and Korea. Japan is shown in a horizontal position, a typical representation of the islands during the seventeenth century. The title cartouche is framed by two indigenous peoples with bows and arrows (left) and two Asian traders (right). While the interiors of the landmasses are detailed, the emphasis of the chart is on the Indian Ocean itself, a seaway vital to the success of the European overseas empires, especially the Dutch.

Unfinished coastlines on the islands east of Java suggest the unknown lands still to be encountered by Europeans. New Guinea is a long thin island that extends into the eastern edge of the chart. It is very close to another coastline that we now know is the York Peninsula in Australia. Although Torres had sailed through the strait now named for him in 1606, the Spanish government suppressed news of the voyage. Interestingly, Abel Tasman's voyages to New Zealand and around the southern coast of Australia are also not included on this chart, although he had sailed nearly a decade before it was made. The VOC was still deciding the value of the geographic information they had gathered, and therefore did not share it widely until later in the century.

Janssonius includes a rough outline of Australia, or *Terre del Zur* as written here, chronicling the early Dutch voyages that tentatively sailed along the western coast of the continent. The information for portions of the coasts in New Guinea and northern Queensland, Australia, for example, come from the voyage of the Dutch vessel *Duyfken* in 1605-1606, the first recorded European contact with Australia.

Chartmaker Biography

*Born in Arnhem, **Jan Janssonius (also known as Johann or Jan Jansson or Janszoon)** (1588–1664) was the son of a bookseller and publisher. In 1612, Jan married the daughter of Jodocus Hondius, who was also a prominent mapmaker and seller. Jonssonius's first maps date from 1616. In the 1630s, Janssonius worked with his brother-in-law, Henricus Hondius. Their most successful venture was to reissue the Mercator-Hondius atlas.*

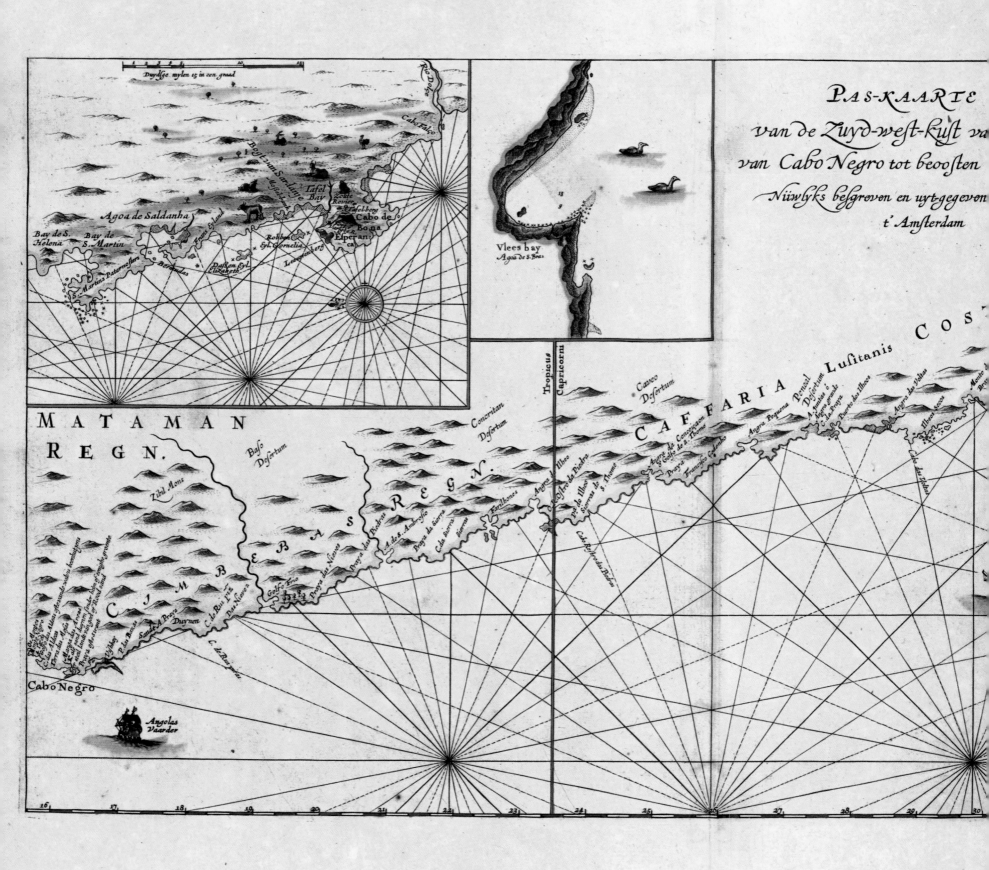

PAS-KAARTE
van de Zuyd-west-kust va
van Cabo Negro tot beoosten
Nüwlyks beschreven en uyt-gegeven
t'Amsterdam

Vlees bay
Agoa de S. Bras

COS

CAFFARIA   Lusitanis

MATAMAN
REGN.

Tropicus
Capricorni

Cabo Negro

Angolas
Vaarder

50

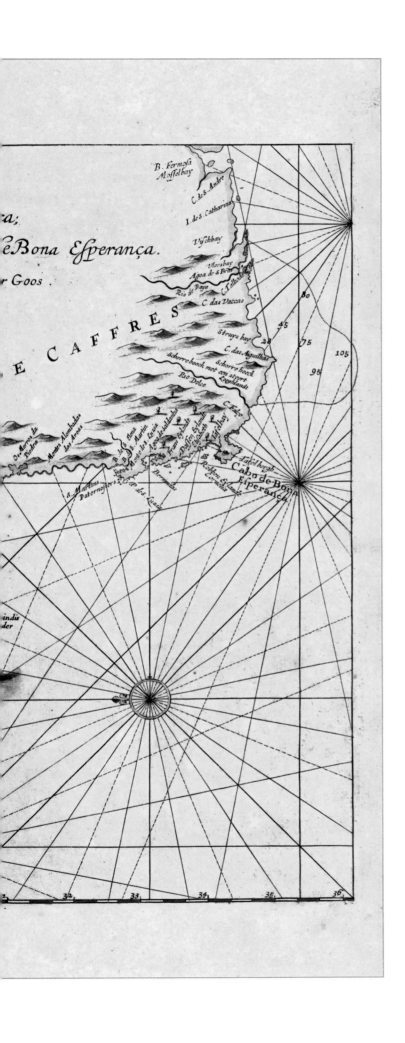

Pas-Kaarte van de Zuyd-west-kust van Africa...

Rather than a large overview of an entire sea or ocean, this chart zeroes in on a specific stretch of coast, Cape Negro to the Cape of Good Hope. There are also insets of the Cape of Good Hope with Table Mount and Vlees Bay. At sea, two ships sail by. One is labeled as a VOC ship, the other an English trader; the English were the Dutch's main rival for East Indies trade by 1660, when this chart was published in Amsterdam.

In 1652, a VOC expedition under Jan van Riebeeck established a Dutch colony at the Cape. It was to act as a supply point for ships on the East India route. Near Table Mount is the VOC fort, and on the coast is the settlement of Leeuwenberg. The land was already occupied, however, by the KhoiKhoi and San peoples, whose pastoral lifestyle was disrupted by the farming and construction of the Dutch settlers.

This chart was published by Pieter Goos in Amsterdam in 1660, but it was first released in 1652 by Jodocus Hondius in a pamphlet trumpeting the voyage of Van Riebeeck. Far from plagiarism, this reprinting of copper plates was common among chartmakers and mapmakers of the early modern period. Copper plates were expensive, thus engravers typically would reuse or correct existing plates, rather than start afresh. Publishers would often sell plates when in financial difficulties, and entire collections of plates could be auctioned when a chartmaker died or went out of business. Thus, the same chart often appeared with different publishers over time.

Chartmaker Biography

Pieter Goos (ca. 1616–1675) was a Dutch map and chart maker, whose father, Abraham Goos (approx. 1590–1643), had already published numerous globes, maps, and charts together with Jodocus Hondius and Johannes Janssonius. Known for his sea charts, in 1666 he published De Zee-Atlas ofte Water-Weereld, *which is considered one of the best sea atlases of its time.*

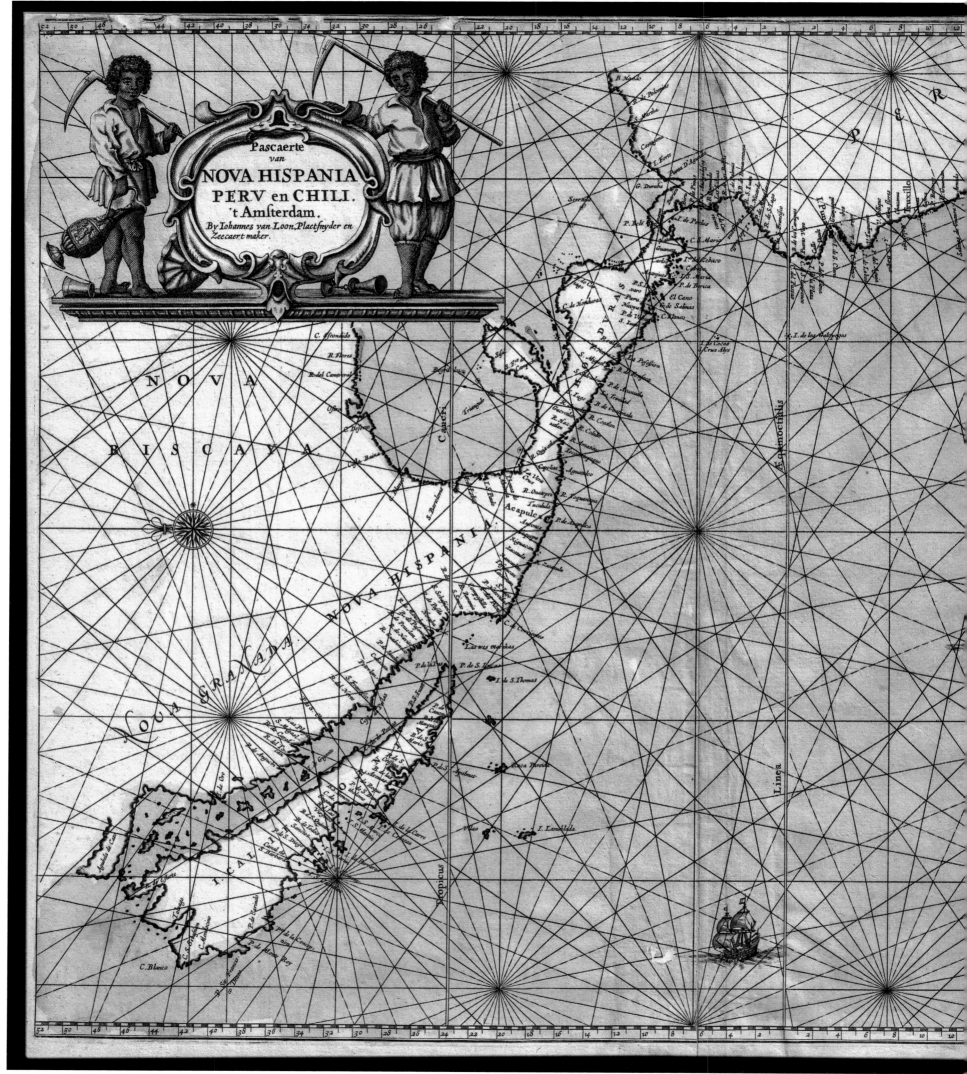

Pascaerte
van
NOVA HISPANIA
PERV en CHILI.
't Amsterdam,
By Iohannes van Loon, Plaetfnyder en
Zeecaert maker.

NOVA

BISCAYA.

NOVA GRANADA

NOVA HISPANIA

CHILI

Pascaerte van Nova Hispania Peru en Chili

This detailed chart (Amsterdam, ca. 1661) outlines the western coasts of North and South America, which were the epicenter of the cross-Pacific galleon trade in silver and commodities that enriched the Spanish empire. Silver mined in Potosi and other mines shipped to Acapulco and then across the Pacific to Manila, which was founded in 1571. From Manila, the silver would underwrite Spanish, and European, trading with China. Asian goods would then return on a northerly route to Acapulco, completing the circuit. This trade was made possible in 1565, when Urdaneta and Legazpi led the first west-east transit of the Pacific.

While the galleon trade is certainly the feature of most world-historical importance referenced in this chart, the most curious detail is the depiction of California as an island. From its first portrayal on a printed map by Diego Gutiérrez, in 1562, California was shown as part of North America by mapmakers, including Gerard Mercator and Abraham Ortelius. In the 1620s, however, it began to appear as an island in several sources.

This was most likely the result of a reading of the travel account of Sebastian Vizcaino, who had been sent north up the shore of California in 1602. A Carmelite friar who accompanied him later described the land as an island, a description first published in Juan Torquemada's *Monarquia Indiana* (1613) with the island details curtailed somewhat. The friar, Fray Antonio de la Ascensión, also wrote a *Relación breve* of his geographic ideas (around 1620). The ideas spread about Spain and, eventually, most likely via Dutch mariners and perhaps thanks to stolen charts, to the rest of Europe. By the 1620s, many mapmakers chose to depict the peninsula as an island. Even after Father Eusebio Kino published a map based on his travels refuting the claim (Paris, 1705), the island remained a fixture until the mid-eighteenth century.

Chartmaker Biography

Johannes van Loon *(ca. 1611–1686) worked as an engraver and chartmaker, but he was also a mathematician. He is known for his nautical atlas Klaer-Lichtende Noort-Ster ofte Zee Atlas of 1661, as well as for engraving for Andreas Cellarius, Jan Jansson, and others.*

Paskaerte van Nova Granada, en t'Eylandt California

This highly detailed map by Goos is one of the best illustrations of the island of California and one of only a couple of large-format maps to focus so minutely on the feature. It is also one of the first sea charts of the island. To the north is a large island with an open border to the west, perhaps denoting that it could be a continent. It is labeled as "*Terra Incognita*," with the Dutch equivalent, "*Onbekendt Landt*," below. Separating this unknown land from the North American mainland is the Strait of Anian.

Anian derives from Ania, a Chinese province on a large gulf mentioned in Marco Polo's travels (ch. 5, book 3). The gulf Polo described was actually the Gulf of Tonkin, but the province's description was transposed from Vietnam to the northwest coast of North America. The first map to do so was Giacomo Gastaldi's world map of 1562, followed by Zaltieri and Mercator. The Strait then became shorthand for a passage to China—i.e., a Northwest Passage. It appeared on maps until the mid-eighteenth century.

The map first appeared in 1666 in Goos's *De Zee Atlas ofte Water-Weereld* (Amsterdam). The *Zee Atlas* was re-issued in 1668, 1669, 1670, 1672, 1675, and 1676. It was also published in a French edition in 1679 and 1697, with an English edition in 1668 and a Spanish in 1669. The reissues and translations underline the popularity and utility of Goos's charts.

Chartmaker Biography

Pieter Goos (ca. 1616–1675) was a Dutch map and chart maker, whose father Abraham Goos (approx. 1590–1643) had already published numerous globes, maps, and charts together with Jodocus Hondius and Johannes Janssonius. Known for his sea charts, in 1666 he published De Zee-Atlas ofte Water-Weereld, *which is considered one of the best sea atlases of its time.*

TERRA INCOGNITA.

Onbekent Landt.

Straet Anian

Paskaerte
Van
NOVA GRANADA.
en t'Eylandt
CALIFORNIA.

t'AMSTERDAM
by Pieter Goos op't Waater inde
Vergulde Zeespiegel A.º 1666

Aguchila de Cato

C. Blanco

C. de S. Sebastian

C. de Mendocino

P. de los Reyes

P. de los Reys

P. S. Francisco

Drace

P. de Carinde

P. de la Conception

CALIFORNIA

Canal de S.
Barbara

P. de la Conception

P. de S. Diego

I. S. Cathalina

I. S. Clement

I. S. Martin

I. de Parraros

I. S. Aarco

I. de Ceintes

I. de la Cerros

B. de S. Quinin

B. de las
Virgines

C. de Engano

B. de S.
Francisco

C. de S.
Bartholom

B. de S.
Simon

C. de S.
Bartholom

Sierra Pintada

B. de las Armas

C. de S.
Christoval

P. de S. Diego

P. de Agtimes

B. de S. Martin

B. de la
Magdalena

P. de
Antigua

B. de Canoal

P. de la Paz

C. de S. Lucas

B. Barnabe

B. S. Iuan

NOVA GRANADA

I. de Oro

R. de Angustu

R. del Tecon

R. de Coral

Xignal

Las Playas

B. de S. Clara

I. de Gigante

Costa del trueno

Golfo de California

R. del Norte

S. Francisco

Patestan

Culiacan

R. Chalon

R. de los Ramalhas

R. de Cahuatemas

B. de los Pintados

Enerno de Mar

Laguna de Calderon

B. de S. Sebastian

Macoá

I. Baxax

Aacoá

S. Miguel

Piastla

B. de los
Catshores

B. de Culiacan

S. Sebastian

Yª de Macatlan

R. del Spiritu Santo

R. Bannia

Sierra de Xalisco

NOVA
GALICIA.

pª de Tentoque

L. del Pilota

Macatlan

pª Natividad

S. Iago

Colima

Malacca

R. Grande

Tuilapam

Las tres Marias

I. de S. Andrea

C. de Corrientes

I. de S. Thomas

Tropicus Cancri

La Vezina

Los Monges

La Desgraciada

Vllao

Roca Partida

Ilha Amblada

55

Paskaarte Vertonende alle de Zekusten van Europa

Harking back to the reference map of Europe with which this chapter began, this large and sumptuously decorative chart of Europe and the eastern Atlantic is by Van Keulen and Goos (Amsterdam, ca. 1680). It is a reissue of an original chart by Willem Blaeu (after 1621) and was a milestone in his career.

The chart captures the entire western coastline of Europe and the shores of much of the Mediterranean Sea. It also extends deep into the North Atlantic to feature Iceland, Greenland, Spitsbergen, and the Azores. The latter is important as the location of the Dutch prime meridian of longitude (before it was changed later in the century to 'Pico' in Tenerife, and then to Greenwich in the nineteenth century), and as an important marker for ships sailing to the West Indies and South America.

The chart is oriented with west at the top and assumes a portolan-style appearance. What embellishment the interior areas do have are elaborate national coats of arms, including those of Russia, Sweden, Denmark-Norway, the Holy Roman Empire, England, France, Spain, and the Ottoman Empire. Four scale cartouches adorn the corners, while a magnificent title cartouche, topped by the Blaeu family's symbol of an armillary sphere and with their motto *"Indefessus Agendo"* ("Act Steadily"), graces the lower-center of the chart. The seas are further embellished with sailing ships and seals, while on the land roam Inuit hunters, goats, bears and elephants.

In about 1650, Pieter Goos acquired the original Blaeu chart. He added his name to the central cartouche at the bottom of the chart, erasing Blaeu's in the process. In Greenland, Goos added another large cartouche, which covered the polar bears that were on Blaeu's original chart. The bears, here colored darkly, were then added to the scale cartouche nearby. Goos's edition was subsequently acquired by Johannes van Keulen, circa 1680. He reprinted the Goos plate, as seen in this example, with his own name inserted in the cartouche in the upper right.

Chartmaker Biography

Johannes van Keulen (1654–1715) was a maritime publisher who came to revive and dominate the Dutch sea atlas trade in the 1680s. He set up shop in 1678 and obtained a privilege for printing sea atlases and pilot guides in 1680. As many of his rivals were dying or selling their businesses, van Keulen was able to obtain many plates and build a large business. The van Keulen family continued to sell charts for two centuries.

OCCID ENTALIS

GROENLANDT

Gedruckt
t'AMSTERDAM
Bij
PIETER GOOS
Op't Water inde Vers
gulde zee-Spiegel.
Syn nu te Bekoomen
by Iohannes van Kuekren

YSLAND

YRLAND

SCOTLAND

ENGE L

SPAN

Portugal

Navarra

Valentia

VRANCRIJCK

NEDERLANDT

Duytschland

NOOR WEGEN

Mecklenborgh
Pomeren

Provence

DENEMARKEN

SWE DEN

Finmarcken

Lombardia

Pruyssen

Coerlandt

LAPLANDT

POLEN

LITTAVWEN

Oostvin
landt

SPITSBERGE

HVNGARIA

Lyflandt

Istria
Croatia

Dalmatia

RVS LANDT

PASKAARTE
Vertonende alle de Zekusten van
EVROPA.
Nieulyes aldus uytgegeven.
Door P. Goos.

No va Zem la

St.
80
79
78
77 St Thomas Smits bay
Blackhuyds Iste
76 Petalas sound
BAFFINS BAY Westerdelms sound
75 S.t Dudley Diges Cape
74 S.t Lennox Lancaster sound
73
72 Hier is varsche visch
71 Sande Romeo doode Walvis, witte Vos-
Eylanden sen en varsche Salm.
70 Steyr land Sandersons tower
C.S. Ioria Cumberlandes Bay Mount Raleigh FREVM DAVIS
69 C.r Bustene J A M E S 8 15 9
68 11 10
NEW NORTH C. Walsingam
67 WALES Corin fort
S.t Smits bay I S S E
66 Monck chese.
Duane Marys Cape Hooy bay
65 Nottlow C.t Cobert Milforts Bruns R. C.t Sabage Goode succes
C.S. Iosuer Summer R.
64 Schaft point Mill Ilss Quene Annes Iland of C. Comfort
Hope avanced C.t Bradrock C. Charles forland good
63 C. Philips BUTTONS FRETUM HUDSON fortuyn
62 C. Southampton I.t Salisbury Ifleg Resolution
Hope Check I.t Notfolc Holds with
61 C Briggs bay Nony fell Hand Diggas I. hoope
60 I.t Hacklyto
Pr. Nelson NOVA
59 Husdson Swanne hook.
58 Bay Schild plaete
BRITANNIA Cardinals hook.
57 New Wales In Hudsons bay, alwaer Hudson oservwinterl I.t Salep
Pr. Nelson heeft, loopt de zee niet boven drie voeten Slapen
56 op, gelyck dat D. Thomas Iacobus in t Iaer bay
1631 waer genomen heeft, t, Iames his Bay waer
55 NEW SOUTH de vloed, met hoogst de twee voetm op swol.
WALES Anthoni hoock of
54 Thomas Button oservwinterde in Pr. Nelson op Iosias his Hollandsche hook
de hooghte van 57 gr heeft in vyler 12 uuren bay bay Souvage Largo baeye
53 waergenomen de Zee vloed op te loopen 15 St Thomas Roo Ilt Grone blanche
voeten, of daer boven, t, hy oock met een Charleton Ite Cousin blanche
52 gewoonlycke Weste winst geven als met Dimby Ite NOVA FRANCIA I. de Brion
een Vollt maen dan meerlap swol. En de K. de Pere Master
51 volghende Zomer heeft hy oock, op de GOLFO Bell Iste
hooghte van 66 gr bevonden diergelycke DE B.S. Basile
50 Zee-vloeden, die haerlui na t Oosten en dan S. LAVRENS TERRA
na t Westen wende. NOVA
49 Lefdovrac
Schipemay B.t de Chaleu
48 I. Breton
NOVELLE BISQUAIE Le Grand R. de Canada I. R.
47
Je de Chile NOVA C.S. Lorenz
46 FRANCIA
20 40 60 80 100 130
45 Duytsche mylen 15 in een graet
20 40 60 80 100 130 140
Spaensche mylen 17½ in een graet
20 40 60 80 100 130 140 160 I. Inskeb L. de Sable
Eng en Fra. mylen 20 in een graet

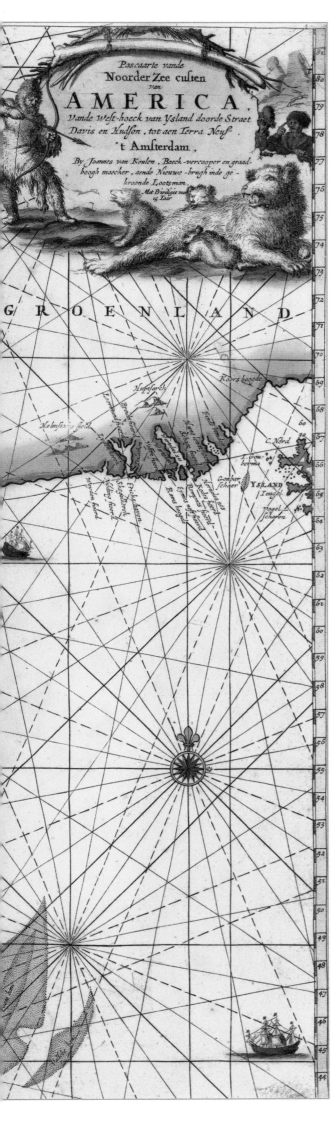

Pascaarte vande Noorder Zee custen van America...

This is a second state of Gerard van Keulen's chart of Hudson Bay and the Arctic. When copper plates needed to be corrected, rather than re-engrave the entire plate—which would be prohibitively expensive—most publishers would simply bang and rub out the incorrect information and re-engrave or add the correct details. In this case, the second state of the chart includes van Keulen's privilege information, saying that he had a monopoly on the printing of this item. The chart originally was published in Amsterdam in 1680, with this second state issued in 1681.

The chart emphasizes the search for the Northwest Passage, a geographic chimera that is still a hot topic today. This chart shows what was then known of Greenland, Hudson Bay, and Baffin Bay, with explanatory notes remarking on some famous voyages. These include the voyages of Henry Hudson, who went on four Arctic expeditions between 1607 and 1611; he disappeared on the final voyage, when some of his crew mutinied and set him adrift. Another voyage that is mentioned is that of Thomas Button, a Welshman who was tasked with finding Henry Hudson in 1612. He did not find Hudson, but he did push the boundaries of what Europeans knew of Northeast Canada.

The cartouche in the lower left corner is particularly interesting on this chart. The cartouche around the scale bar has indigenous Americans helping Europeans to load materials; this is a general cartouche that could be inserted on many charts. Indeed, here it is out of place, given the frigid geography of the area shown. The title cartouche is less anomalous, as it is Arctic in subject and would only be at home on charts of the Far North. It features a fur-clad hunter shooting at a polar bear and her cubs with a bow and arrow. Above the title is a hanging whale bone.

Chartmaker Biography

Gerard van Keulen (1678–1726) was the son of Johannes van Keulen, who founded the van Keulen cartographic dynasty. Gerard continued his father's work, producing new editions of their charts and creating new items as well. In 1706, Gerard was named hydrographer to the VOC.

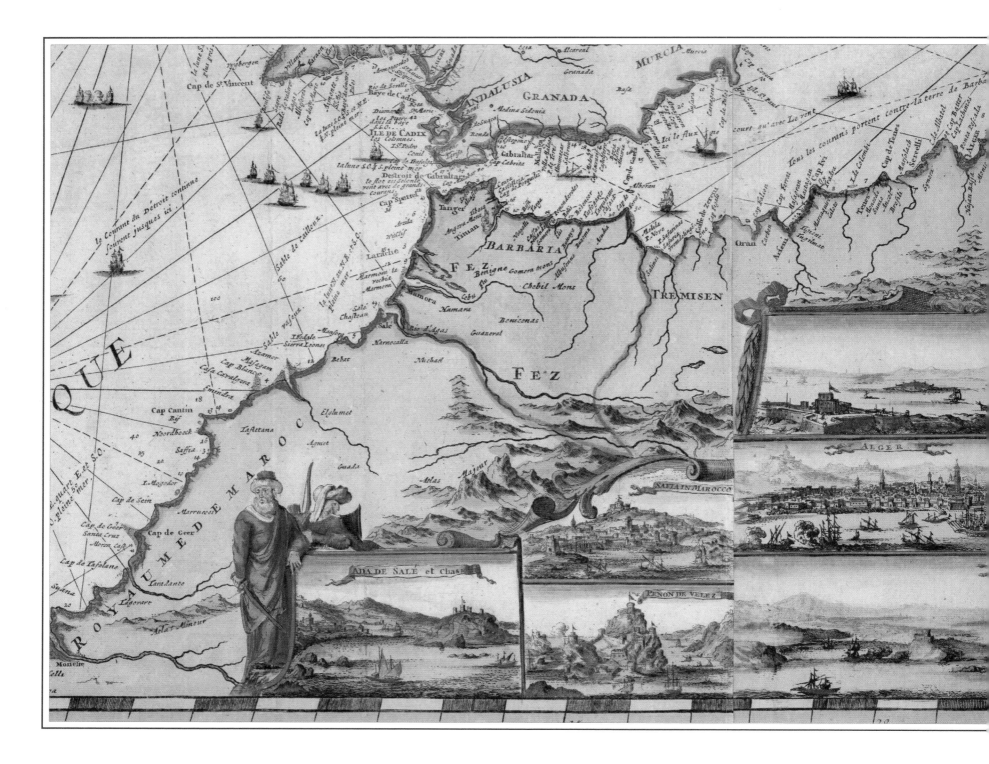

Carte Nouvelle De La Mer Méditerranée...

Chartmaker Biography

Pierre Mortier (1661–1711) obtained a privilege in 1690 to publish French geographers in the Low Countries. His wife and his son, Cornelis (1699–1783), continued the business. In 1721, Cornelis forged a partnership with Johannes Covens (1697–1774), who had recently married his sister. They published under the joint name of Covens & Mortier. The partnership was one of the largest and most successful publishing firms in Dutch history.

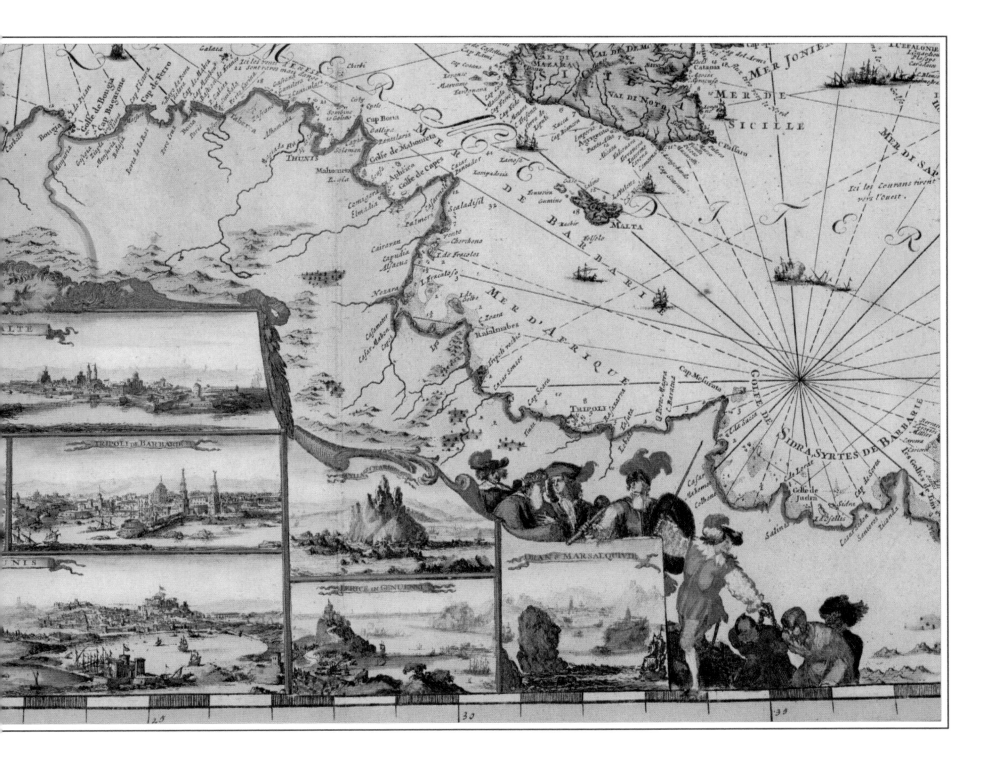

One of the most lavish charts to come out of Amsterdam in the seventeenth century, this chart was published as part of a select section of the Mortier atlas, the *Neptune François*, first published in Amsterdam in 1693. One of nine charts in the atlas engraved by Romeyn de Hooghe (1645–1708), a respected artist, the section in which it appeared was titled "*Cartes Marines a l'Usage des Armées du Roy de la Grande Bretagne*," or Marine Charts for the Use of the Armies of the King of Great Britain.

A massive chart, the work is three sheets joined together and nearly 56 inches across. It contains 38 insets, showing important ports and harbors around the Mediterranean. The sea itself is covered in rhumb lines and has sailing directions printed on many coasts. To the right (seen on pages 62–63) is an elaborate cartouche decorated in classical motifs bearing a dedication to De Wildt, a Dutch official.

Although the chart bears a dedication to another, the entire atlas was meant as a compliment to William III, recently crowned King of England. Pierre Mortier likely sought to curry favor with the monarch, who was Dutch in origin. The huge size and expensive artistry behind the charts, including this one, signal that this sea atlas was intended to impress on land, not navigate at sea. It was reprinted several times, with this fourth state of the chart bearing the imprint of Covens & Mortier.

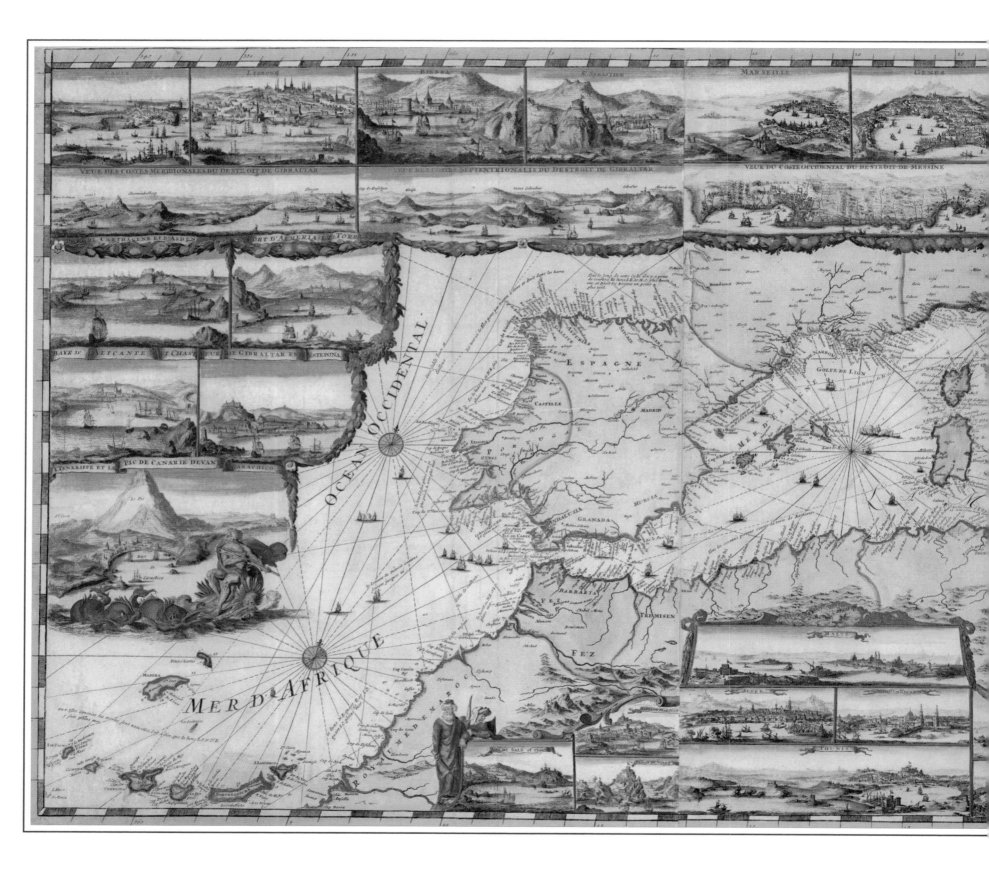

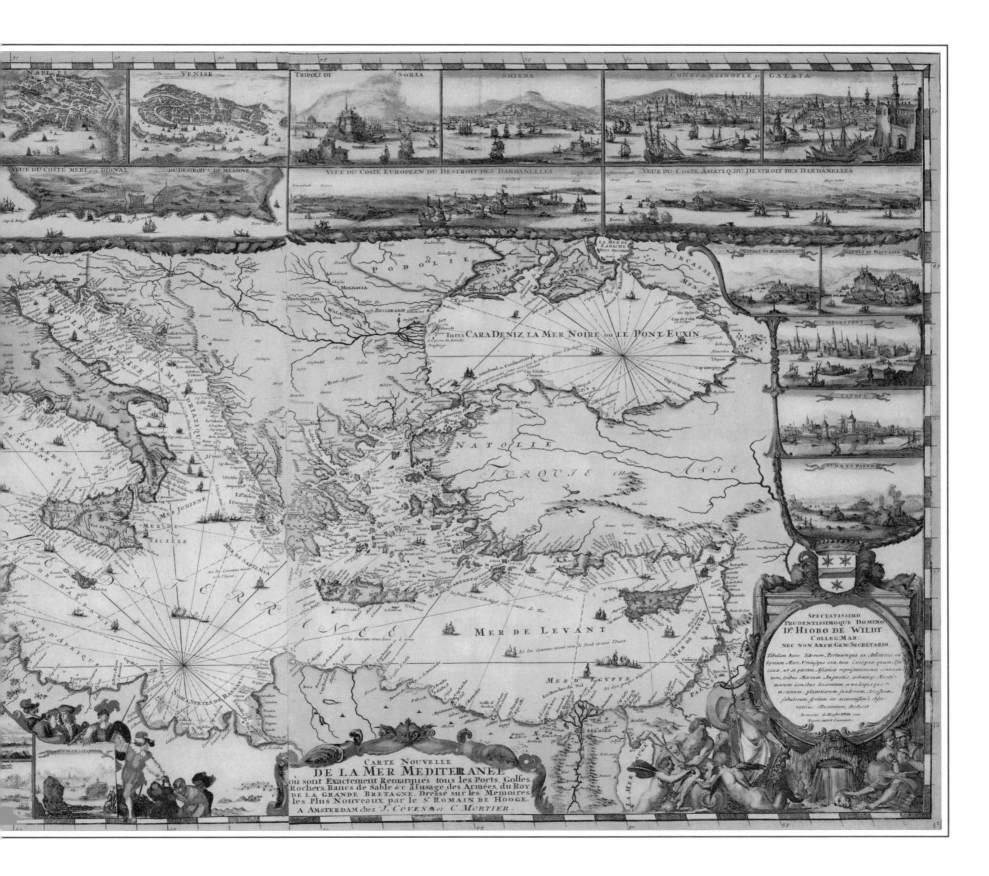

63

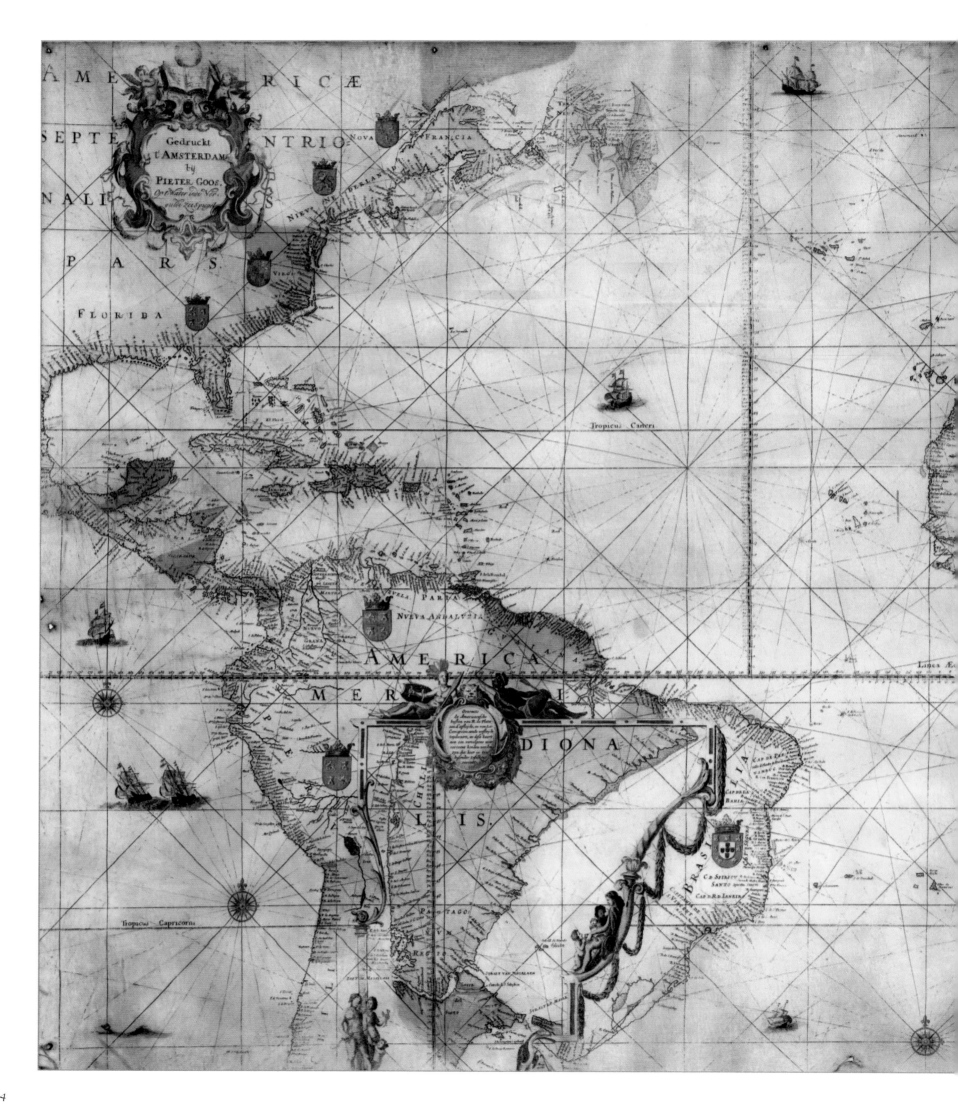

West Indische Paskaert...

One of the most iconic charts of the Dutch Golden Age, this is a ca. 1695 Loots reissue (Amsterdam) of Willem Blaeu's masterful chart of the Atlantic. Printed on durable vellum, it was the first sea chart relating to North America to use the Mercator projection. Although it covers a huge geographic area, it could be used to calculate bearing and distance along straight loxodromes. The geographic area is actually extended even farther, as Patagonia and Tierra del Fuego are ingeniously contained within an inset in Brazil.

Impressively, the chart was printed from a single plate, rather than several plates put together. This was highly unusual for the period and would have necessitated the construction of an entirely new press. The Blaeu workshop was known to have the largest printing presses in the world in the mid-seventeenth century. This chart was intended for voyages from Africa to the Americas, a trade regulated by the WIC, which Blaeu supplied with maps and charts.

The first state of the chart was issued ca. 1626–1630. The plate was then purchased by Jacob Robijn, most likely during the sale of the Blaeu stock in 1674; the Blaeu printing presses had burned in a terrible fire in 1672, and Willem's son and successor, Joan, died in 1673. Then the plate passed to Pieter Goos, whose imprint is still on this state. Around 1693, Johannes Loots acquired the plate and printed this state. This is an excellent example of the shuffling of valuable plates between publishers that was commonplace in the market at this time.

Chartmaker Biography

Johannes Loots (1665–1726) was a publisher of sea charts who was active from 1693 until his death in 1726. Loots began his career as an apprentice to Hendrick Doncker and later set up his own shop on Nieuwebrugsteeg, in Amsterdam, in 1693.

Oost Indien, Wassende-Graade Paskaart...

This impressive and detailed general chart covers a massive area, stretching from Africa to Australia and New Guinea. Published by the van Keulen firm ca. 1699, it broadly captures the VOC's main sphere of influence. This is the second edition of the chart, an updated version of Pieter Goos's sea chart of the same title, issued ca. 1658.

Goos's original chart was one of the first to incorporate the latest VOC encounters with western and southern Australia, including those of Abel Tasman. While Tasman's voyage was planned, most Dutch ships in Australia arrived there because they had been caught by the roaring forties, the harsh winds in farther southern latitudes, and blown onto the continent's western shore. In this updated edition, the west coast of Australia is further updated with soundings; such updates are important, as many ships had been lost to rocks and obstructions in coastal waters.

This chart also includes the 1696 de Vlamingh voyage, which was sent to western Australia to look for survivors of the *Ridderschap van Holland*, wrecked in 1694. They found no survivors, but added significantly to the geography of western Australia. Van Keulen was able to add such details to his chart so quickly because he was then hydrographer to the VOC.

Chartmaker Biography

Johannes van Keulen (1654–1715) was a maritime publisher who came to revive and dominate the Dutch sea-atlas trade in the 1680s. He set up shop in 1678 and obtained a privilege for printing sea atlases and pilot guides in 1680. As many of his rivals were dying or selling their businesses, van Keulen was able to obtain many plates and build a large business. The van Keulen family continued to sell charts for two centuries.

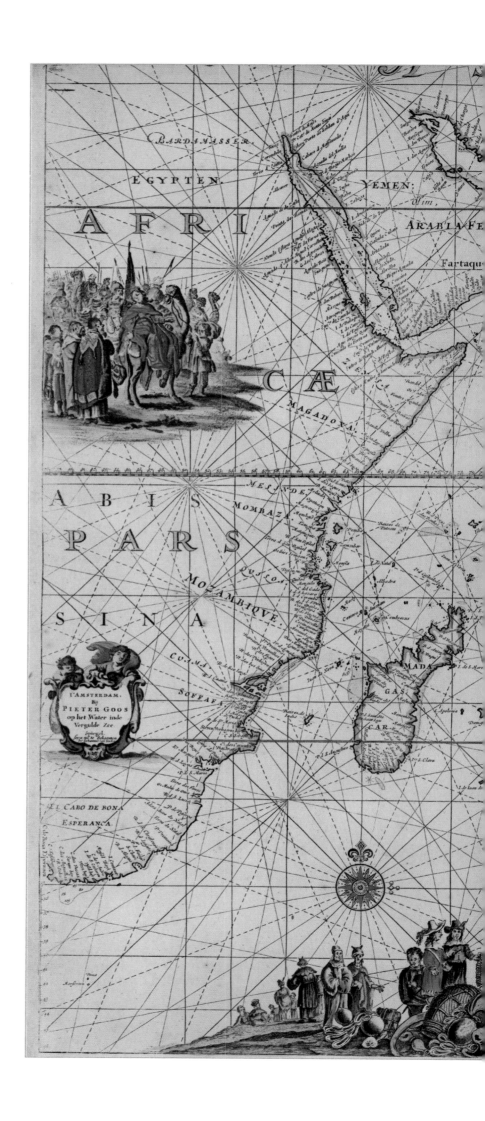

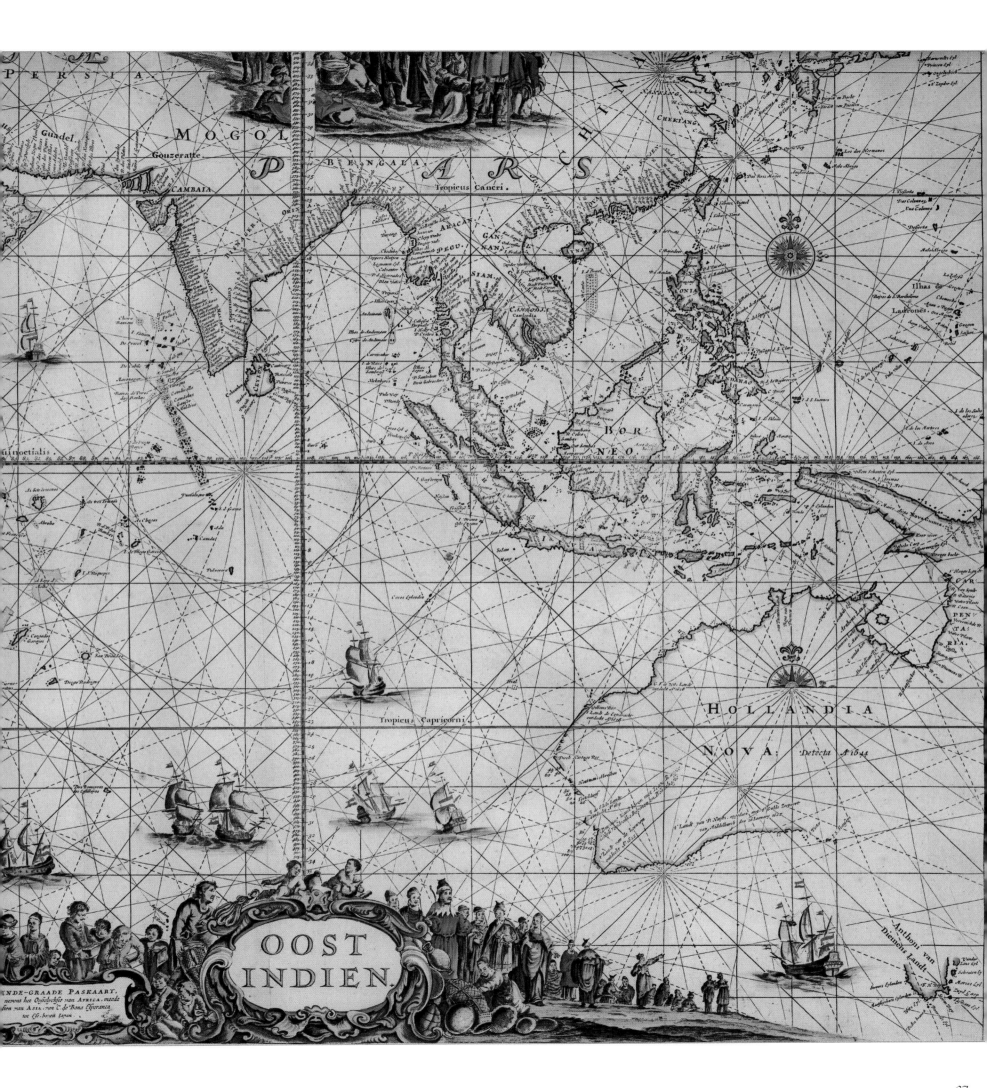

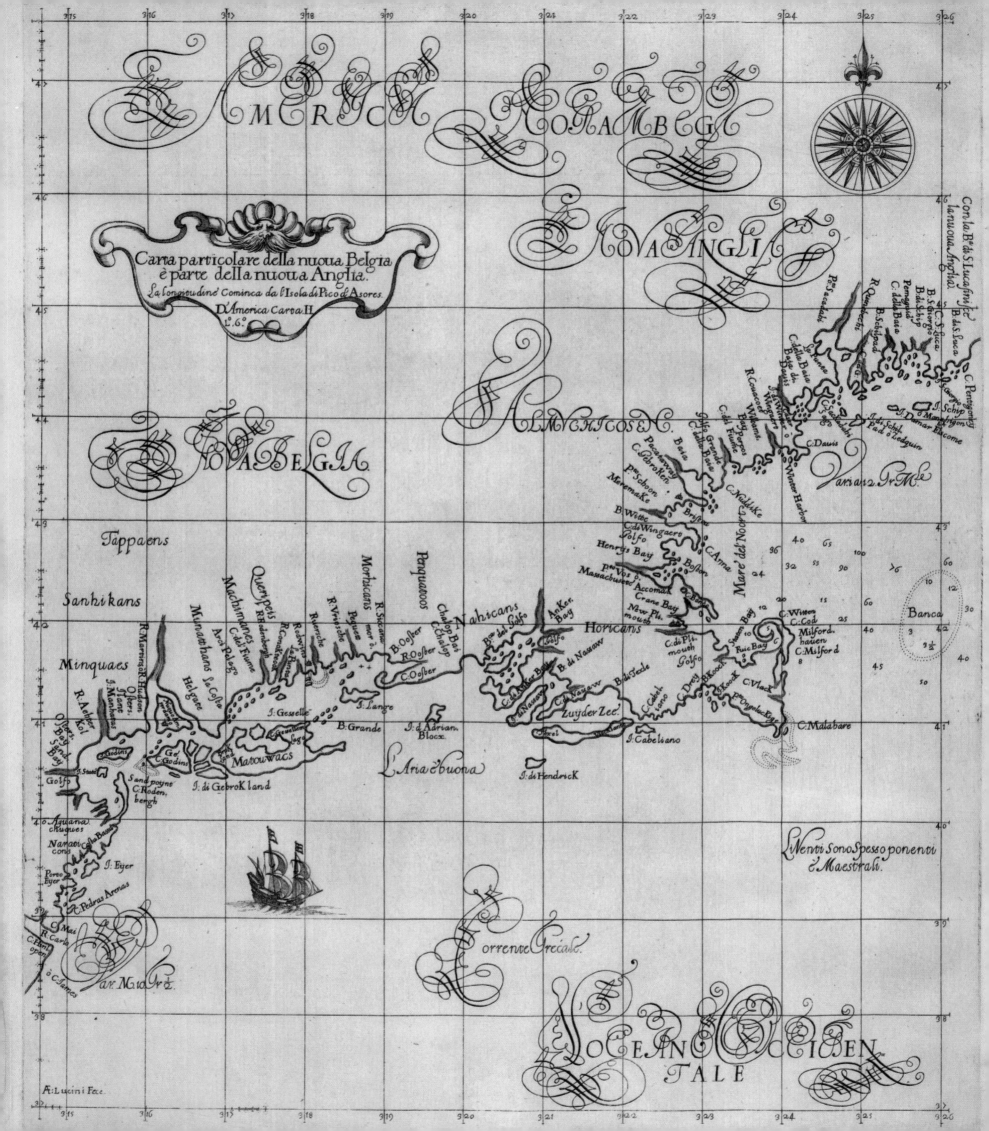

Carta particolare della nuova Belgia è parte della nuova Anglia

While Amsterdam and the Low Countries were undoubtedly the epicenter of chart publication and innovation in the seventeenth century, it was certainly not the only place to produce exciting and beautiful new charts. This is a second state (1661) of Robert Dudley's chart of New Netherlands and New England; the original (1646) was the first printed sea chart of the area. Dudley's sea atlas, *Arcano del Mare*, published in Florence, was the first sea atlas prepared by an Englishman and the first to use a Mercator projection.

Dudley's charts are easily recognizable due to their graceful, characteristic lettering. It loops and curves artistically around the chart's features. Other decorative components include a cartouche around the title that has a mustachioed man peeking out and a ship sailing serenely south of Long Island (*Matouwacs*). There is a large compass rose in the upper right corner and sounding depths near Cape Cod, both useful for navigation. Readers will recognize many place names, including New Amserdamo (New Amsterdam, or New York), Brok Land (Brooklyn), Milford, Cape Cod, and Boston.

The *Arcano del Mare* was the result of decades of compilation of notes on sailing and navigation. The title translates as "the secret of the sea," and it includes charts of the coasts of the then-known world. Dudley finished the manuscript in 1636 and published the work in 1646–1647, at age 73.

The chart was compiled and drawn by Dudley, but it was engraved by Anton Francesco Lucini (1610–ca. 1661). Lucini, a Florentine, did the engravings for Dudley's entire *Arcano del Mare*. The fine scrollwork and distinctive style of Dudley's charts are due to Lucini, who spent twelve years and 5,000 pounds of copper in making the 200 plates and 146 charts.

Chartmaker Biography

Robert Dudley (1574–1649) was the illegitimate son of the Earl of Leicester, a favorite of Queen Elizabeth I. In 1603, Dudley entered into a court battle to establish his legitimacy, but the Star Chamber ruled against him, forcing him into self-exile in Florence. There, he served Ferdinand I, Grand Duke of Tuscany, as a ship designer and chartmaker.

The Proliferation and Rationalization of Charts in the Eighteenth Century

*I*n the Medieval period, charts, like all written works, were the purview of the elite. Only rulers, scholars, and some clergy and officials could access the written word, including the language and symbolism of cartography. Navigators who used portolan charts might only be able to read the names of the ports that clustered along the inside shoreline. In the sixteenth and seventeenth centuries, those that could access charts expanded slightly to include much of the merchant class, including the masters of many ships. A hallmark of the Dutch Golden Age was the high degree of literacy among the middling sort, the burghers of the Low Countries' cities and towns who prized maps and charts as symbols of their upwardly mobile and worldly existence.

In the eighteenth century, the subject of this chapter, map conscious-ness, a term used to describe both the ability to read maps and to under-stand their symbolic power and quotidian utility, expanded greatly relative to previous periods. While literacy was still only available to a portion of the population, the middle classes across Europe could not only read, but also could for the first time afford maps and charts. Accordingly, the number of cartographic objects exploded. Maps appeared in newspapers and books in growing numbers, while people could purchase sheet maps and charts; pocket maps, atlases, and globes, map games and toys, as well as larger atlases, globes, and instruments at a variety of price points.

Coincident with the growth in map consciousness and consumption was the expansion of European empires. Britain expanded its hold over India and eastern North America, while Britain, France, and Spain vied for supremacy in the middle of that continent. Spain extended their presence south and to the interior of South America, while they also built up their colony in the Philippines. The Portuguese penetrated ever deeper into Brazil, even as they lost influence in the East Indies, where the Dutch still held sway in competition with other European trading companies. Toeholds on the African coast foretold further European interference in the nineteenth century. Additionally, Russia stretched toward the Northern Pacific, while several powers kept an eye on the Arctic and a possible passage to China.

In contrast to formal imperial presence, European empires also marked out their influence via exploration. The eighteenth century was the century of Pacific voyages of encounter, when the Spanish, French, Russians, and especially the British planned large state-sponsored expeditions to find, record, and survey new islands, seas, and, hopefully, continents. Expeditions also probed the far reaches of northeast North America and the coasts of southern Patagonia. The Indian Ocean was *crossed by hundreds of ships a year en route to Middle Eastern, Indian, and East Asian ports. Geographic knowledge was a goal and an output of exploration, and all these shores were charted with greater frequency and in more detail than ever before.*

Whereas the Dutch had been the undisputed leaders of both chart production and design in the seventeenth century, the eighteenth century witnessed a maturity in chartmaking skill across Europe. Nevertheless, there were still hubs of production and sale, particularly Paris and London, as well as Amsterdam. In the former, state-recognized and supported savants worked under the title of geographe du roi. *They tended to draw their own maps and charts, which were sent to specialized engravers and then printed under the name of the* geographe *who had designed them. As in Amsterdam and most of Europe, certain families tended to carry on the tradition of cartography for several generations, often intermarrying and combining collections of plates and map stores.*

In London, production was slightly different. Chart and mapmakers tended to be engravers in their own right. Their geography was self-taught, and the state had a decidedly hands-off approach to the production of cartographic objects, although military officers, officials, and bureaucrats were some of the most frequent customers of map and chart printers and sellers. Whereas natural philosophers, what we would now call men of science, were certainly interested in geography, few made their own maps. Unlike in France, where geographers were recognized experts, cartography tended to be treated as an artisan skill, albeit one with a mathematical and technical component, with few chart and mapmakers included in the ranks of the Royal Society, Britain's premier scientific body.

The eighteenth century was also the century of the Enlightenment, an intellectual and cultural movement focused on the application of rational thought to all aspects of human existence, including cartography and hydrography. As cosmopolitan networks shared ideas and material culture, charts took on an ever more uniform appearance with standardized symbols and a pared-down, less-ornate style. As navigational instruments improved, charts also became more inclusive and precise with information such as latitude and longitude coordinates, wind direction, tidal flows, and sounding depths. In the same vein, charts were now firmly accepted as an indelible tool of the skilled navigator; a master or captain would not leave on a voyage without a variety of charts, while commanders, directors, and merchants alike were often depicted in portraits poring over detailed charts, which were a symbol of profit, knowledge, and power.

Carte Particuliere d'une Partie d'Asie ou sont les Isles...

This chart also appeared in the *Neptune François*, a sea atlas first mentioned in the previous chapter. Originally published in France in 1693 by Alexis Hubert-Jaillot (ca. 1632-1712), *geographe du roi*, the initial atlas showed the coastlines of Europe from Norway to Gibraltar. The project had been at the behest of Jean Colbert, who ordered that astronomers and mathematicians from the state scientific body, the *Académie Royale des Sciences*, work with French naval hydrographers to draft an atlas of western Europe's shores. In the same year as Jaillot's edition appeared in Paris, Mortier used his privilege, or monopoly, on publishing French charts in the Low Countries to release a newly engraved edition of the work—he could not acquire the original plates from Jaillot.

This chart appeared in an expanded section of the *Neptune François*. Published in Amsterdam, this third part of the work, *Suite du Neptune François, ou Atlas Nouveau des Cartes Marines*, contained charts prepared for the king of Portugal.

The two-sheet chart extends from Saudi Arabia and the Horn of Africa in the west to the Straits of Malacca, with the focus centered on the busy Indian Ocean. Each portion of the chart, east and west, contains a simple title in an oval (west) or octagonal (east) cartouche. Together, the two sheets highlight the major trading islands and entrepots which were then the gateways for European traders to Asian goods. It also shows areas under Ottoman control, highlighting the disputes that often erupted over trade rights and access and which were underwritten by religious difference.

Chartmaker Biography

Pierre Mortier (1661–1711) obtained a privilege in 1690 to publish French geographers in the Low Countries. His wife and his son, Cornelis (1699–1783), continued the business. In 1721, Cornelis forged a partnership with Johannes Covens (1697–1774), who had recently married his sister. They published under the joint name of Covens & Mortier. The partnership was one of the largest and most successful publishing firms in Dutch history.

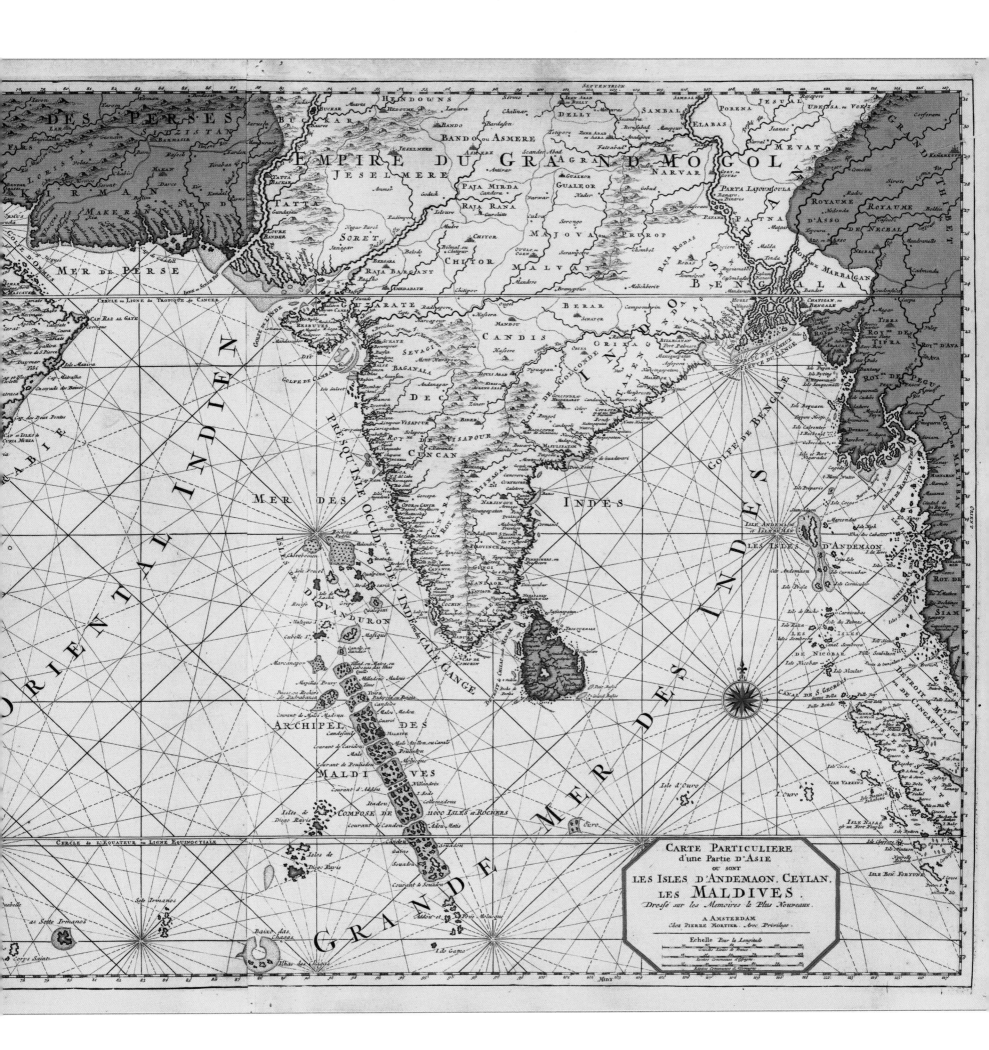

CARTE PARTICULIERE
d'une Partie D'ASIE
OU SONT
LES ISLES D'ANDEMAON, CEYLAN,
LES MALDIVES,
Dressé sur les Memoires le Plus Nouveaux.
A AMSTERDAM
Chez PIERRE MORTIER, Avec Privilege.

73

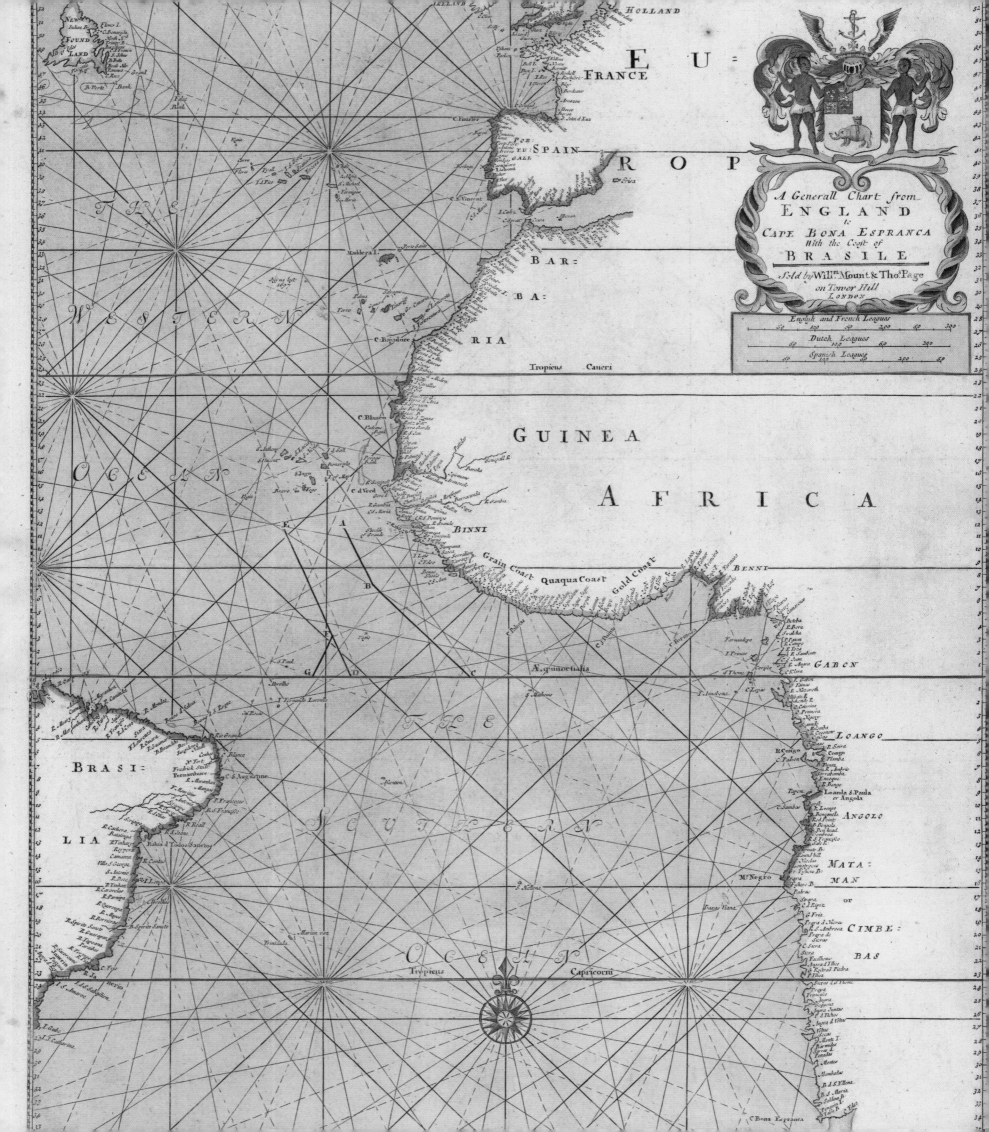

A Generall Chart from England to Cape Bona Espranca With the Coast of Brasile

This chart would have been useful for voyages between West Africa and Brazil, the coasts of which are pictured, or for depicting a portion of the voyage between the Atlantic and Indian Oceans. The transatlantic trade in enslaved Africans is referenced by the two black men in the decorative cartouche in the upper right corner.

Off of Western Africa are two roughly parallel lines labeled with the letters A through G. These show the *Karrepad* or *Wagenweg*, a Dutch term that translates to "wagon way." The lines indicate a corridor through the Doldrums, an area near the equator where weather patterns often cause large areas of hot temperatures with little wind. The system originated on Dutch charts and was sometimes included on charts from other countries, as seen here.

The chart was included in the third book of the *English Pilot*. The *English Pilot* was originally a project hatched by John Seller (1632–1697). Seller knew that English sailors would prefer English charts, but to date they had been dependent on the superior products of the Dutch geographers. Seller released the first volume of the *Pilot* in 1671. Shortly thereafter, he was granted a royal privilege that protected his work against the import of foreign waggoners for thirty years. Ironically, this English project with an English privilege was actually the result of the reissuing of altered Dutch plates.

Seller fell into financial difficulties, as did many chartmakers embarking on large projects. William Fisher and John Thornton acquired the plates and released a third volume. Fisher's apprentice, William Mount, took over after Fisher died and worked with Thornton and, after Thornton's death, with his apprentice-turned-partner, Thomas Page. Mount and Page republished editions of the *English Pilot* throughout the eighteenth century; this chart dates to ca. 1703.

Chartmaker Biography

*The partnership of **Mount & Page** dominated sea-atlas publishing in Britain throughout the eighteenth century, thanks in large part to the* English Pilot. *William Fisher (1631–1692) partnered with his former apprentice and son-in-law William Mount (1654–1722). After Fisher's death, Mount turned to his own son-in-law and apprentice Thomas Page (d. 1733); their descendants continued the partnership.*

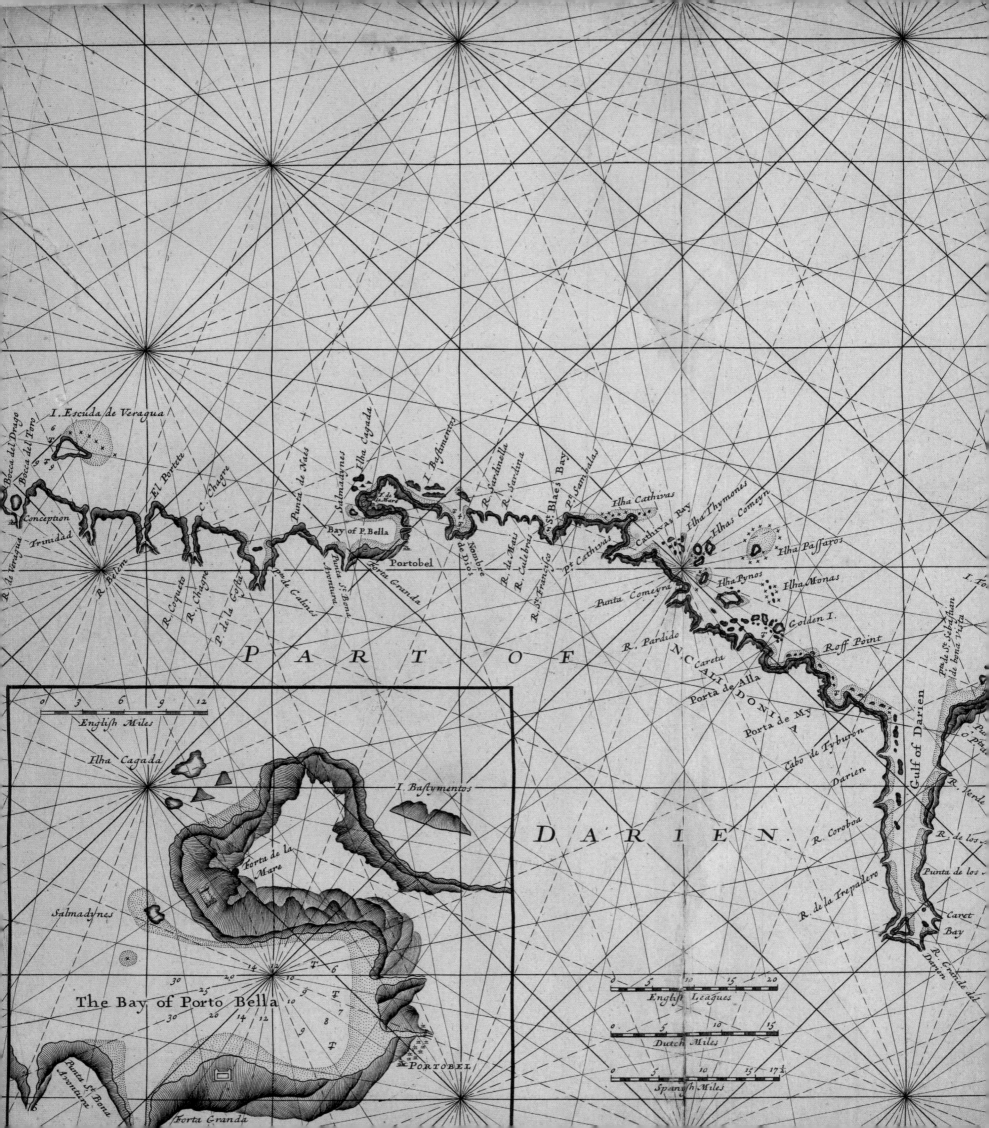

I. Escuda de Veragua

Bocca del Drago
Bocca del Toro

Conception
Trinidad

R. de Veragua
R. Belem

El Porbete
C. Chagre
R. Coqueto
R. Chagre
P. de la Gorda
P. de Calines

Punta de Naes
Punta S. Bona
Aventura

Salmadynes
Ilha Cagada
I. de la Mare

Bay of P. Bella
Portobel
Porta Granda

Nombre de Dios

I. Bastmentos

R. Jardinello
R. Jardina
R. de Mai
R. Culebra
R. St. Francisco

St. Blaes Bay
P. Sambalas
Pt. Cathivas

Ilha Cathivas
Cathivas Bay

Ilha Thymones
Ilhas Comeyn

Ilha Passaros

Punta Comeyra
Ilha Pynos
Ilha Monas

Golden I.

R. Pardido
Careta
Porta de Alla

Caret
Porta de My

Roff Point

Cabo de Tyburon
Darien

Pta de St. Sebastian
de bona vista

Gulf of Darien

PART OF

NCALIDONIA

DARIEN.

R. Coroboa

R. de los

Punta de los

R. de la Trepadero

Caret
Bay

R. Crebado del
Darien

Inset map

0   3   6   9   12
English Miles

Ilha Cagada

I. Bastymentos

Porta de la
Mare

Salmadynes

The Bay of Porto Bella

30   25   20   14   10   T   6
          10   9   T
30   20   14   12   10   8   7
                     9   T

PORTOBEL

Porta Granda

Punta S. Bona
Aventura

0   5   10   15   20
English Leagues

0   5   10   15
Dutch Miles

0   5   10   15   17½
Spanish Miles

A Chart of the Coast of America. From Cartagena to Bocca del Drago

Interestingly, this chart was also published in an edition of the *English Pilot*, this one published by Jeremiah Seller and Charles Price in London in 1703. After Jeremiah's father, John Seller, fell on hard times and could not finish the *Pilot*, he turned to other mapmakers for financial support. This resulted in a dispersal of his plates and charts; most went to Fisher and Mount, but some fell into the hands of his son, Jeremiah, when Seller died in 1697.

Seller and Charles Price, Jeremiah's partner in chart and instrument making, issued a further volume of the *Pilot* focused on the coasts of Africa in 1701. They also reissued some of John Seller's charts, including this one. It shows the eastern coastline of Panama and the coast of Colombia, extending to Cartagena. There is good detail of rocks, shoals, islands, and anchorages off the shore. Rivers, bays, points, and ports are named all along the coast.

This chart was published in London during a particularly pitched period of interest in the area, due to the activities of pirates and colonizers. As just one example, a large inset shows the bay of Portobello, protected by two forts: *Forta de la Mare* and *Forta Granda*. William Parker captured the city in 1601; the (in)famous pirate/privateer Captain Henry Morgan did so again in 1668; and John Coxon did so yet again in 1680. Later in the eighteenth century, the port would serve as the site of large naval sieges, but at this time it was better known as a buccaneer target.

Chartmaker Biography

Charles Price (1679?–1733) was apprenticed to John Seller, Jeremiah's father. Jeremiah and Charles were made free of the Merchant Taylors Guild on the same day, September 1, 1703. The two were already in partnership by then. After breaking with Seller, Price worked with other mapmakers. He was still working in the 1720s, but was in Fleet Prison in 1731 for debt and died in 1733.

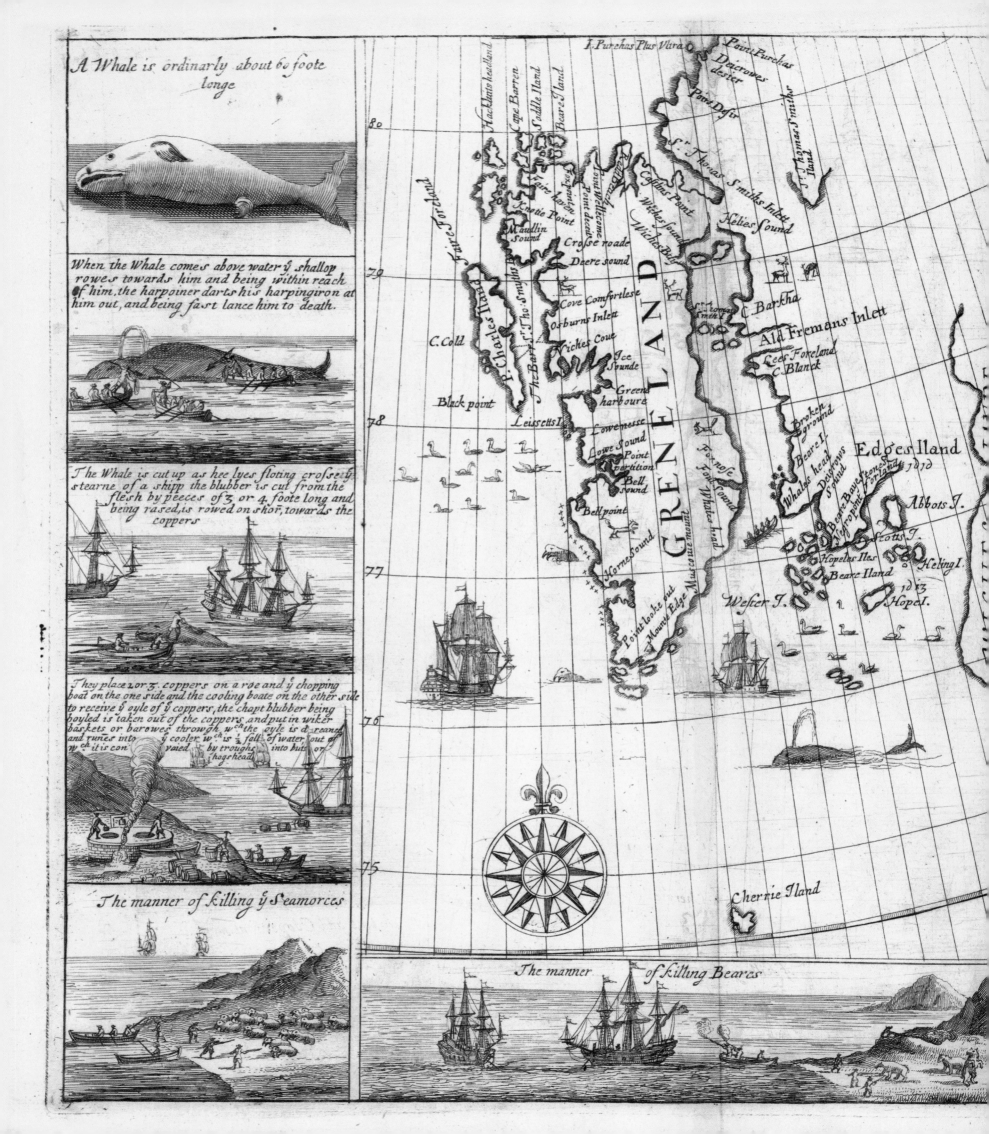

A Whale is ordinarly about 60 foote longe

When the Whale comes above water ẙ shallop rowes towards him and being within reach of him, the harpoiner darts his harpingiron at him out, and being fast lance him to death.

The Whale is cut up as hee lyes floting crosse ẙ stearne of a shipp the blubber is cut from the flesh by peeces of 3 or 4 foote long and being rased, is rowed on shor, towards the coppers

They place 2 or 3 coppers on a roe and ẙ chopping boate on the one side and the cooling boate on the other side to receive ẙ oyle of ẙ coppers, the chapt blubber being hoyled is taken out of the coppers, and put in wiker baskets or barowes through wᶜʰ the oyle is dreaned and runes into ẙ cooler wᶜʰ is ½ full of water, out of wᶜʰ it is conuoied by troughs into buts or hogsheads

The manner of killing ẙ Seamorces

I. Purchas Plus Vltra
Point Purchas
Deicrowes de iter
Point Defir
Sᵗ Thomas Smithes
Sᵗ Thomas Smiths Inlett
Sᵗ Thomas Smiths Iland
Hacklants headland
Cape Barren
Saddle Iland
Beare Iland
Foxnoese
Fowle Isle
Costlins Point
Withers Sound
Withes Bay
Point deceit
Loud Wellecome
Fair harbor
Helies Sound
Sᵗ Thomas Smith
C. Barkha
Ald Fremans Inlett
Lees Foreland
C. Blanck
Knotie Point
Maullin Sound
Crosse roade
Deere sound
Cove Comfortlese
Osburns Inlet
Nickes Coue
Ice Sounde
Greene harboure
Lowenesse
Lowe Sound
Point Pertition
Bell sound
Bellpoint
Broken ground
Beare I.
Whales head
Fox noese
Fox Sound
Whales head
Deicrows Sound
Edges Iland 1616
Beare Bay
Negro point
Abbots I.
Stones Forland
Scotts I.
Hopeles Iles
Beare Iland
Heling I.
Hornesound
Whales mount
Wester I.
Hopel. 1613
C. Cold
P. Charles Iland
The Brase Sᵗ Tho: Smiths
Black point
Leissetts I.
Point looke out
Mounts Edge Muscoue mount
GRENELAND

Cherrie Iland

The manner of killing Beares

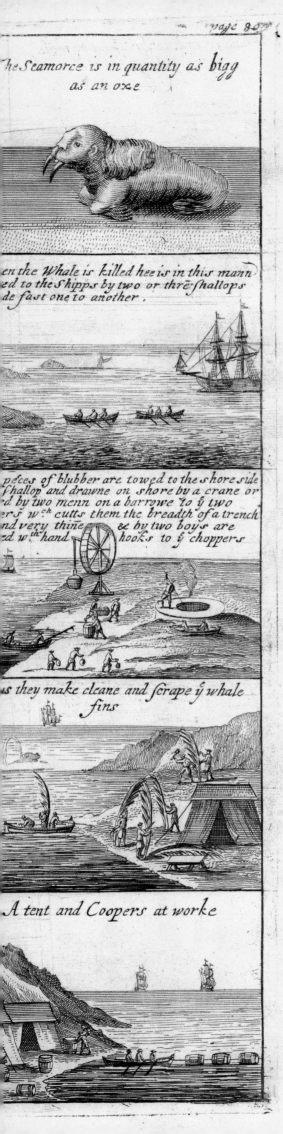

Page 80

The Seamorce is in quantity as bigg as an oxe

en the Whale is killed hee is in this mann ed to the shipps by two or three shallops de fast one to another.

peces of blubber are towed to the shore side shallop and drawne on shore by a crane or d by two menn on a barrowe to ý two ers wᶜʰ cutts them the breadth of a trench nd very thinne & by two boys are d wᵗʰ hand hooks to ý choppers

as they make cleane and scrape ý whale fins

A tent and Coopers at worke

[The Svalbard Archipelago]

Although the large island at the center of this chart is labeled "Greneland," it actually depicts Spitsbergen and the Svalbard archipelago, north of Norway. English sailors in the seventeenth century called the landmass Greenland, which was also the name for the world's largest island, due west from Svalbard. This chart shows just how far north the islands are, as the lines of longitude are very close together.

The island is replete with pictures of foxes and reindeer, but the main animal of interest to Europeans in the seventeenth and eighteenth centuries was the whale. Eleven images surround the chart, depicting how to recognize, hunt, and process whales. They were sought for their oil, a by-product of their fatty blubber. Two of the eleven images also show how to hunt the "seamorce," or walrus, which is typically "as bigg as an oxe." The long image under the chart also discusses hunting polar bears, underlining how important the island's wildlife was to the European economy.

This chart and flanking images were originally published as part of Samuel Purchas's famous travel collection, *Purchas his Pilgrimes* (London, 1625). It was then republished in the travel collection of the Churchill brothers, published in London in 1704. The illustrations derive from the voyages of the Muscovy Company in the early seventeenth century. While working for the Muscovy Company in 1607 and 1608, Henry Hudson reported numerous whales around Spitsbergen. Other voyages in the following years confirmed this finding, and whalers from around Europe were soon seeking the giants of the sea in the archipelago.

Chartmaker Biography

The Churchill brothers, Awnsham (1658–1728) and John (ca. 1663–ca. 1714), were publishers in London who catered to an affluent clientele, and they were from a prominent family of politicians themselves. In 1704, they released A Collection of Voyages and Travels, *but they are perhaps best known as the publisher of John Locke. Locke is supposed to have written the introductory discourse of the voyage collection.*

[Straits of Magellan/Patagonia]

This chart shows the important Straits of Magellan, as charted by John Narborough in 1669 to 1671. An inset of Patagonia and Tierra del Fuego is fitted into the interior of South America, while the Straits are shown in detail. Notes about the coasts and surrounding terrain are included along the Straits, as are profile views of the mountains and hills, sounding depths, and magnetic variation compass roses at either end of the Straits.

Narborough's chart was one of the first detailed charts of the Straits to be published. Prior to the eighteenth century, only tens of ships had even tried to pass through the Straits. This is partially because the Straits were part of the trade monopoly of the Dutch East India Company; only Company ships were supposed to traverse the Straits, although their imperial rivals, the Spanish, never recognized this monopoly. Narborough was sent on a mission to establish trade with indigenous peoples and settlers in Patagonia in 1669. He made it through the Straits and to Valdivia, Chile, where four of his men were seized, his guide abandoned ship, and he was forced to return through the Straits to England.

The chart was first printed in 1673 by John Thornton, who helped Narborough to improve his manuscript charts, which contained many illustrations and more textual notes. It was modified and reduced to be included in the first publication of Narborough's journal, part of a voyage collection published by the Fellows of the Royal Society in 1694. This second state of the map, dedicated to the Earl of Oxford, was in the second edition of the voyage collection, published in 1711.

Chartmaker Biography

Sir John Narborough (1637–1688) entered the Royal Navy as a midshipman and served during the war with the Dutch in 1664. In 1669, he led the first state-sponsored expedition by the English into the South Seas. He was made Rear Admiral and knighted in 1673, and was appointed as a Commissioner of the Admiralty in 1680, a post he held until his death in 1688.

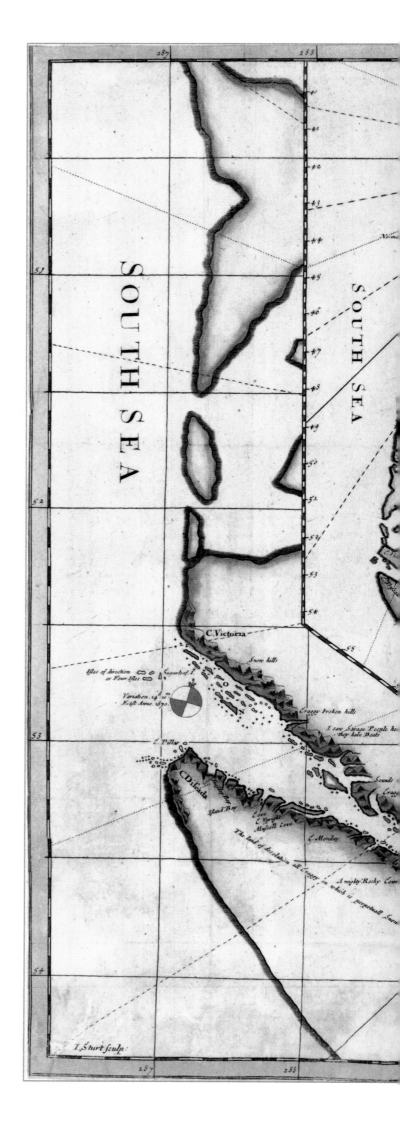

A large chart of part of the coast of Guzaratt & India from Diu head to Bombay

This chart, a second state published ca. 1716 by Mount & Page, shows the Gujarat coast of India and the vicinity of what is today Mumbai and which was then known as Bombay. The shoreline is shown from roughly Somnath and Diu to Vadodara, and south to Mumbai, which is shown on one of the three islands off the main coast. There is a tiny British flag near Mumbai; the city had passed into British hands in 1661, and this is one of the first charts or maps to show this political shift.

Bombay had long been a Portuguese possession; they had arrived in the 1530s and had successfully fought off Dutch and English attempts to unseat them from the wealthy entrepot. In 1661, however, the islands of Bombay were transferred to England as part of the dowry of Catherine of Braganza, who was marrying England's King Charles I. In practice, the Portuguese stayed in possession of some islands, while the English holdings were leased to the English East India Company.

This chart was one of the first to show the area in detail and was used for over a century. It was issued as part of John Seller's *Atlas Maritimus*, first published in 1675, but was most likely drawn by Samuel Thornton in ca. 1703. Samuel's father, John, had acquired many of Seller's plates after Seller had encountered financial problems. This was a composite atlas, wherein buyers could specify which charts they wanted to be included. It was only in 1768, when William Nicholson was commissioned to survey the harbour and adjacent coastline, that the chart was superseded.

Chartmaker Biography

Samuel Thornton (ca. 1665–1712) was the son of the prominent chartmaker John Thornton, who was known for his manuscripts and printed works. Samuel inherited his father's successful business in 1708. After Samuel's death only four years after his father's, his stock passed to the firm of Mount & Page, who continued to reprint his chart stock.

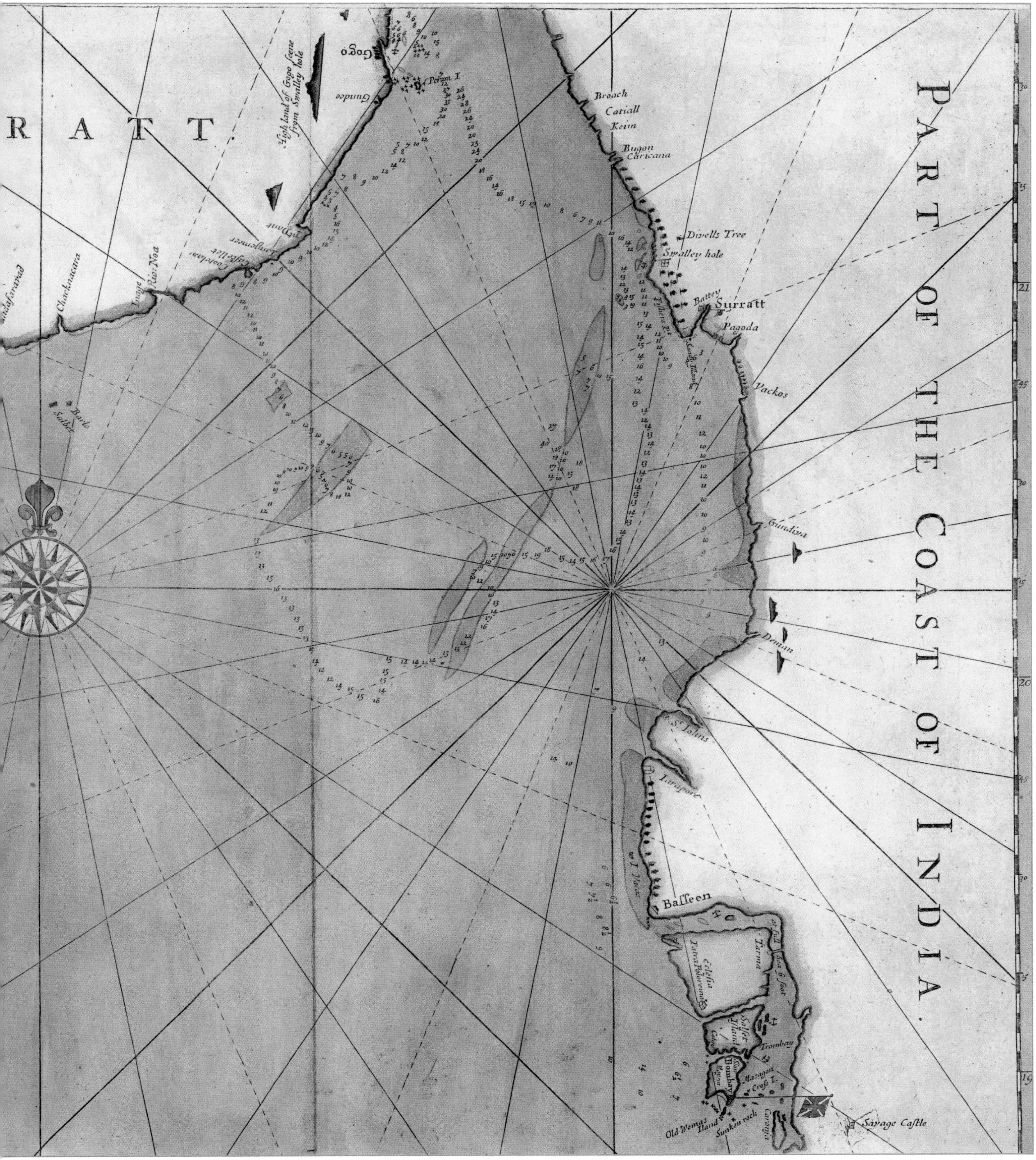

RATT

Gogo

Gundee

Peram I

Broach
Catiall
Keim
Bugon
Curicana

Divells Tree
Swalley hole

Battey
Surratt
Pagoda

Vackos

Gundiva

Dentan

St Johns

Lirapore

Baſſeen

Tarma
Elefta
Trtrot Palorimolty

Salfet
Iland
Caloe
Trombay

Bombay
Mazon

Mazgon
Cros I.

Old Womas
Iland
Sunken rock

Carania

Savage Caſtle

High land of Gogo ſeene
from Swalley hole

Chackmatara

Inuel

Riu: Noa

Lookran

Dant

Loneſpinter

Coſte Ilet

Bark

Saltier

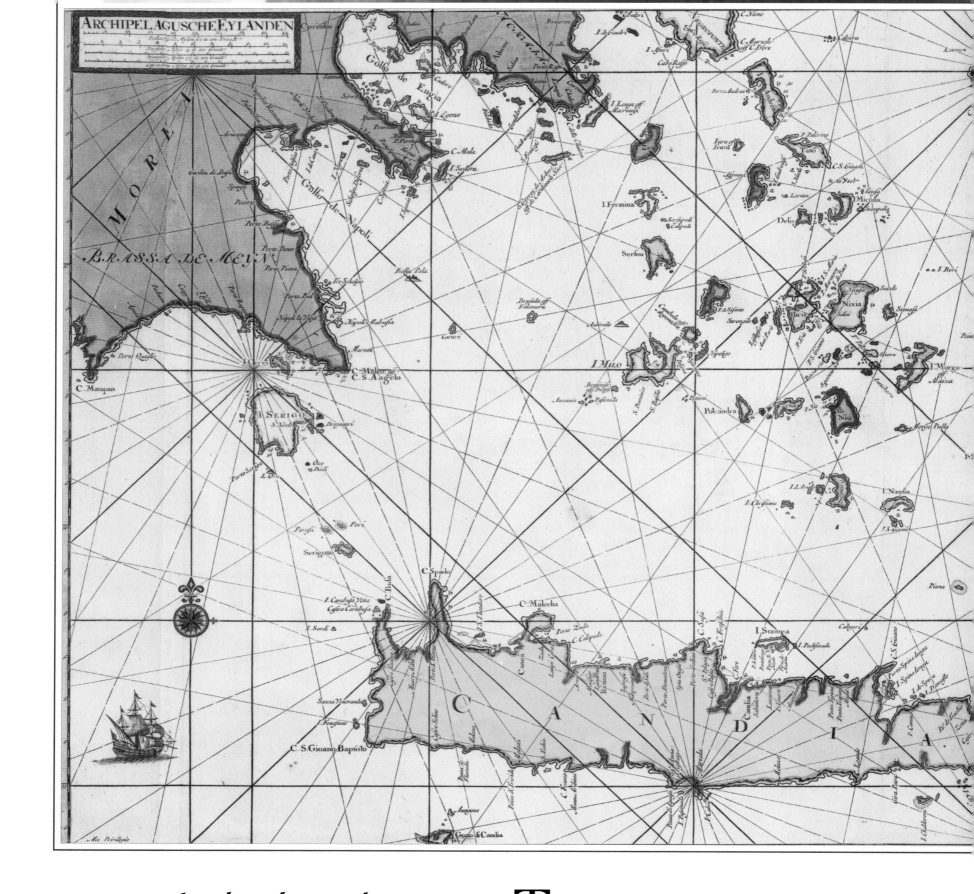

Archipelagusche Eylanden

Chartmaker Biography

Gerard van Keulen *(1678–1726) was the son of Johannes van Keulen, who founded the van Keulen cartographic dynasty. Gerard continued his father's work, producing new editions of their charts and creating new items as well. In 1706, Gerard was named hydrographer to the VOC.*

This highly detailed chart shows the majority of the Aegean Sea, from Morea to the southwestern coastline of Turkey. It extends from Izmir, Bodrum, and Marmaris east to Athens, the Gulf of Egino, and the Gulf of Napoli di Malvasia (Monemvasia), Porto Kagio, and the island of Kithira in the west, with Crete, or Candia, to the south. Other islands shown include Rhodes, Ios, Mikonos, Andros, Tinos, Kea, Kithnos, Siros, Samos, Ikaria, Keros, Kalimnos, Kos, and Mandraki. An inset of Rhodes is integrated into the cartouche.

The cartouche is quite decorative with an Asian man and a European man

eyeing each other over the title. This area is a crossroads of culture and goods, which is referenced by the cartouche. In the lower right corner, the theme of trade and East meeting West is repeated, with a European man bartering over a rug with other transactions and a ship being loaded in the background.

Published in Amsterdam ca. 1717 by Gerard van Keulen, this two-sheet chart was one of the first Dutch charts of the Aegean Sea and is one of two charts to carry this name by the van Keulens. It had first been published by his father, Johannes, in the 1680s, but was reissued well into the eighteenth century.

As has been seen with several of the charts in this chapter, many maps and charts had long afterlives, with some staying in issue and relevance for a century. Maps and charts rely on detailed surveys that are expensive to perform and prepare, meaning that many areas were not systematically or repeatedly surveyed until the state-run surveys that were common from the late-eighteenth century onward. Thus, the eighteenth century is a crossroads of cartographic styles and information, much as the Aegean Sea was a crossroads of commerce and culture.

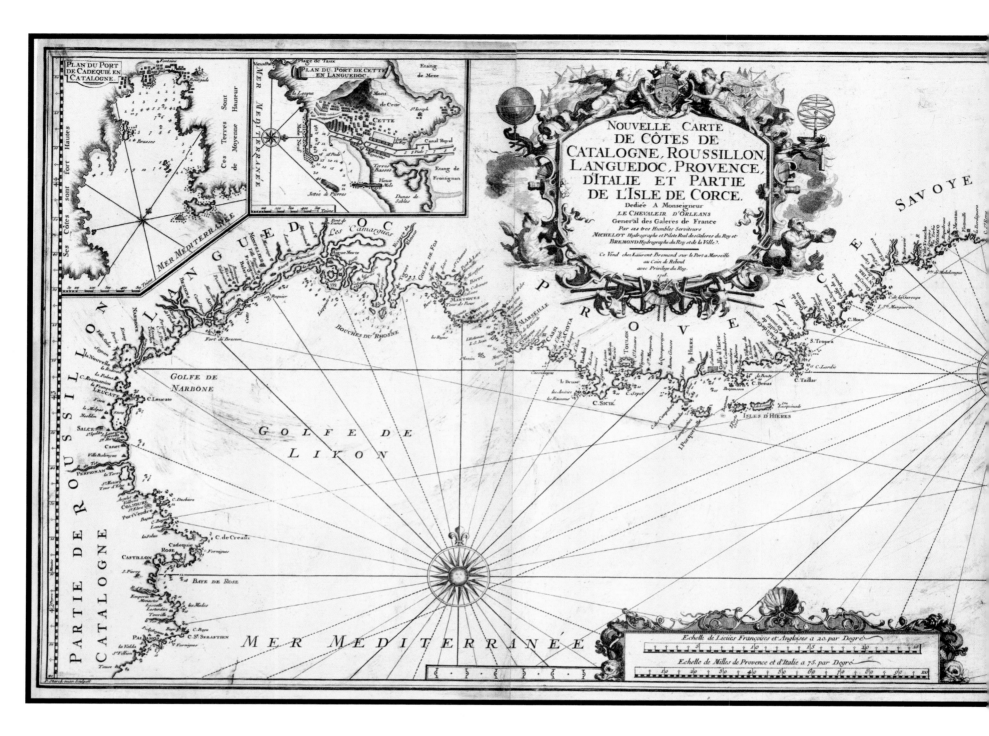

Nouvelle Carte De Côtes De Catalogne, Roussillon, Languedoc, Provence, D'Italie...

Chartmaker Biography

Henri Michelot and ***Laurent Bremond*** *were chart sellers active in the early eighteenth century. They also published a book of port views and profiles,*
Recueil de plusieurs plans des ports et rades de la Mer Mediterranée, *first published in Marseilles in 1727.*

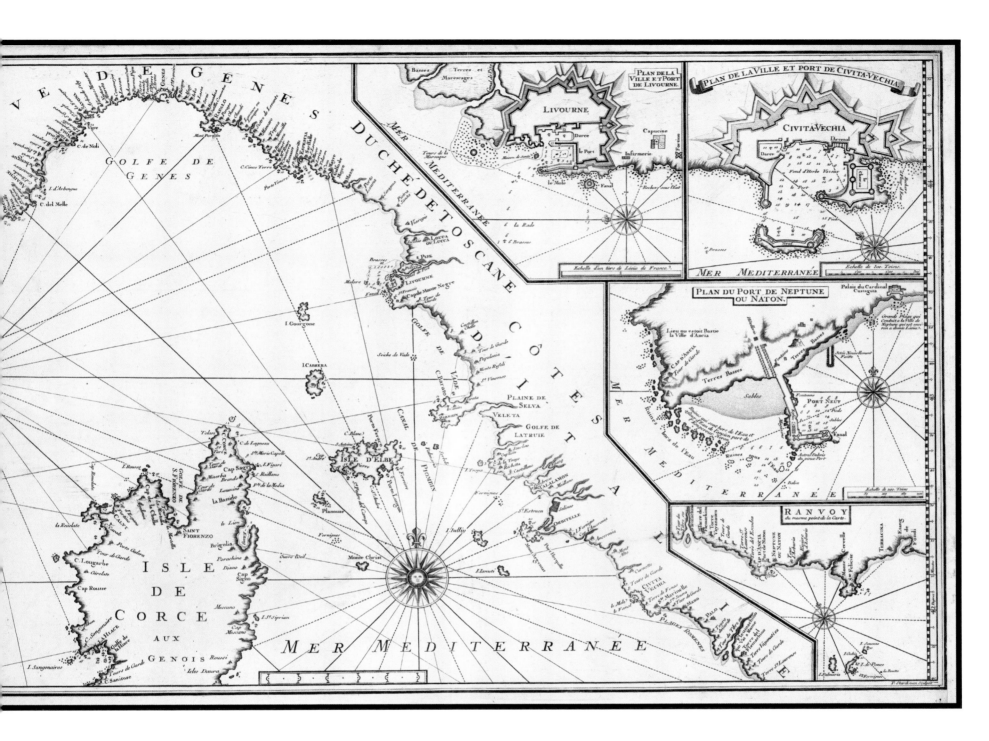

This is a striking two-sheet chart of the Mediterranean coast, from Catalonia to the mouth of the Tiber River in Italy, showing most of Corsica and the island of Elba, with six large insets. It is one of the charts in Henri Michelot and Laurent Bremond's hydrographic atlas, published in Marseilles in 1726.
The charts in the atlas date from 1715 to 1726, with this one dated 1718.
The charts are engraved by P. Starckmann, a skilled engraver about whom little is known.

The emphasis is on the waters of the northwest Mediterranean, which has three compass roses and rhumb lines. Many of the conventions appear similar to those used on portolan charts, but the chart is less busy and more reserved.

There is no decoration inland. Even the cartouches, which are ornate, are contained and general; they are less narrative and sprawling than those seen on earlier maps and charts.

The insets show important ports around the Mediterranean, with sounding depths and anchorages to help a ship to dock. Languedoc includes a mix of profile and plan views, so that a sailor could recognize the waters and land from sea. However, these profiles are sleeker and less conspicuous than on previous charts. Other insets include Catalogne, Ranvoy, Neptune (Naton), Civita-Vechia, and Livourne. Some of these ports, like Civita-Vechia and Livourne, include plans of fortified towns that are studded with bastions.

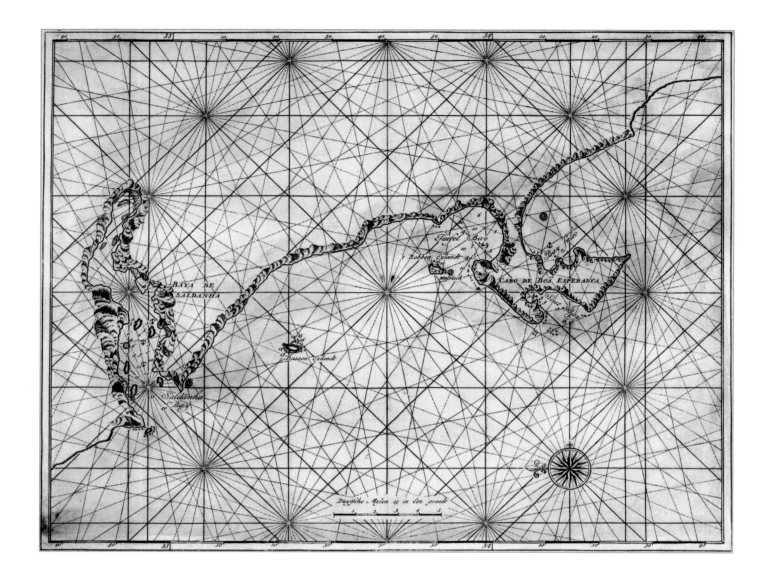

[Cape of Good Hope, South Africa]

This is a nice example of François Valentijn's chart of the coast of South Africa near the Cape of Good Hope and Table Bay. It featured in his *Oud en Nieuw Oost-Indien* (Dordrecht, 1724), a significant history of the Dutch in Maritime Asia and one written with rare access to the Dutch East India Company (VOC) archives and information. Bartolomeu Dias was the first European to reach the Cape in the early modern era. He landed there in 1488 and named the promontory the Cabo das Tormentas, or Cape of Storms. Joan II of Portugal renamed it as the Cape of Good Hope, a decidedly more optimistic name.

Saldanha Bay was initially called Table Bay after the Portuguese encountered it in 1503. In 1601, when nearby Table Bay was named the same thing, the name Saldanha was given to the first bay, after the Portuguese António de Saldanha, who was a captain in the initial expedition. Saldanha also was the first European

to anchor in the actual Table Bay and the first European to climb Table Mountain. The Dutch settled the Cape in 1652 and established a camp near Table Bay. Today, this city is Cape Town, although on this chart settlements are not shown. It quickly became an important stopping point for all ships sailing between the Atlantic and the Indian Ocean.

Valentijn's history of the East Indies, *Oud en Nieuw Oost-Indien*, is regarded as a veritable encyclopaedia on maritime Asia. It is considered a useful collection of sources, from the eighteenth century and earlier, drawn from the closely-monitored Dutch East India Company archives and personal papers. Some of his maps, particularly those of Australia, are drawn from manuscript sources now lost, making his history the lone surviving record of endangered knowledge.

Chartmaker Biography

François Valentijn *(1666–1727) was a clergyman and writer who worked for the Dutch East India Company as a minister. He lived in the East Indies for sixteen years over two separate trips before returning to Dordrecht to write* Oud en Nieuw Oost-Indien, *or the Old and New East-India.*

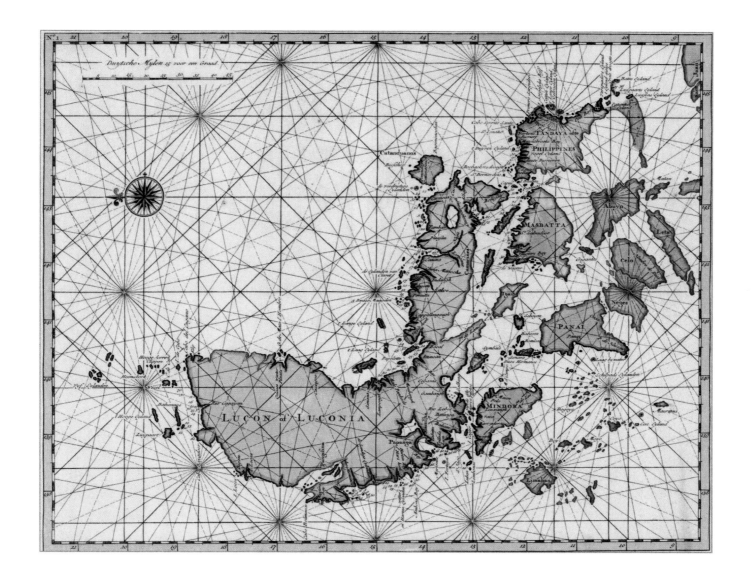

[Philippine Islands]

Oriented with east at the top, Valentijn's map encompasses Luzon and its associated islands to the immediate south. The chart is criss-crossed with rhumb lines, with one decorative compass rose in the waters north of the islands. Sounding depths are included near shore, as are sandbanks, shoals, and obstructions. A scale is in the upper left corner. Port cities are also included.

Luzon is the main focus of this chart, an appropriate emphasis as it is the largest island in the Philippines archipelago and the most populous. It also contains one of the most important ports in the entire Pacific, Manila, which was part of a cross-oceanic trade route linking Acapulco in New Spain to Manila and the markets of Asia.

Luzon has always maintained strong trading and exchange ties with neighboring island groups and mainland Asia. Magellan arrived in 1521 and nominally claimed the islands for Spain. However, the Spanish exercised no real control until 1565, when Miguel López de Legazpi began the first Spanish settlements near Cebu; here the island called "Celo." The Spanish declared Manila the capital in 1571. When this chart was made, the islands were still under Spanish control, as they would be until 1898.

Valentijn's *Oud en Nieuw Oost-Indien* was divided into five parts spread over eight volumes. It had over a thousand illustrations, including some of the most accurate maps of the region published to that date.

Chartmaker Biography

François Valentijn *(1666–1727) was a clergyman and writer who worked for the Dutch East India Company as a minister. He lived in the East Indies for sixteen years over two separate trips before returning to Dordrecht to write* Oud en Nieuw Oost-Indien, *or the Old and New East-India.*

A Chart of the Atlantick Ocean [four-sheets]

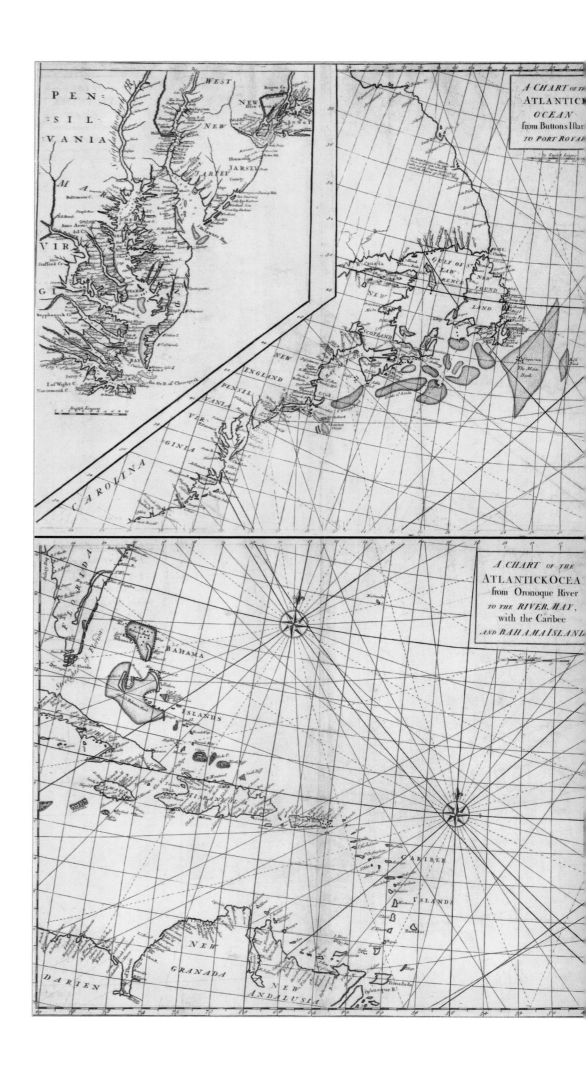

Chartmaker Biography

*Little is known about **Nathaniel Cutler.***

***Edmund Halley** (ca. 1656–1742) was one of Britain's foremost astronomers and natural philosophers. He was also an explorer and mapmaker famous for his late-seventeenth century voyages to study magnetic variation. In 1721, Halley was named as the second Astronomer Royal and moved to Greenwich, where he died in 1742.*

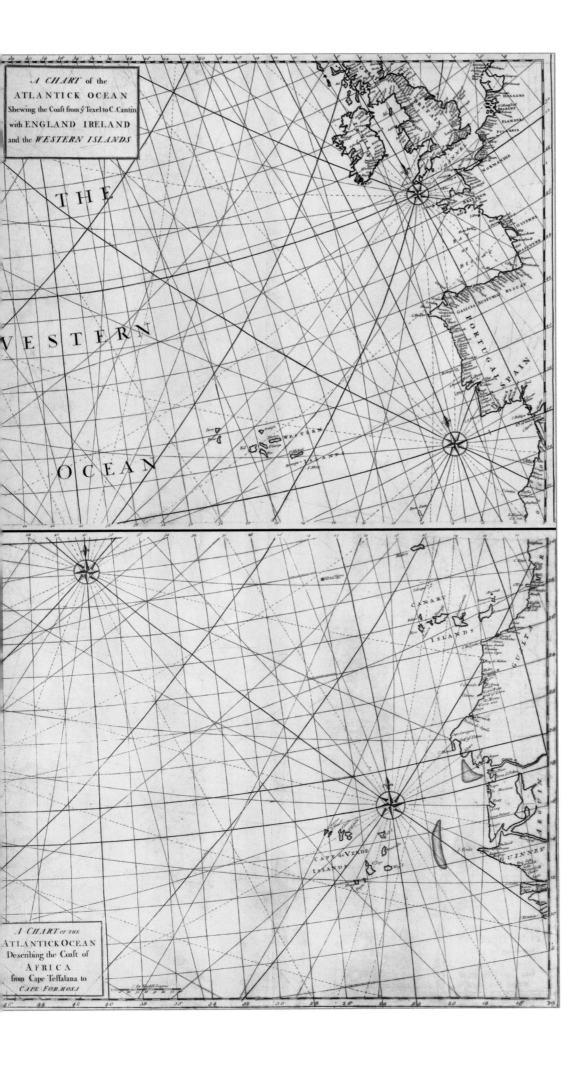

T his four-sheet chart of the North Atlantic is
actually four charts in one. In the top left is the Eastern
Seaboard with the fish-rich Outer Banks and an inset
of Chesapeake Bay—one of the most detailed printed
depictions of the area to date. In the top right are the
coasts of Ireland, Britain, France, and Portugal, with
a bit of Northern Africa as well. In the lower right is the
tip of Western Africa and the Cape Verde Islands. Finally,
in the lower left, is Hispaniola, Cuba, the Bahamas,
a stumpy Florida, and, to the south, a portion of
Central and South America.

The charts are starkly simple, with the defining
feature the grid of latitude and longitude and curved
rhumb lines. They appeared in *Atlas Maritimus et
Commercialis*, published in London in 1728, as a
competitor to Mount & Page's *English Pilot*. These
charts were designed by Nathaniel Cutler and explained
by Edmund Halley, and Daniel Defoe is supposed to have
written part of the text.

Focused on commercial trade, the first part of the
atlas contained a description of all the countries of the
world, their resources, and economy. The second part
consisted of Cutler's 52 exacting sea charts, of which
these are four. Unlike the *English Pilot*, the *Atlas
Maritimus et Commercialis* condensed the entire
world, including coasts of the Americas not included
in the *Pilot*, into one volume.

A Chart of Part of ye Sea Coast of England, Holland & Flanders &c

This chart is stuffed with immense amounts of information. It is still unadorned; there are no decorative cartouches or illustrations, but every open space is filled with information useful to sailors. The chart shows the English Channel and the North Sea. Sea routes from England to Holland, France, and Flanders are noted, as are soundings, shoals, and other navigational hazards. There are also historical notes, including the landing of King William in Yarmouth in 1694, as well as the loss of the *Gloucester* on the "Lemmon Sand" in 1682. This large-scale chart also includes legends to place water and coastal features in inland England and Flanders, allowing even more information to be shared.

In the title cartouche of this ca. 1730 chart, Moll mentions that he based it on information from a "Capt. G. Collins." This refers to Captain Grenville Collins, an officer in the Royal Navy. Collins surveyed the majority of the coastline of the English Isles in the 1680s. His charts were rushed to publication, as they were in high demand, and then published collectively as a sea atlas, the *Coasting Pilot*, in 1693. He was recognized as Hydrographer to the King in 1683 and as one of the elder brethren of Trinity House in 1693. Collins's charts remained a respected authority on the English coastline, even though he died in 1694.

Chartmaker Biography

Herman Moll (ca. 1654–1732) was likely born in Bremen, Germany, but moved to London to escape conflict. His first original maps appeared in the early 1680s, and he opened his own shop in the 1690s. Moll was part of a group that congregated at Jonathan's Coffee House, which included Robert Hooke, Jonathan Swift, and Daniel Defoe. He became known especially for his maps and charts in South Seas voyage accounts.

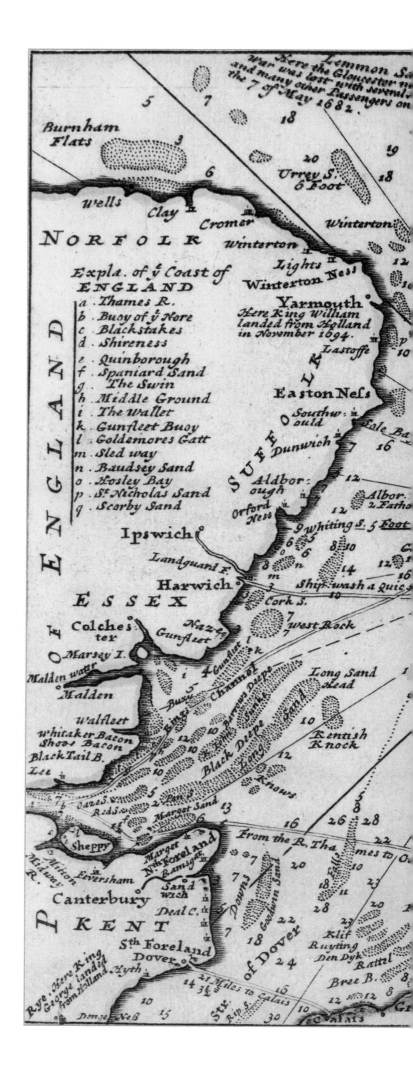

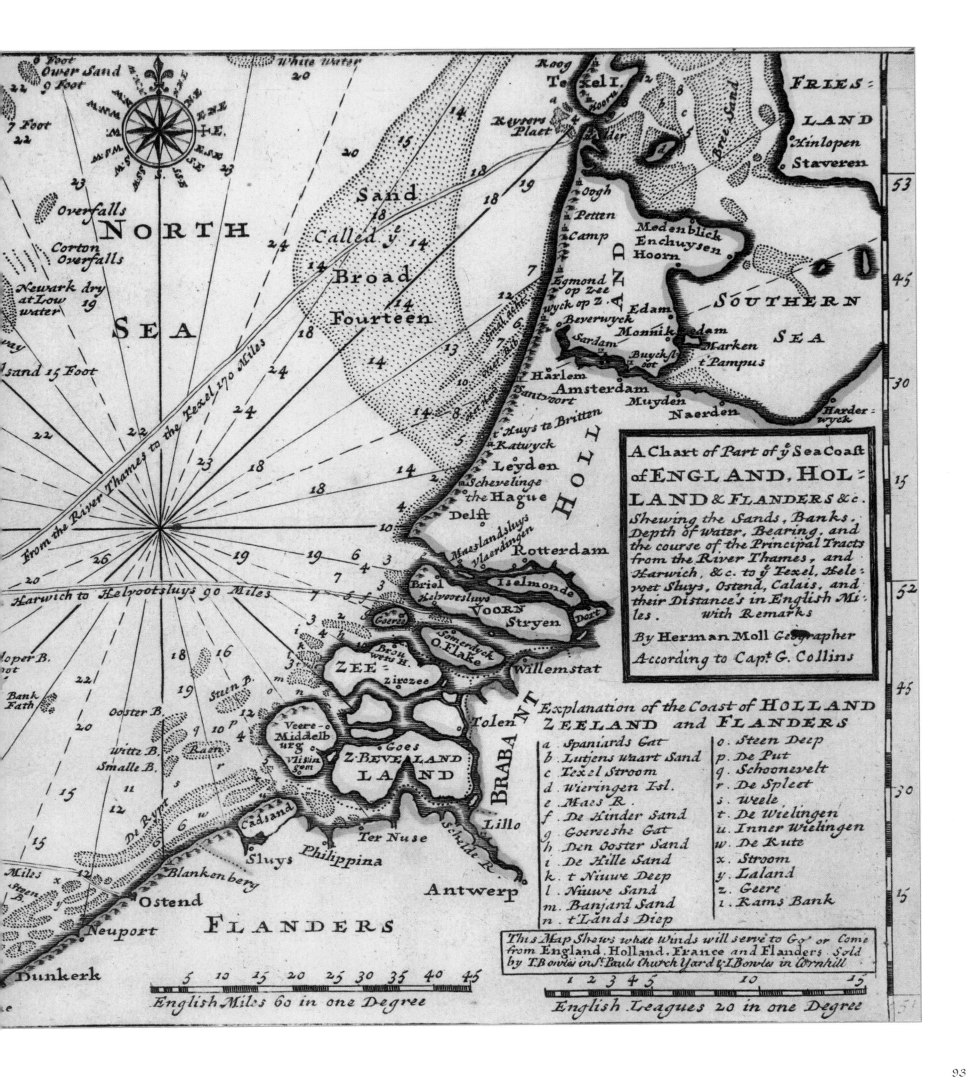

A Chart of Part of ye Sea Coast of ENGLAND, HOL=LAND & FLANDERS &c. Shewing the Sands, Banks, Depth of water, Bearing, and the course of the Principal Tracts from the River Thames, and Harwich, &c. to ye Texel, Hele=voet Sluys, Ostend, Calais, and their Distances in English Mi=les. with Remarks

By Herman Moll Geographer

According to Capt. G. Collins

Explanation of the Coast of HOLLAND ZEELAND and FLANDERS

a. Spaniards Gat
b. Lutjens waart Sand
c. Texel Stroom
d. Wieringen Isl.
e. Maes R.
f. De Hinder Sand
g. Goereeshe Gat
h. Den Ooster Sand
i. De Hille Sand
k. t Niuwe Deep
l. Niuwe Sand
m. Banjard Sand
n. t'Lands Diep

o. Steen Deep
p. De Put
q. Schoonevelt
r. De Spleet
s. Weele
t. De Wielingen
u. Inner Wielingen
w. De Kute
x. Stroom
y. Laland
z. Geere
1. Rams Bank

This Map Shews what Winds will serve to Go or Come from England. Holland. France and Flanders. Sold by T. Bowles in St Pauls Church Yard & I. Bowles in Cornhill

NORTH SEA

HOLLAND

FRIES=LAND

SOUTHERN SEA

ZEE LAND

Z. BEVELAND LAND

BRABANT

FLANDERS

English Miles 60 in one Degree

English Leagues 20 in one Degree

A Correct Chart
of St. Georges Channel

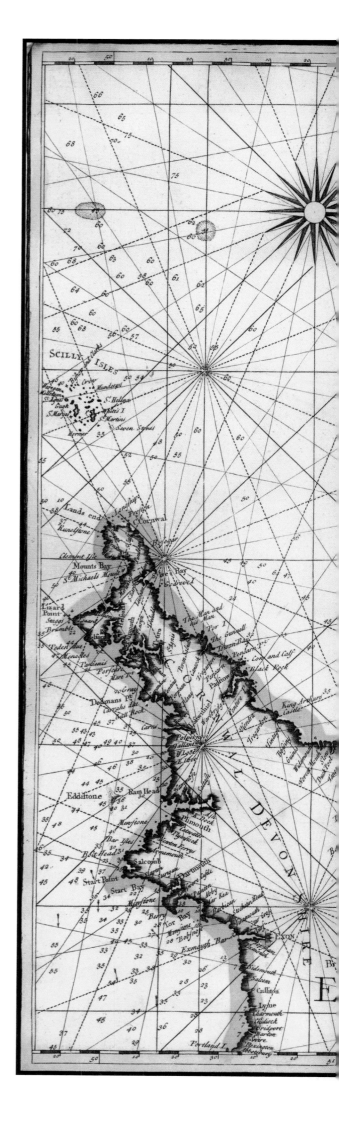

Charles Price included this chart in his extremely rare *Atlas maritimus, or, A new sea atlas,* published in London. Price had announced his intent to publish the atlas in 1730, but he went to debtors' prison in 1731. It was long thought an unfinished project, but it seems that Price did publish a set of over twenty charts of the English coast by 1732. This was not the completion of his vision; rather, the entire project was likely rushed to market to allow Price to pay off his debts. The chart was previously unrecorded, and the only known institutional example is in the Bancroft Library at UC Berkeley.

The chart shows the St. George's Channel connecting the Irish Sea and the Celtic Sea and is based on the work of Grenville Collins. The chart is thick with rhumb lines, suggesting the high volume of trade that traveled the Channel. Sounding depths are spread widely, while sandbars and shoals blanket many of the shores. A seashell adorns the scale bar in the interior of Wales. The title cartouche, in Ireland, is more ornate, with a scrollwork frame, putti, and a coat of arms. It carries a dedication to Sr. Thomas Jones KT (1614–1692), Member of Parliament and judge.

Chartmaker Biography

Charles Price (1679?–1733) was apprenticed to John Seller, Jeremiah's father. Jeremiah and Charles were made free of the Merchant Taylors Guild on the same day, September 1, 1703. The two were already in partnership by then. After breaking with Seller, Price worked with other mapmakers. He was still working in the 1720s, but was in Fleet Prison in 1731 for debt and died in 1733.

A New Chart of the Bahama Islands
And the Windward Passage

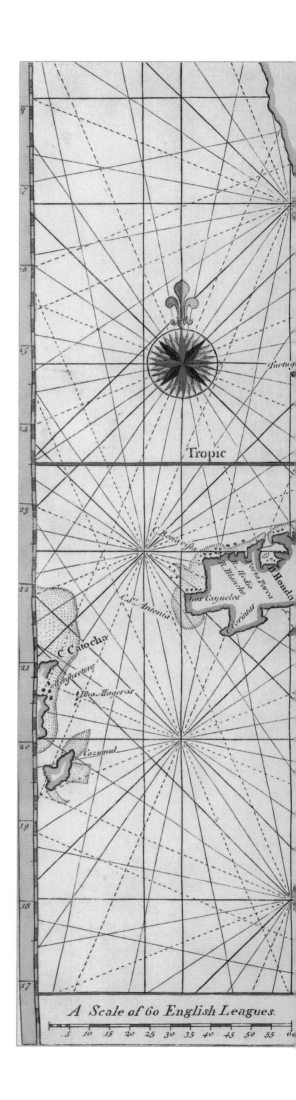

This chart by Mount and Page includes the tip of Florida, the Cayman Islands, Cuba, Jamaica, the western part of Hispaniola, and Cozumel to the far west. The treatment of Florida is quite distinctive, as there are two large bays on the west coast. In the upper right corner is a simple, yet attractive, title cartouche proclaiming the area covered, the Bahamas and the Windward Passage, and the publishers' names and shop location.

The Bahamas are shown in great detail, particularly with regard to the banks and sandbars that can be so treacherous for sailing vessels. Indeed, this is one of the largest-scale treatments of the region to appear in the first half of the eighteenth century. The Bahamas garnered such attention due to their importance, or infamy, for piracy in the Caribbean region.

Colonists, most seeking religious freedom, sought to settle the Bahamas during the English Civil War, although the islands had been visited by Europeans since Columbus's voyages. After the war, however, many settlers returned to Bermuda. They were replaced by exiled criminals, free blacks and runaway enslaved peoples, and pirates. After 1670, the islands were under the control of the Lords Proprietors of the Carolinas, but they exerted little actual influence there. For thirty years, the Bahamas were synonymous with anarchy and alternative living outside the reins of imperial power.

In 1718, the British government attempted to halt the lawlessness by diminishing the Proprietors' powers and sending in a military governor. They chose Captain Woodes Rogers, a man famous for his recent circumnavigation and capture of a Spanish treasure galleon in the Pacific. Rogers was armed with a one-time pardon for the pirates; 1,000 outlaws took the offer, while eight who did not were hanged. By 1728, the Bahamas were considered a safe and potentially prosperous colony.

This chart was originally included in the *English Pilot* in 1689, during the height of piracy. This fourth state was included in 1737, just after the Rogers period, when the Bahamas were being integrated into the larger Caribbean economy.

Chartmaker Biography

*The partnership of **Mount & Page** dominated sea-atlas publishing in Britain throughout the eighteenth century, thanks in large part to the* English Pilot. *William Fisher (1631–1692) partnered with his former apprentice and son-in-law William Mount (1654–1722). After Fisher's death, Mount turned to his own son-in-law and apprentice Thomas Page (d. 1733); their descendants continued the partnership.*

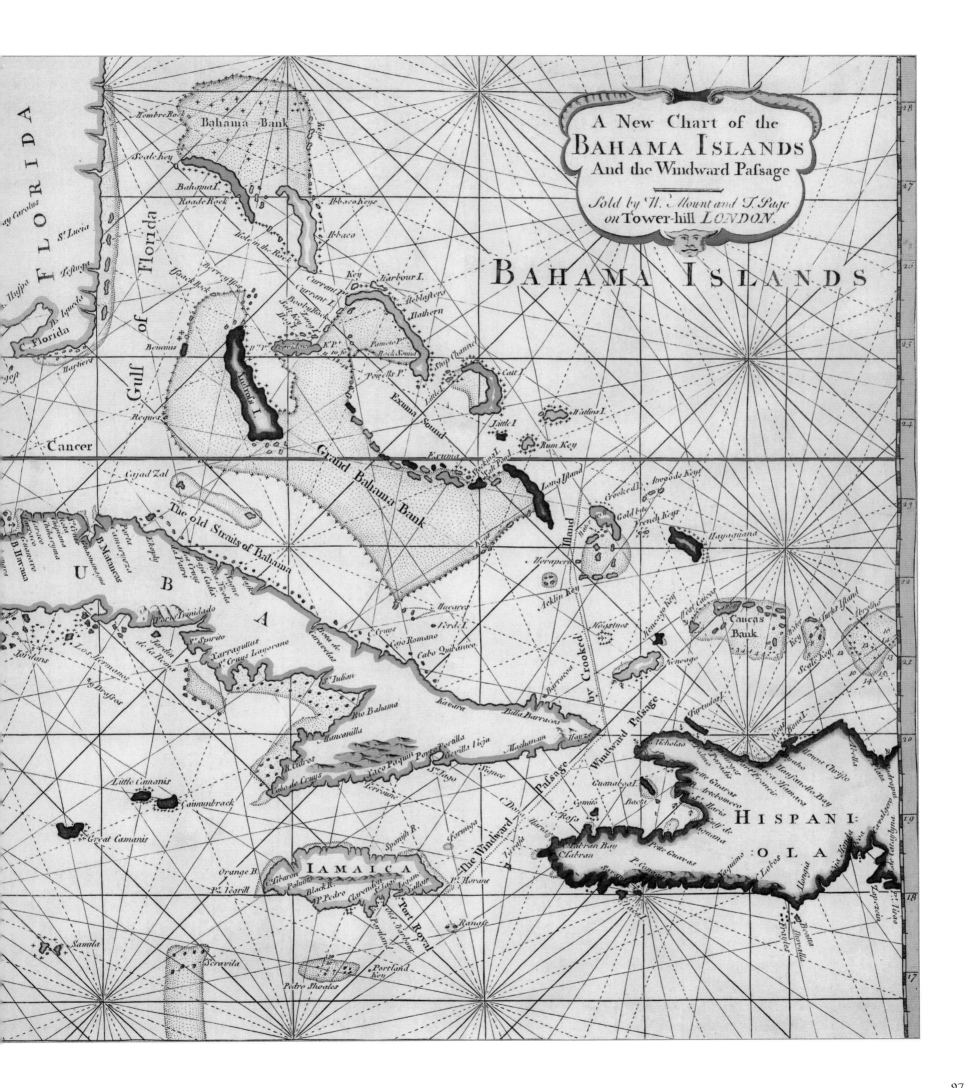

A Correct Chart of the Baltick or East Sea from ye Sound to Petersburg From the latest and best Observations

Achart of the Baltic Sea, this work shows the waterway between what was then Sweden, Russia, and Poland. In the lower right corner is an inset of the harbor of St. Petersburg, which was less than fifty years old when this chart was published. The city was founded by Peter the Great in 1703, when he replaced the captured Swedish settlement of Nyenskans with a new fortress, the Peter and Paul Fortress. In addition to the conventions typical of nautical charts, this chart includes a legend to identify types of city, running from imposing "Imperial Cities" to villages and castles.

The chart featured in a history of England, which was originally the work of Paul de Rapin de Thoyras (1661–1725). Fleeing persecution after the revocation of the Edict of Nantes, Rapin found work tutoring Lord Woodstock, the son of the first Earl of Portland. Rapin lived in London and the Hague. After Woodstock married, Rapin began working full-time on his long-term ambition of writing a history of England. In 1723, he published the first eight volumes, with two more in 1725, the year he died.

His work was translated and published in London by Nicholas Tindal (1687–1774) in fifteen volumes between 1725 and 1731. Later, Tindal offered a continuation of the history to go with his translation, published in 1744–1745. This chart was featured in this continuation.

Chartmaker Biography

*The chart was made by **Richard William Seale** (before 1732–1785). Seale engraved the maps for many books, especially those published by the Knaptons, who published Tindal's translation. He also created many of the maps for magazines of the era, which increasingly featured maps and charts to illustrate their stories.*

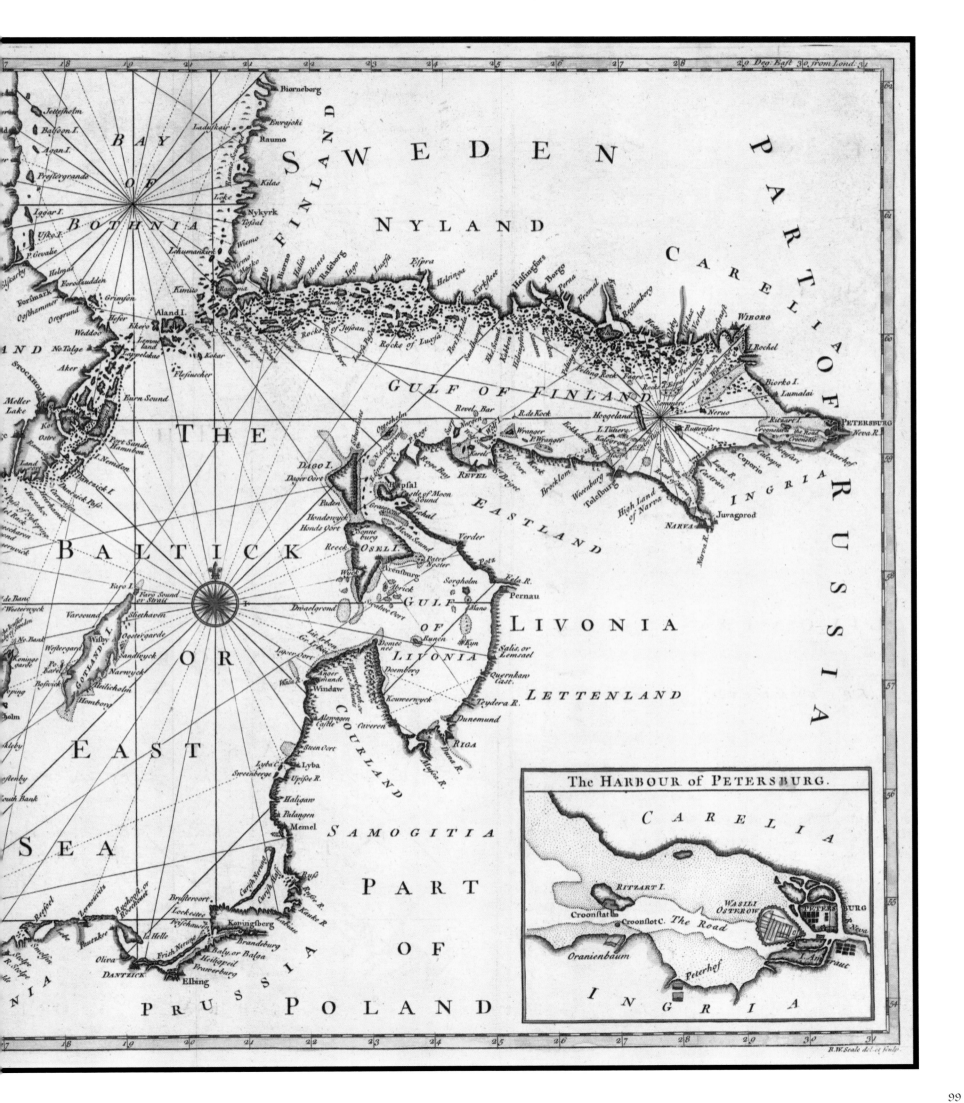

A New Chart of the Coast of New England, Nova Scotia, New France or Canada...

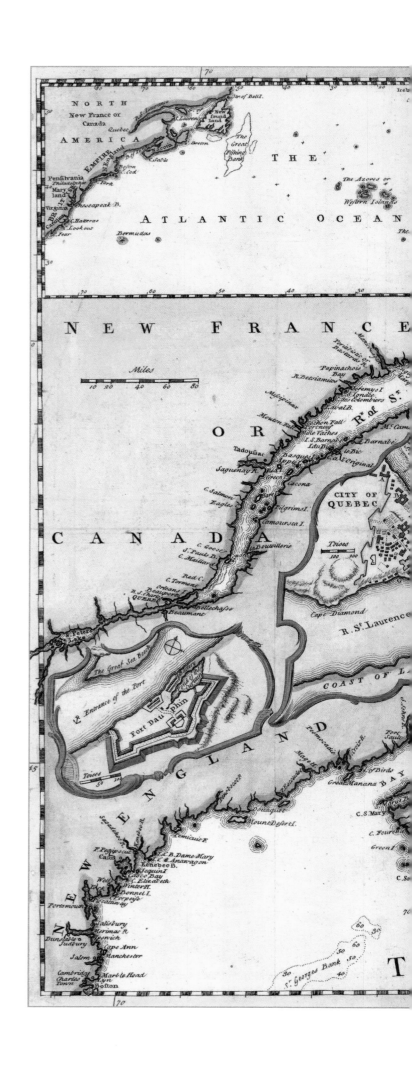

This chart was published in the *Gentleman's Magazine* in January 1746. It shows Newfoundland and Nova Scotia, with portions of New England and Canada. Insets artistically fitted within New France show the North Atlantic and a plan of fortified Louisbourg, Nova Scotia. Insets in New England show Fort Dauphin and Quebec City. A sculpted cartouche in the bottom right corner contains the title and a dedication to the British merchants at work in the English colonies in North America. A naval battle is depicted next to the cartouche.

This chart was designed to appeal to the readers of the *Gentleman's Magazine*, and it was also intended to mimic the style of Jacques-Nicolas Bellin, who published the original version of the chart in 1744. The *Gentleman's Magazine* was a British publication that helped to normalize the use of maps in support of articles and features. It was founded in 1731 by the prominent London publisher Edward Cave, a pioneer in periodical journalism. The magazine continued in print for nearly two centuries, shuttering production in 1922.

This was the publication that first used the word "magazine," from the French for storehouse. Cave wanted to create a storehouse of knowledge, and he employed some of London's best writers to fill his pages: Samuel Johnson gained his first regular employment by writing for the *Gentleman's Magazine*. Other famous contributors included Jonathan Swift.

The publication covered a broad range of topics, from literature to politics, and, from 1739, frequently used maps as illustrations. The first map they printed was a woodcut of Crimea; the second was a fold-out map of Ukraine by Emanuel Bowen. Maps were used to show battle lines, to chronicle voyages, and to educate about areas with which Britain traded. Certain geographers, like Thomas Jefferys, who created this chart, contributed several illustrations to the publication.

Chartmaker Biography

Thomas Jefferys (ca. 1719–1771) was apprenticed to Emanuel Bowen, a prominent mapmaker and engraver, even though Jefferys's own father was a cutler. Jefferys was a prolific map and chartmaker and was named the Geographer to Frederick Prince of Wales and, from 1760, to King George III. Upon his death in 1771, his workshop passed to his partner, William Faden, and Jefferys's son, Thomas Jr.

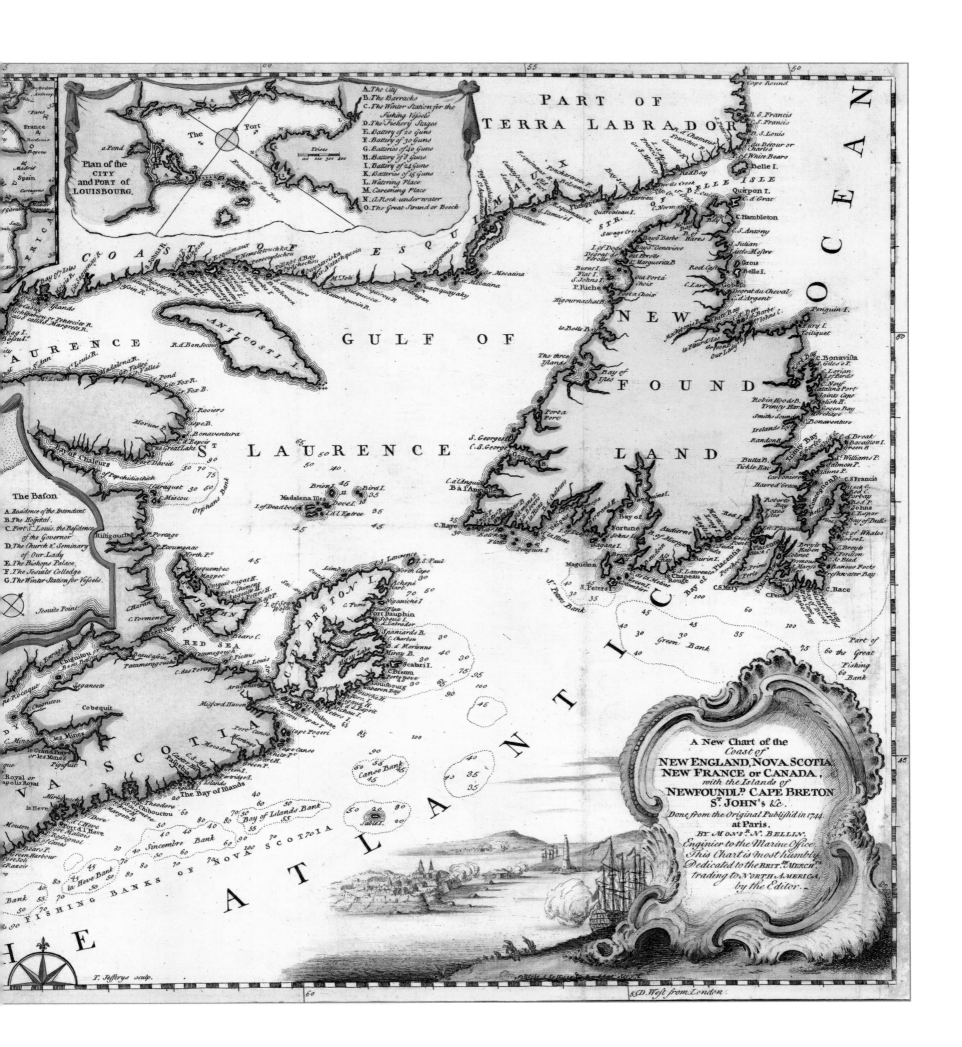

Plan of the CITY and PORT of LOUISBOURG.
a Pond
The Port
Entrance of the Port
Toises

A. The City
B. The Barracks
C. The Winter Station for the Fishing Vessels
D. The Fishery Stages
E. Battery of 20 Guns
F. Battery of 30 Guns
G. Batteries of 10 Guns
H. Battery of 8 Guns
I. Battery of 14 Guns
K. Batteries of 15 Guns
L. Watering Place
M. Careening Place
N. a Rock under-water
O. The Great Strand or Beech

PART OF TERRA LABRADOR

COAST OF ESQUIMAUX

BELLE ISLE

NEW FOUND LAND

O C E A N

GULF OF ST LAURENCE

ANTICOSTI I.

St JOHN

CAPE BRETON I.

RED SEA

NOVA SCOTIA

The Bason
A. Residence of the Intendant
B. The Hospital
C. Fort St Louis, the Residence of the Governor
D. The Church & Seminary of Our Lady
E. The Bishops Palace
F. The Jesuits Colledge
G. The Winter Station for Vessels
Jesuits Point

Green Bank

St Peters Bank

FISHING BANKS OF NOVA SCOTIA

Bay of Islands Bank

Canso Bank

la Heve Bank

Sincomtre Bank

A T L A N T I C

Part of the Great Fishing Bank

A New Chart of the
Coast of
NEW ENGLAND, NOVA SCOTIA,
NEW FRANCE or CANADA,
with the Islands of
NEWFOUNDL.d CAPE BRETON
St JOHN's &c.
Done from the Original Publish'd in 1744.
at Paris,
BY MONS.r N. BELLIN,
Enginier to the Marine Office.
This Chart is most humbly
Dedicated to the BRIT.sh MERCH.ts
trading to NORTH AMERICA,
by the Editor.

T. Jefferys sculp.

55 D. West from London.

101

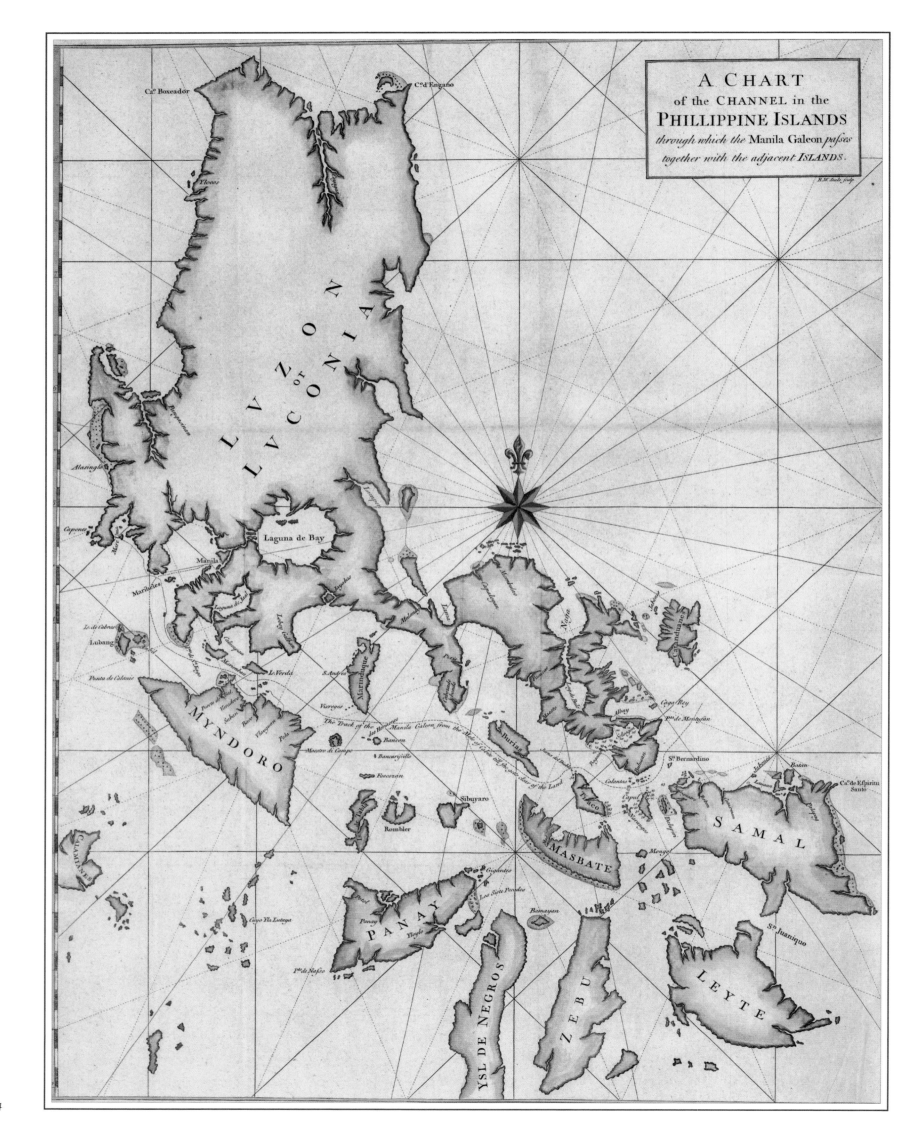

A CHART
of the CHANNEL in the
PHILLIPPINE ISLANDS
through which the Manila Galeon *passes
together with the adjacent* ISLANDS.

R.W.Seale,sculp

A Chart of the Channel in the Phillippine Islands...

This is one of three charts included in George Anson's bestselling *Voyage round the World* (London, 1748). It shows the area from Luzon to Leyte, to Zebu and Ysle De Negros [*sic*]. The track of the transpacific treasure galleon is noted and ends near the island of Samar, written here as Samal, where the galleons enter into open water.

In 1739, resentment over Spanish raids on British ships in the Caribbean sparked the War of Jenkin's Ear, which would widen into the larger War of the Austrian Succession. The Commissioners of the British Admiralty planned a global strategy to harass Spanish trade and weaken its over-stretched navy and merchant marine. Anson's voyage was part of this strategy. He set out in 1740 with a squadron of six ships and 1,900 men.

By 1743, Anson had crossed the Pacific after raiding the west coast of South America. Prior to crossing, he had waited off the Mexican coast for the Acapulco galleon, full of silver, to appear, but he only succeeded in blocking the ship from leaving port. Meanwhile, he had also lost five of his ships and 1,400 of his men, primarily to scurvy; only his own ship, *Centurion*, remained intact. After repairing at Macao, Anson let Chinese officials know that he was headed for Britain; in reality, he sailed to the Philippines to await the entrance of the Acapulco galleon. Remarkably, considering the voyage prior to that point, the *Centurion* took the galleon *Nuestra Señora de la Covadonga* with only light casualties.

The chart was not intended to illustrate the entirety of the Philippines; rather, it was supposed to offer a geographic snapshot of the route of the galleon from Manila. The chart, drawn by Richard William Seale, was also intended to communicate British knowledge of the Spanish-controlled archipelago, yet the stylized and blocky representation of the islands reveals that there was still much to learn about the coastlines of the Philippines.

Chartmaker Biography

*The chart was made by **Richard William Seale** (before 1732–1785). Seale engraved the maps for many books, especially those published by the Knaptons. He also created many of the maps for magazines of the era, which increasingly featured maps and charts to illustrate their stories.*

Veduta della Città e Porto di Tripoli di Barbaria

This finely-executed chart shows the coastline near Tripoli, with a bird's-eye view of the city below, reflecting one of the final attempts by the Venetian Empire to conquer the pirate stronghold at Tripoli, on the Barbary Coast. The decorative key in the bottom left, shaped like a stone monument, locates approximately fifty points of interest and gives the scale.

This is a close-up chart drawn on a large scale, unlike some of the more general, small-scale charts in this chapter. The bay is included in minute detail, with dozens of sounding depths and sandbars marked, especially those near the line of rocks at the entrance to the bay.

The bird's-eye view includes a squadron of five ships on an expedition to Tripoli in 1766; it was likely published in the same year. They managed to force the *beylerbeyi* of the city to pay for damage to Venetian vessels by privateers, but the pirates stationed there continued unabated. They and their colleagues along the Barbary Coast would continue to operate well into the nineteenth century.

The chart is dedicated to Girolamo Zulian (1730–1795), a Venetian diplomat who served as the Ambassador to the Holy See (1779–1783) and Constantinople (1783–1789). Zulian was a noted antiquarian, who collected Egyptian sculptures.

Chartmaker Biography

*The title indicates that this chart was drawn from a plan drawn from the perspective of **Ignacio Avesani**, a Venetian officer.*

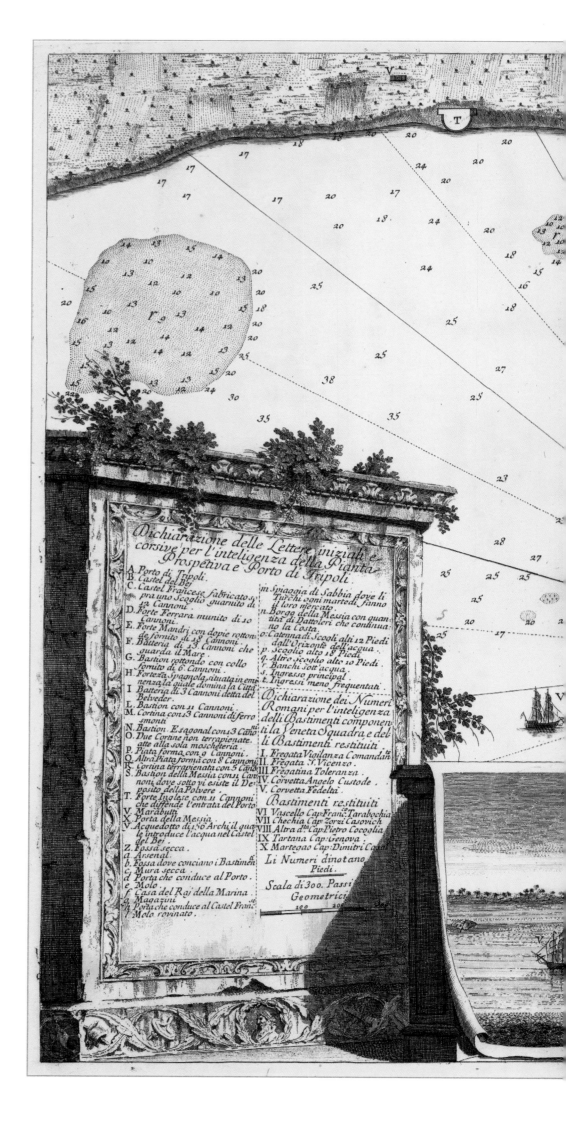

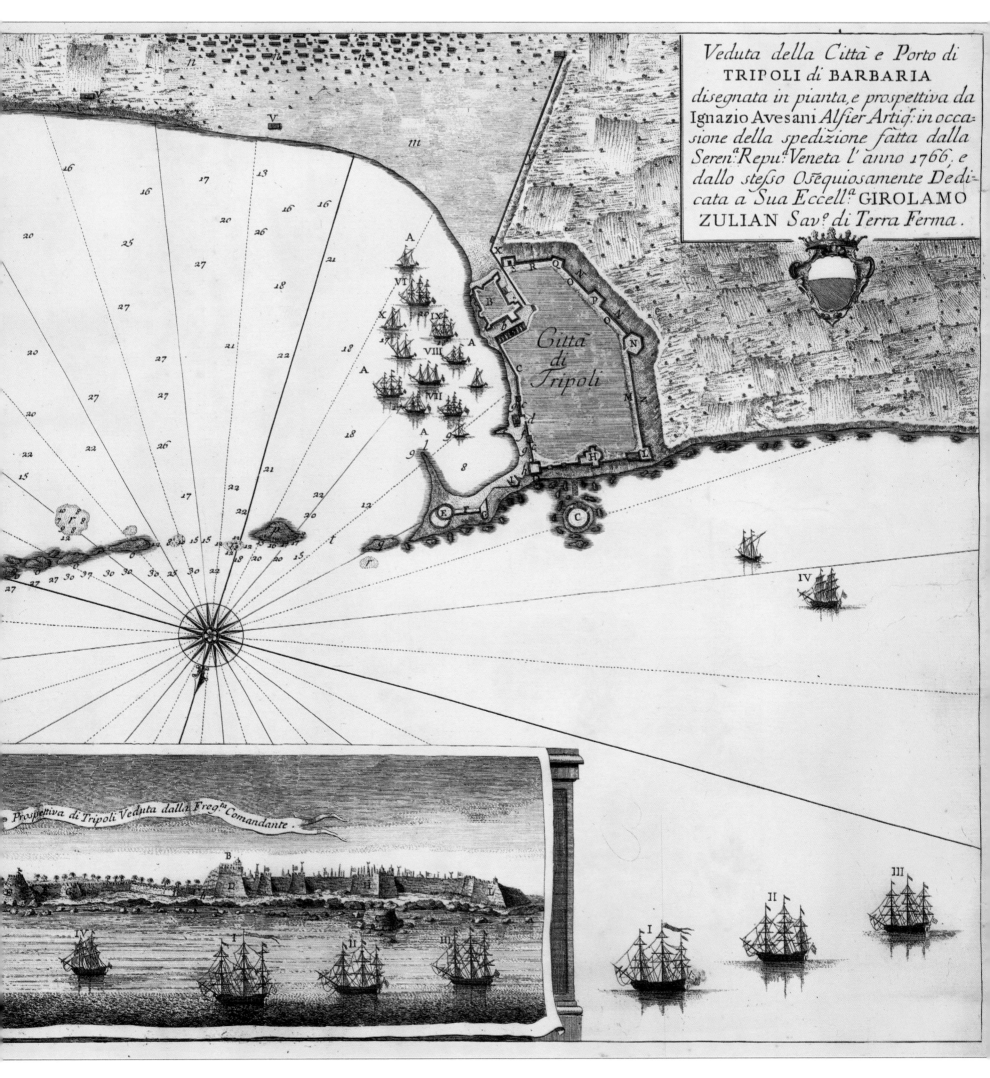

Veduta della Città e Porto di
TRIPOLI di BARBARIA
disegnata in pianta, e prospettiva da
Ignazio Avesani Alfier Artig: in occa-
sione della spedizione fatta dalla
Seren.ª Repu: Veneta l'anno 1766, e
dallo stesso Ossequiosamente Dedi-
cata a Sua Eccell.ª GIROLAMO
ZULIAN Sav.º di Terra Ferma.

Città
di
Tripoli

Prospettiva di Tripoli Veduta dalla Freg.ta Comandante.

ESSAI D'UNE CARTE

Construite d'après toutes les connoissances les plus nouvelles
présentée à l'Académie Royale des Sciences avec un Mémoire approuvé le 24 Mars 1773
par le S.r De VAUGONDY Géographe ordinaire du Roi,
de l'Académie royale de Nanci.

POLAIRE ARCTIQUE

pour servir aux Navigations et aux Découvertes à faire dans la mer Glaciat
et jugé digne d'être imprimé dans le Recueil des Mémoires des Savans étranger
du feu Roi de Pologne Duc de Lorraine et de Bar,
et Censeur royal. 1774.

A PARIS
Chés l'Auteur Quai de l'horloge du Palais
près le Pont neuf.

(a) Naufrage en 1746
(b) ici l'on n'a vu ni terre ni glace
au nord et à l'ouest du Spitzberg, selon le Capit.e Chisgs

Gravé par E. Dussy

Essai D'Une Carte Polaire Arctique

This polar chart was intended to illustrate a presentation made by Didier Robert de Vaugondy to the French Academy of Sciences in August 1773, regarding de Vaugondy's theories on possible sailing routes to the Pacific Ocean via the north polar seas. The chart was part of a decades-long feud between French geographers about the Northwest Passage and internal waterways in North America.

De Vaugondy was convinced that there was no persuasive evidence of a watercourse through the continent. Here, he is presenting theories on possible polar routes, although he did not believe all these were viable. He is attempting to depict competing and contradictory theories in order to assess what could be geographic reality, a technique he perfected.

The chart was ostensibly meant to answer questions of navigation, as the dashed curved lines, representing wind rhumbs, indicate. The chart is on an orthographic polar projection. It represents the scholarly study of geography as it was practiced in the eighteenth century. While geography and cartography had not yet hardened into academic disciplines, a nineteenth-century development, there were complex discussions, as represented by this chart, about hydrography and exploration that defined the mapping of the Enlightenment.

Chartmaker Biography

Didier Robert de Vaugondy *(ca. 1723–1786) was the son of prominent geographer Gilles Robert de Vaugondy, and Didier carried on his father's impressive work. Together, they published their best-known work, the* Atlas Universel *(1757). Like his father, Didier served as geographer to King Louis XV. In 1773, he was appointed Royal Censor in charge of monitoring the information published in geography texts, navigational tracts, and travel accounts.*

National Hydrographic Services and Organizations

*W*hile the high ebb of state-run hydrographic bodies can be said to have occurred in the nineteenth and early twentieth centuries, when they were responsible for near-absolute standardization of chart features and symbols, they have significant antecedents in earlier centuries.

The first known European cartographic repository was the Armazém da Guiné, *which was in place in Lisbon by 1496. A receiver of stores, the* almoxarife, *oversaw the upkeep of a master chart, the* padrao de el-Rei, *as well as monitored the distribution and return of charts, the training of pilots, and the management of the contents of those charts that left the centralized repository. In later centuries, the* Armazém *was responsible for approving the printing of rutters, charts, and other cartographic materials that were to be held in private hands. The* Armazém *was destroyed in the Lisbon earthquake of 1755, along with an irreplaceable archive of manuscript and printed maps and charts.*

Founded in 1503 in Seville, its Spanish counterpart, the Casa de la Contratación, *operated in a similar fashion, wherein cosmographers monitored the master chart and the dissemination of geographic knowledge. Cosmographers were employees of the state, and information was tightly controlled, if not entirely secret. This is a different situation to the Dutch, whose main cartographic archive was held by the Dutch East India Company in Amsterdam and Batavia, as discussed in chapter two. As the Dutch relied on commercial mapmakers to maintain their repository and provide materials, many details made their way onto charts for sale on the open market.*

The centralization of hydrography in France began in earnest when Jean-Baptiste Colbert became First Minister of France in 1661. Under his watch, the first Royal School of Hydrography began operation, as did the first survey of France's coasts (1670–1689). In 1680, Colbert consolidated various collections of charts and memoirs into a single assemblage, forming the core of sources for what would become the Dépôt de la Marine, *known more formally as the* Dépôt des cartes et plans de la Marine. *In 1720, the Navy consolidated its collection with those government materials covering the colonies, creating a single large repository of navigation. By 1737, the* Dépôt *was creating its own original charts and, from 1750, they participated in scientific expeditions to determine the accurate calculation of longitude. In 1773, the* Dépôt *received a monopoly over the composition, production, and distribution of navigational materials, solidifying their place as the main producer of geographic knowledge in France.* Dépôt-approved charts were distributed to official warehouses in port cities and sold by authorized merchants. The Dépôt *continued to operate until 1886, when it became the Naval Hydrographic Service.*

By contrast, the British did not set up their state-run hydrographic body until the end of the eighteenth century. Prior to that time, captains and masters, including Royal Navy officers, were required to supply their own charts and instruments before sailing. Individual officers skilled in hydrography, like James Cook and George Vancouver, produced charts that were sold on the open market, but the Navy itself did not yet publish or regulate their own charts.

In 1795, King George III appointed Alexander Dalrymple, a pedantic geographer, to consolidate, catalogue, and improve the Royal Navy's charts. He oversaw production of the Admiralty's first chart in 1800; the Hydrographic Office (HO) sold its first charts to the public in 1821. By 1825, the HO was offering over seven hundred charts and views through direct sale and approved vendors. It also began to participate in exploratory and surveying expeditions. The first was a joint French-Spanish-British trip to the South Atlantic, a voyage organized in part by the Royal Society of London. The most famous were the three voyages of the HMS Beagle (1826–1830, 1831–1836, 1837–1843), on the second of which sailed Charles Darwin.

In 1829, Rear Admiral Sir Francis Beaufort was appointed Hydrographer Royal. Under his management, the HO introduced the wind-force scale named for him, as well as began issuing official tide tables in 1833. Later in the nineteenth century, the HO supported the Challenger expedition, which is credited with helping to found the discipline of oceanography. The HO also participated in the International Meridian Conference held in Washington D.C. in 1884, which decided on the Greenwich Meridian as the Prime Meridian. Regulation and standardization of oceanic and navigational measures continued into the twentieth century.

Throughout the nineteenth century, other nations began to found their own hydrographic bodies, modeled for the most part on those of France and Britain. In the United States, President Thomas Jefferson created a coastal surveying service in 1807, which became the U.S. Coast Survey in 1832.

Like their counterparts in Europe, the U.S. charting body explicitly combined chartmaking with surveying and scientific experimentation, for example in studies of the Gulf Stream and tidal prediction.

Thanks to the large-scale production of the national charting agencies, and the global spread of their empires, charts became standardized as never before. With an increase in shipping, thanks to new developments in steam and shipbuilding technology and a more-globalized economy, the demand for charts was growing as well. More charts were available to more buyers at lower prices than ever before. While some luxury atlases were still being produced, the increased frequency of chart correction and updating meant that charts were ever more ephemeral, even as they were more plentiful.

Despite the overarching trend toward international standardization, there were some idiosyncratic elements to charting that distinguished different national and regional traditions. This problem was addressed in an international conference held in Washington, DC in 1899. This led to two more conferences in St. Petersburg, the International Congress on Navigation in 1908 and the International Maritime Conference in 1912. Finally, in 1919, at the International Hydrographic Conference in London, attendees decided to create a permanent, international hydrographic body dedicated to ensuring the high quality and uniformity of nautical charts. In 1921, this body, the International Hydrographic Bureau, was established; its headquarters are in Monaco, thanks to an invitation from HSH Prince Albert I, who was deeply interested in marine science and navigation. In 1970, they changed their name to the International Hydrographic Organization (IHO), which is still the governing body of hydrographic standards today.

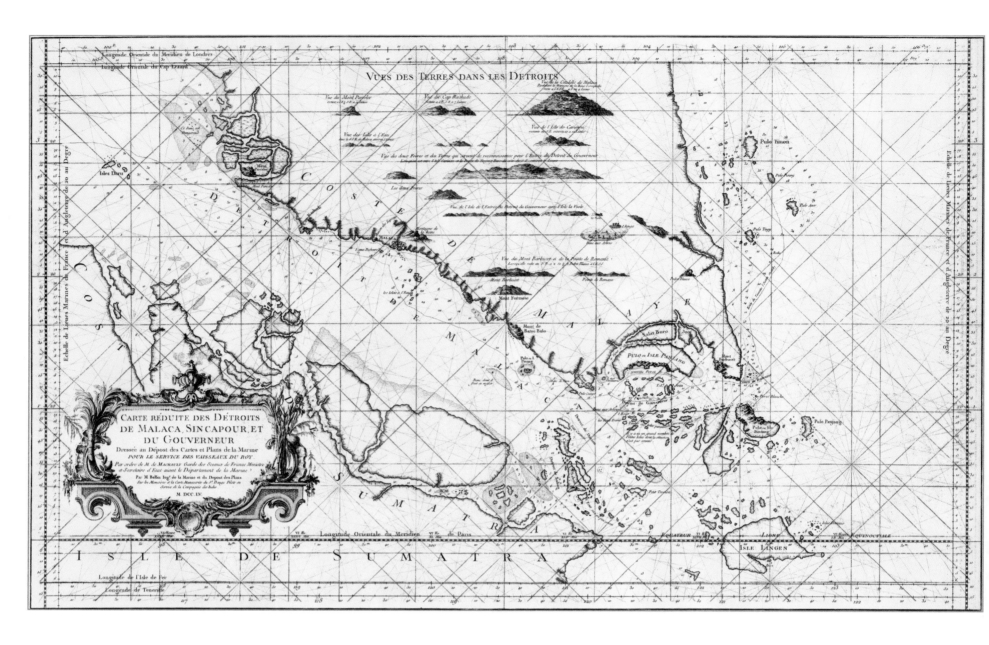

Carte Reduite des Detroits de Malaca, Sincapour, et Gouverneur

Chartmaker Biography

*At age eighteen, **Jacques-Nicolas Bellin** (1703–1772) was appointed hydrographer to the French Navy. In August 1741, he became the first* Ingénieur de la Marine *of the* Dépôt de la Marine *and was named Official Hydrographer of the French King. During his term as Official Hydrographer, the* Dépôt *was the single most active center for the production of sea charts and maps.*

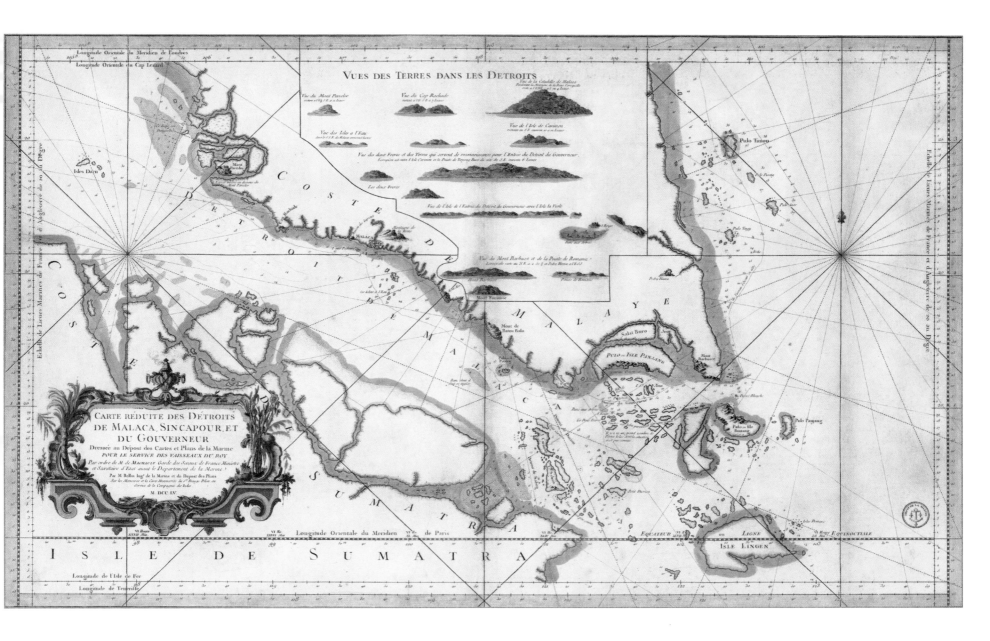

This exceptionally-rendered early sea chart (right) of the Strait of Malacca shows the southern part of Malaysia, the island of Singapore, and the eastern part of Sumatra. The Malaysian coastline on this chart is extraordinarily detailed, a testament to the diligence of Jacques-Nicolas Bellin and his fellow cartographers at the *Dépôt de la Marine*. The chart contains several illustrated profile views of land as seen from the straits.

Included in the floral cartouche in the bottom left is a note that the map has been drawn from the records and manuscript map of *"Sr. Dauge, Pilote du Service de la Compagnie des Indes,"* a ship captain in service to the *Compagnie française pour le commerce des Indes orientales* (the French East India Company) who had travelled through the region.

This map includes the route of the vessel *Oiseau*, known to have completed two trips from France to Siam (Thailand) between 1685 and 1688. In 1685, the ship carried six Jesuit monks from France headed to China. The monks disembarked at the Siamese capital, and the following year the ship returned from Siam with members of a diplomatic mission to the French court. In 1687, the Siamese diplomats returned home aboard the *Oiseau*, accompanied by M. de la Loubere, French envoy to the King of Siam. The ship returned to France later that year. The 1687 voyage is shown here, providing an example of a successful route to sailors viewing this chart.

The colored state of the map is paired here with an enhanced first state of the chart (left); both were printed in 1755. This state is overprinted with rhumb lines and does not include the box around the insets or the printed rhumb lines, which were added to the plate in later states.

Carte Reduite des Mers Comprises Entre l'Asie et l'Amerique...

This fine chart, issued by the *Depôt de la Marine* in 1742, corrected to 1756, depicts the Pacific world as it was known by Europeans in the 1750s, a time of their renewed interest in the world's largest ocean. The chart depicts the entire west coast of the Americas up to roughly 40 degrees north latitude. California is correctly shown to be a peninsula, but Japan retains its horizontal depiction, a representation typical of mid-eighteenth-century maps. The Korean Peninsula takes on an exaggerated size, and the area where Japan's Hokkaido should be located is left blank; the area had not been extensively explored and was subject to diverse cartographic interpretations.

In line with changing cartographic standards that preferred fewer decorative additions, especially for working charts, this chart has few embellishments. The exception is the ornate title cartouche situated in the center of the South Pacific. A large frame surrounds the title. It is topped with various items which Europeans associated with the Pacific and Southeast Asia, including a parasol, a conical hat, a feathered headdress, and a parrot.

The depiction of Australasia is reflective of the European interest in and ignorance of the area. The north coast of Australia up the western shores of the Gulf of Carpentaria reveals the discoveries of various Dutch explorers, particularly Willem Janszoon's voyage of 1605–1606 in what is today Queensland. Also included is the information gathered by Abel Tasman, who was the first European to encounter both Tasmania (which was named for him, but was called Van Diemen's Land by Tasman) and New Zealand.

The cartographers at the *Depôt* have added a dotted line between Van Diemen's Land and the southern coast of Australia, as well as between Van Diemen's Land and the east coast of Carpentaria and New Guinea. Van Diemen's Land would not be proven to be an island until the very end of the century in which this chart was made.

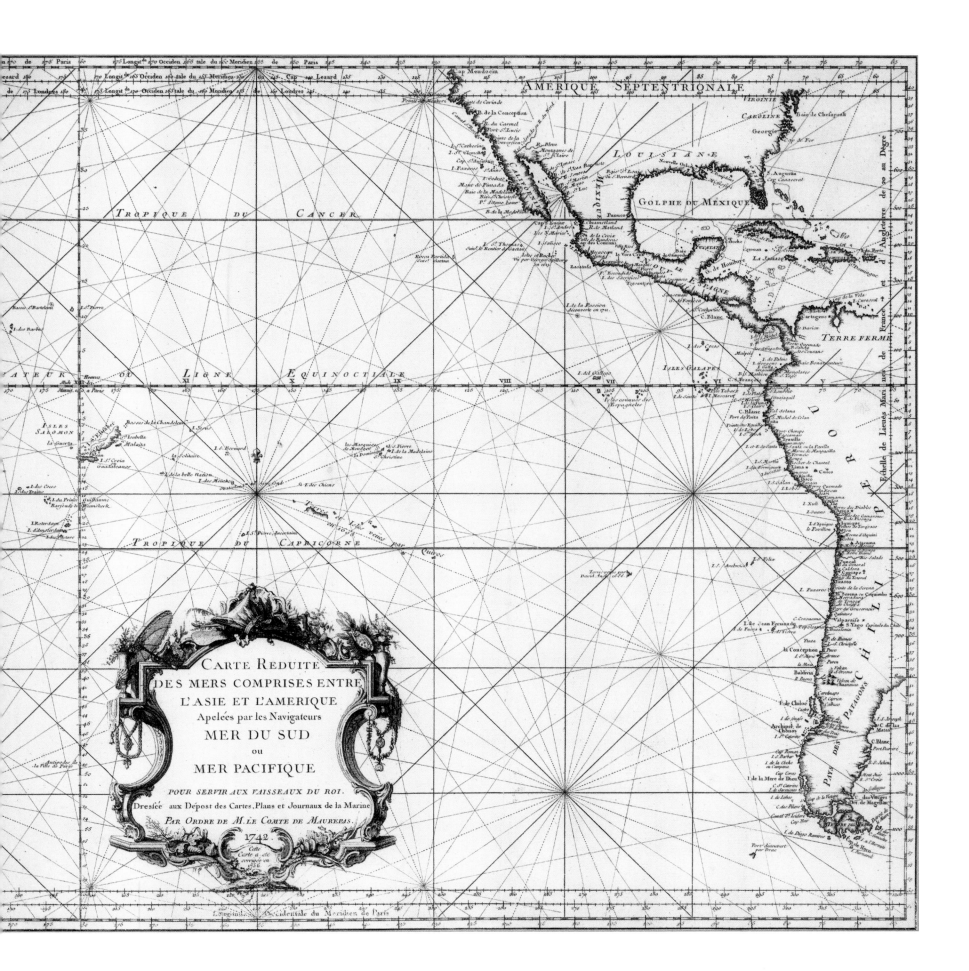

115

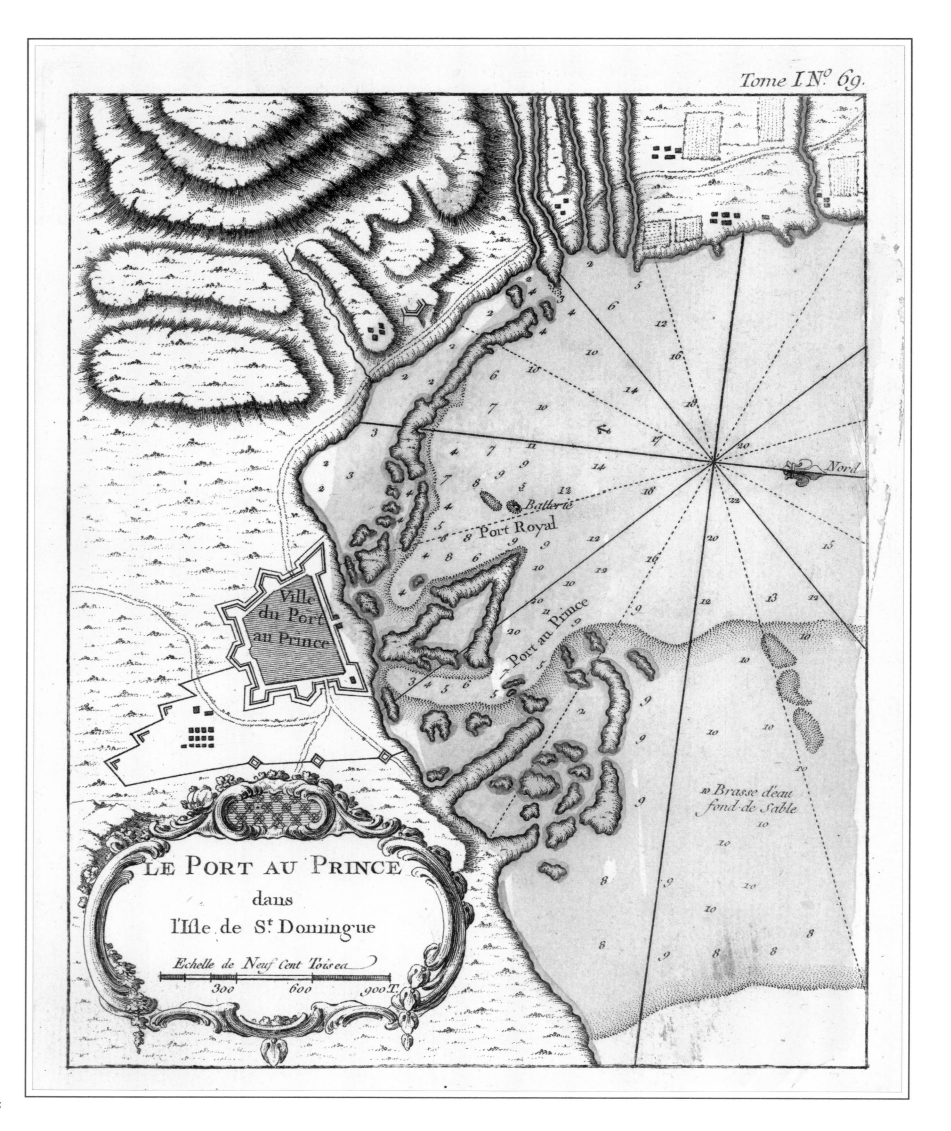

Nord

Batterie

Port Royal

Port au Prince

Ville du Port au Prince

10 Brasse d'eau
fond de Sable

LE PORT AU PRINCE
dans
l'Isle de St. Domingue

Echelle de Neuf Cent Toises

300   600   900 T.

Le Port au Prince dans l'Isle S. Domingue

This detailed chart of Port au Prince Bay in Haiti, then called Saint Domingue, was published in 1764 in Bellin's *Petit Atlas Maritime*. The chart is oriented with west at the top. The plan shows the town, fortifications, anchorages, soundings, buildings, and topographical details. The bay is filled with rhumb lines and a scattering of sounding depths. These are especially important because of the many islands in the bay and its large sandbars.

Only six years after this chart was published, Port au Prince became the capital of Saint Domingue. Although initially colonized by the Spanish, the French took over the western third of the island of Hispaniola in 1697 with the Treaty of Rijswijk. As in the rest of the Caribbean, they developed large-scale plantations worked by enslaved Africans, with coffee plantations in the interior and sugar on the northern plains.

The slave regime in Saint Domingue is considered by scholars as one of the most extreme. Slave mortality was high and violence common; the French imported over 800,000 men and women to the colony, practically double the total number imported to North America. This economic system built on the forced labor of thousands made Saint Domingue the most lucrative colony in the world. In 1791, Saint Domingue witnessed the largest and most successful slave revolt in history and was renamed Haiti.

Chartmaker Biography

*At age eighteen, **Jacques-Nicolas Bellin** (1703–1772) was appointed hydrographer to the French Navy. In August 1741, he became the first* Ingénieur de la Marine *of the* Dépôt de la Marine *and was named Official Hydrographer of the French King. During his term as Official Hydrographer, the* Dépôt *was the single most active center for the production of sea charts and maps.*

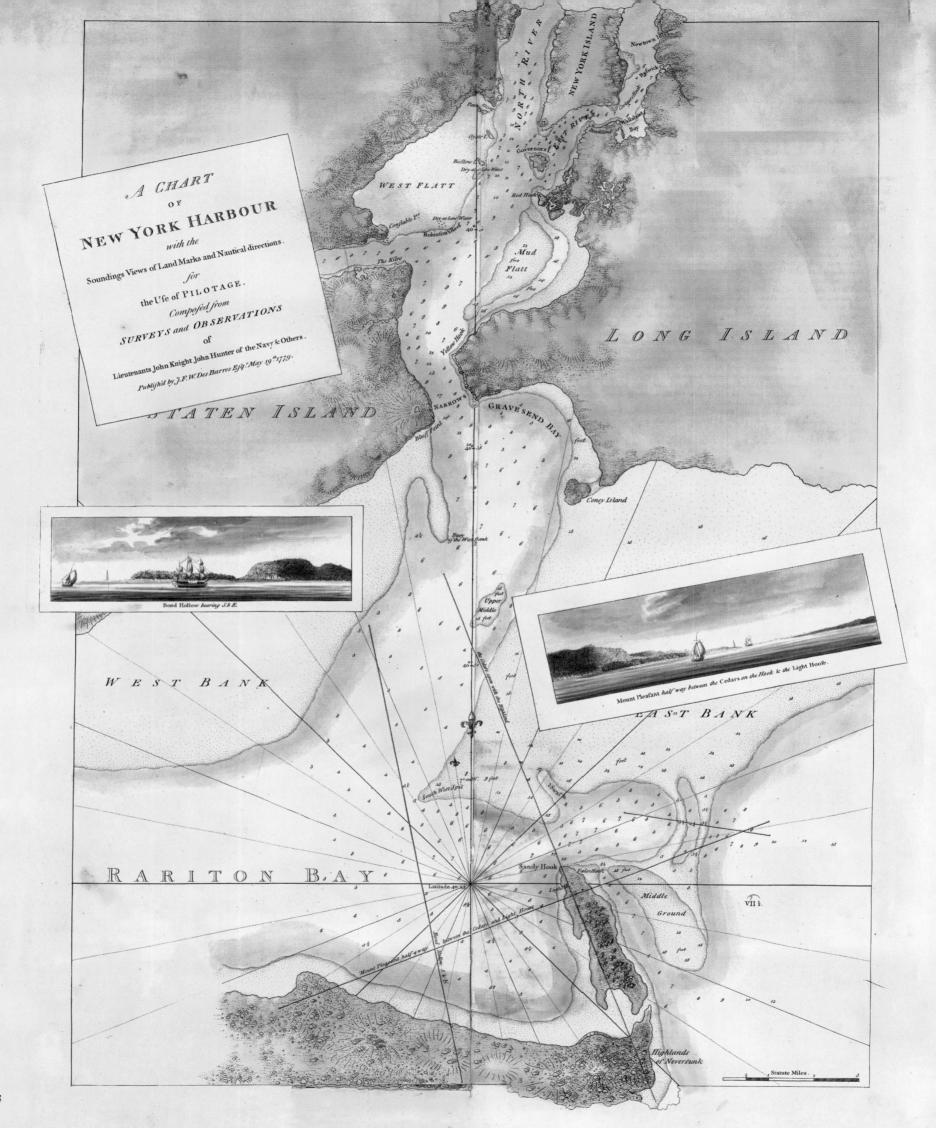

A CHART
OF
NEW YORK HARBOUR
with the
Soundings Views of Land Marks and Nautical directions.
for
the Use of PILOTAGE.
Composed from
SURVEYS and OBSERVATIONS
of
Lieutenants John Knight John Hunter of the Navy & Others.

Publish'd by J.F.W. Des Barres Esq.r May 19th 1779.

NORTH RIVER

NEW YORK ISLAND

EAST RIVER

Newtown

Bytwick

Wallabout Bay

Governors I.

Oyster I.

Bedlow I.

Dry at Low Water

Red Hook

WEST FLATT

Constable P.t

Dry at Low Water

Robinsons Hook

Mud for Flatt

The Kilns

Yellow Hook

LONG ISLAND

STATEN ISLAND

NARROWS

GRAVESEND BAY

Bluff Point

Coney Island

River of the West Bank

Bond Hollow bearing S.b.E.

Upper Middle

WEST BANK

Mount Pleasant half way between the Cedars on the Hook & the Light House.

EAST BANK

South West Spit

Shrews

RARITON BAY

Sandy Hook

False Hook

Light H.

Middle Ground

VII ½.

Latitude 40.

Mount Pleasant half way between the Cedars and Light House.

Highlands of Neversunk

Statute Miles.

A Chart of New York Harbour...

This Revolutionary War–era chart of New York Harbor was included in the significant nautical atlas, Joseph DesBarres's *Atlantic Neptune*. This example is different from others because it is attached to a set of sailing directions, a highly unusual inclusion for a DesBarres chart. The directions instruct a sailor on how to navigate into New York Harbor, the East River, and Long Island Sound.

The chart covers Manhattan Island to modern-day 42nd Street. It shows Hunters Point in Queens, Williamsburg down to Coney Island in Brooklyn, part of New Jersey bordering the harbor, part of Staten Island, and the Sandy Hook area of New Jersey. There are also two stylized landscape coastal profiles showing Bond Hollow and Mount Pleasant.

DesBarres's *Atlantic Neptune* was the first sea atlas to contain a systematic survey of the east coast of North America. After the Seven Years' War, DesBarres was enlisted to survey the coastlines of Nova Scotia, Newfoundland, and the Gulf of St. Lawrence. With these remarkably accurate surveys in hand, DesBarres returned to London in 1774, where the Royal Navy charged him with producing the atlas. The finished product was a four-volume sea atlas containing over 250 charts.

Chartmaker Biography

Joseph Frederick Wallet DesBarres (ca. 1721–1824) was a Swiss mathematician who immigrated to Britain, where he trained at the Royal Military College, Woolwich. In 1756, he joined the British Royal American Regiment as a military engineer, where his charts came to wider attention. After the war, DesBarres continued surveying and released the famous Atlantic Neptune. Later, he became lieutenant governor of Prince Edward Island.

Chart of the Sandwich Isles

Hawai'i was first encountered by Europeans when Captain James Cook led his crew there on his third, and final, voyage, arriving in early 1778. Cook was tasked with searching for the much-desired Northwest Passage, and Hawai'i proved a useful wintering stop when the ships, the *Resolution* and the *Discovery*, sailed south for the winter. They stayed for over two weeks at the end of January 1779, where they interacted peacefully with the native Hawai'ians. Unexpectedly, Cook had to return to Hawai'i after setting off because of a broken mast. An altercation broke out on the beach at Kealakekua Bay and Cook was killed on February 14, 1779. This bay is the subject of the inset in the bottom left of this chart.

The chart is a reprint of the first chart of the islands, which was released along with the account of the third voyage in 1784. It was drawn by Lieutenant Henry Roberts under the direction of Cook. The chart was also included in subsequent editions of Cook's popular account; this example was engraved for William Anderson's folio-sized edition of Cook's expeditions and other Pacific voyages, published in 1784.

The chart also includes the track and anchorages of Cook's ships, *Resolution* and *Discovery*. The inset has soundings and anchorage points, in addition to a macabre note marking where Cook died. Both the archipelago and the inset carry a good deal of topographic info as well as navigational; they would have been European readers' first glimpse of what were soon to become the most famous islands in the world.

This chart continued to serve as the basis for the Admiralty chart of the area, first issued in 1841. The insets would change over time, but the basic layout of the chart was unvaried for a century after Cook first landed on Hawai'i.

Chartmaker Biography

James Cook (1728–1779) was a surveyor, navigator, and explorer. He originally served in the merchant marine, before volunteering for the Royal Navy. There, he impressed his superiors with his skills for surveying, a skill that got him the command of a Pacific voyage to view the Transit of Venus in 1768. He led two other Pacific voyages, and created many excellent charts, before being killed in Hawai'i on his third voyage.

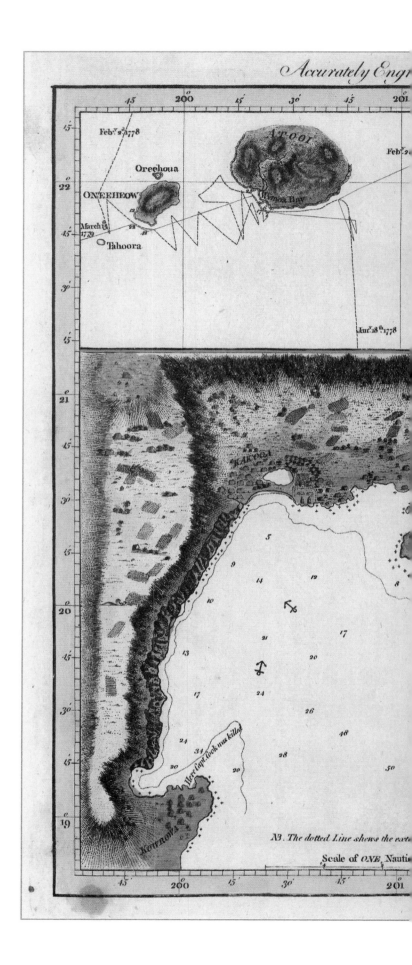

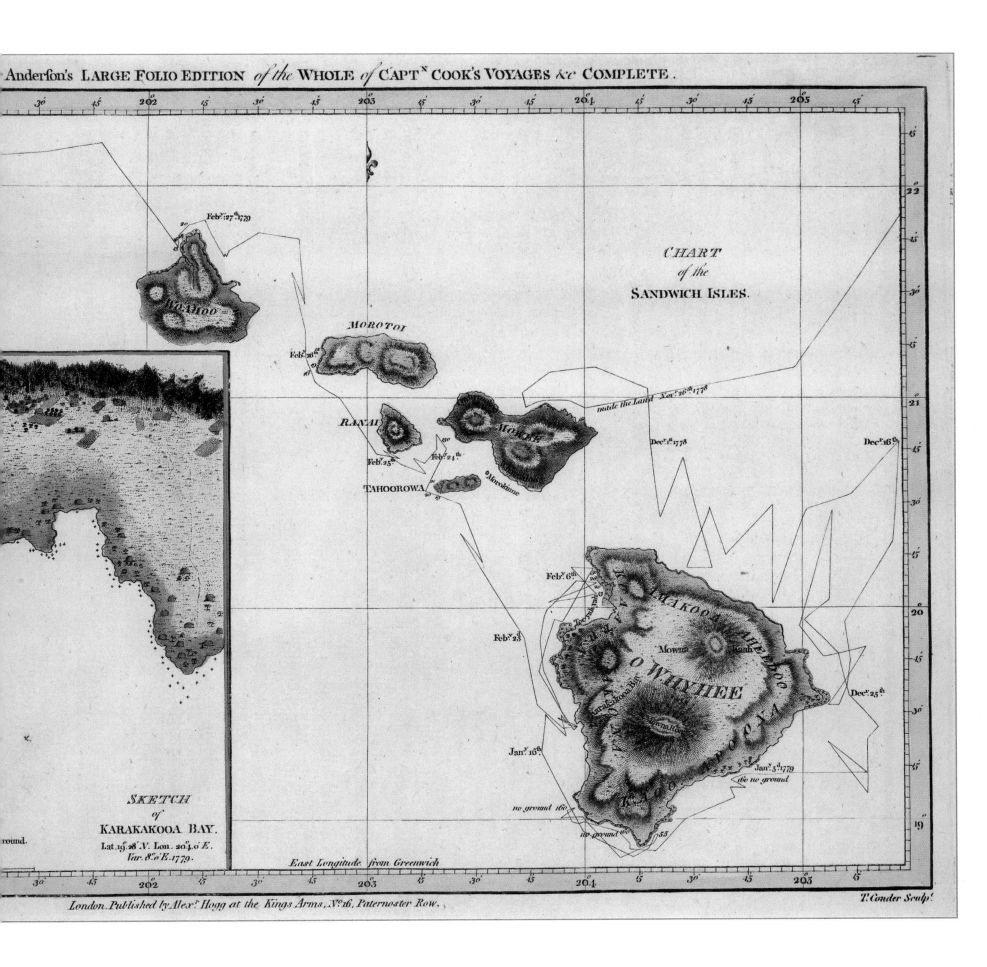

CHART
of the
SANDWICH ISLES.

WOAHOO

Feb.ʳ 27.ᵗʰ 1779

MOROTOI

Feb.ˢ 26.ᵗʰ

made the Land Nov.ᵗ 26.ᵗʰ 1778

RANAI

MOREE

Feb.ʳ 25.ᵗʰ   Feb.ʳ 24.ᵗʰ

TAHOOROWA   ⁰Morokinne

Dec.ʳ 1.ˢᵗ 1778   Dec.ʳ 16.ᵗʰ

MAKOO   AHEEDOO

Feb.ʳ 6.ᵗʰ

Toeahyah B.

Mowna

WHYHEE

Karakakooa Bay

Feb.ʳ 23.ᵈ

Dec.ʳ 25.ᵗʰ

Mowna Roa

Jan.ʳ 16.ᵗʰ

Jan.ʳ 5.ᵈ 1779

160 no ground

no ground 160

no ground 160   55

East Longitude from Greenwich

SKETCH
of
KARAKAKOOA BAY.
Lat.19°.28'.N. Lon. 204°.0'.E.
Var. 8°.0' E. 1779.

... round.

London. Published by Alex.ʳ Hogg at the Kings Arms, N.º 16, Paternoster Row.

T. Conder Sculp.ᵗ

121

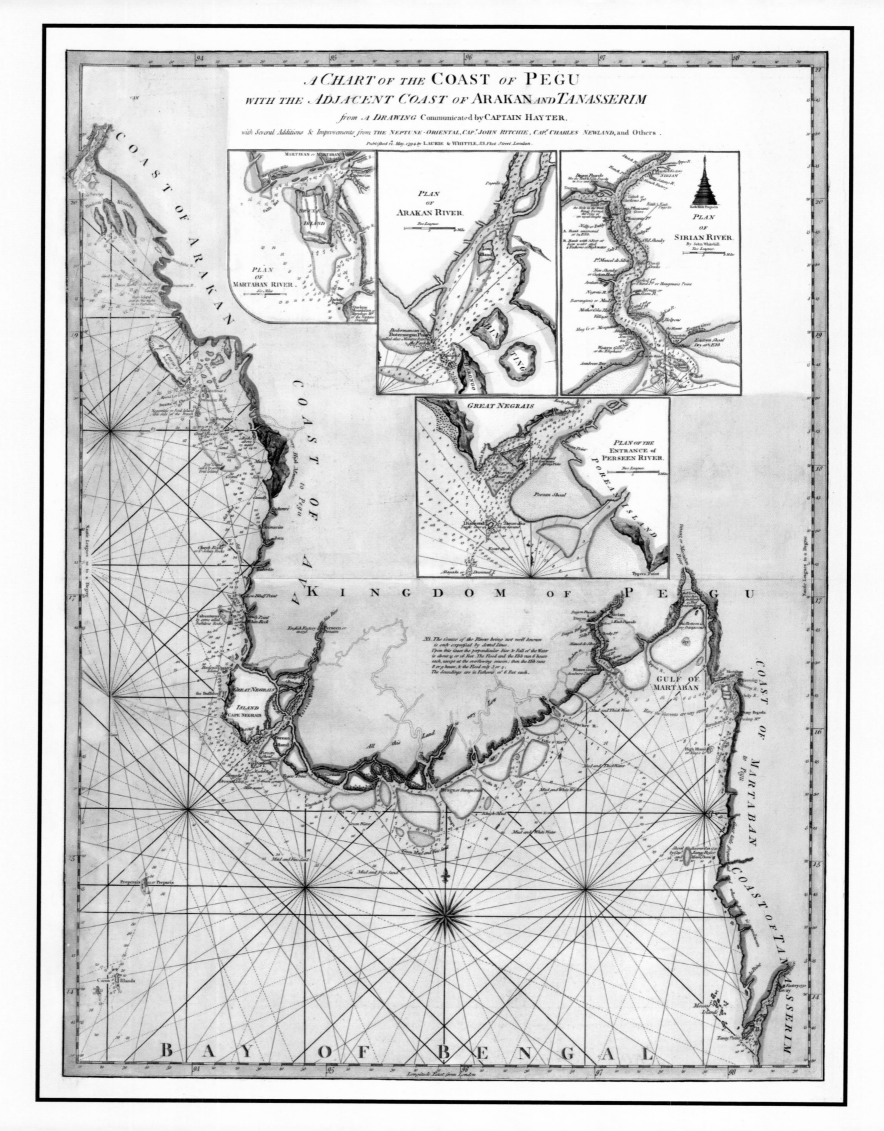

A Chart of the Coast of Pegu with the Adjacent Coast of Arakan and Tanasserim

Prior to the creation of the British Hydrographic Office, opened in 1795, private chartsellers were the only option for naval officers and ship's captains headed to sea. Laurie & Whittle forged a successful firm, largely thanks to the sale of nautical charts. Even after the Hydrographic Office began producing their own charts, they depended on authorized agents for the sale of the charts to the public.

This chart shows the coast of the Burma Peninsula from the Bay of Bengal to the Gulf of Martaban. Set into the peninsula are four insets showing the Martaban River, the Arakan River, the Sirian River, and the entrance of the Perseen River. Sailing notes accompany sounding depths and navigational obstructions along the shoreline.

The chart has a long history. It is based on a 1745 French chart included in the *Neptune Oriental* of Jean Baptiste Nicolas Denis d'Apres de Mannevillette. The English edition was updated with content from East India Company and merchant marine captains, who are named in the title. This chart dates to 1794, which was before the British colonized Burma, today Myanmar, in 1824.

Chartmaker Biography

*Laurie & Whittle refers to the partnership of **Robert Laurie** (ca. 1755–1836) and **James Whittle** (1757–1818), engravers and map publishers. Both men were employed by Robert Sayer (ca. 1724– 1794). When Sayer died, his business was taken over by his assistants. The two worked together as Laurie & Whittle until 1812, when Laurie retired.*

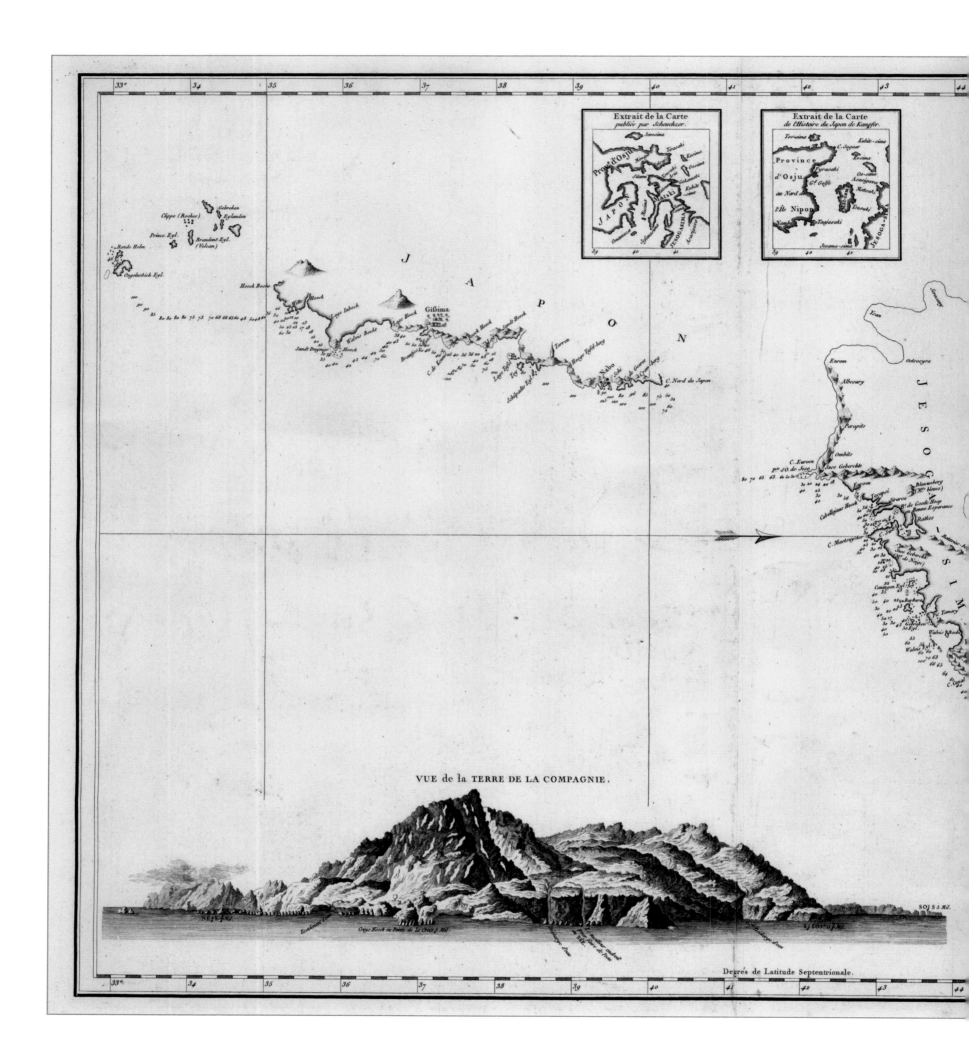

Extrait de la Carte
publiée par Scheuchzer.

Extrait de la Carte
de l'Histoire du Japon de Kæmpfer.

VUE de la TERRE DE LA COMPAGNIE.

Degrés de Latitude Septentrionale.

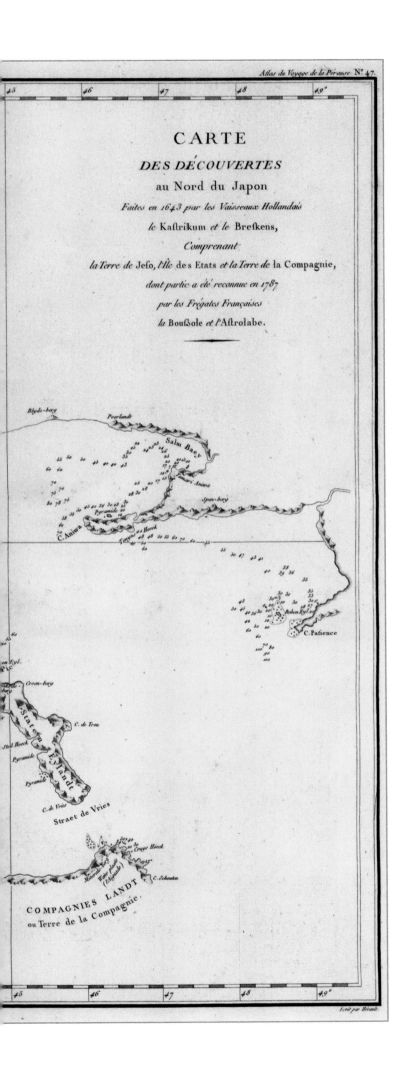

CARTE

DES DÉCOUVERTES

au Nord du Japon

Faites en 1643 par les Vaisseaux Hollandais

le Kastrikum et le Breskens,

Comprenant

la Terre de Jeso, l'Ile des Etats et la Terre de la Compagnie,

dont partie a été reconnue en 1787

par les Frégates Françaises

la Boußole et l'Astrolabe.

COMPAGNIES LANDT
ou Terre de la Compagnie.

Carte Des Découvertes au Nord du Japon

A feature of the state-sponsored expeditions that sailed in the late eighteenth century was the testing of geographic chimeras. One of these was Compagnies Land and Yesso in the northern Pacific. Oriented with west at the top, this chart shows the supposed discoveries made by the Dutch ships *Kastrikum (Castricum)* and *Breskens* in 1643 in the northern parts of Japan. It was published in 1797 from the papers of Jean-François de Galaup, the comte de La Perouse, France's most famous explorer. To the left is the coast of Japan, while to the right (north) are coastlines labeled as *Jesoga-Sima, Staten Eylandt,* and *Compagnies Landt.* Below is a view of the latter as seen from on deck a ship.

Jesoga-Sima is a reference to Jesso, a feature included on many eighteenth-century maps. Historically, Eso (Jesso, Yedso, Yesso) refers to the island of Hokkaido. It varies on maps from a small island to a nearly continent-sized mass that stretches from Asia to Alaska. La Perouse also mentions Dutch discoveries in 1643, which indicates that his understanding of Jesso is tied to two other North Pacific chimeras, Gamaland and Compagnies Land.

Juan, the grandson of Vasco da Gama, sailed from Macau to Japan in the later sixteenth century. He then struck out east, across the Pacific, and supposedly saw lands in the North Pacific. Several voyagers sought out da Gama's lands, including the Dutchman Maarten Gerritszoon Vries in 1643. Vries commanded the *Castricum,* while Hendrick Cornelisz Schaep was in charge of the *Breskens.* Compagnies Land, along with Staten Land, were islands sighted by Vries and named for the VOC and the Dutch States General (Staten Land). In reality, he had rediscovered two of the Kuril Islands.

In the mid-eighteenth century, Vitus Bering, a Danish explorer in Russian employ, and James Cook would both check the area and find nothing. La Perouse also sought the huge islands, but found only the small islands shown here, putting to rest the myth of the continent-sized dream lands.

Chartmaker Biography

Jean-François de Galaup, comte de La Perouse (1741–ca. 1788) joined the French Navy as a marine and served in the Seven Years' War and the American Revolution, traveling from the Indian Ocean to Hudson's Bay. He was selected to lead France's largest exploratory voyage to the Pacific in 1785. La Perouse and his two ships disappeared at sea in early 1788, but not before he sent a shipment of his papers back to France.

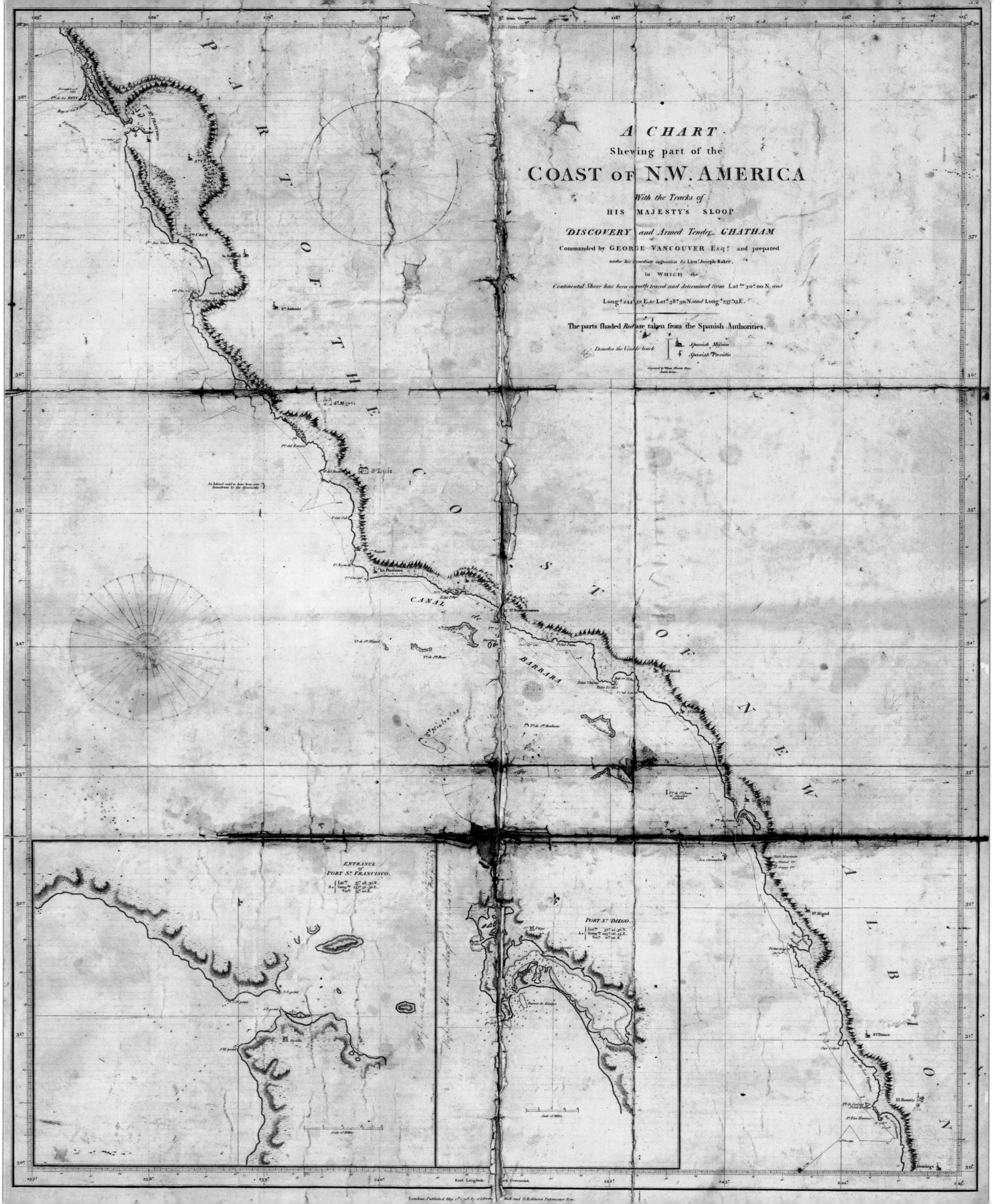
A CHART
Shewing part of the
COAST OF N.W. AMERICA
With the Tracks of
HIS MAJESTY'S SLOOP
DISCOVERY and Armed Tender CHATHAM
Commanded by GEORGE VANCOUVER Esq.r and prepared
under his immediate inspection by Lieu.t Joseph Baker,
in WHICH the
Continental Shore has been correctly traced and determined from Lat.de 30°. 00. N. and
Long.d 244°. 32 E. to Lat.d 38°. 30 N. and Long.d 237°. 13 E.
The parts shaded Red are taken from the Spanish Authorities.
Denotes the Vessels track
Spanish Mission
Spanish Presidio
PART OF THE COAST OF NEW ALBION
CANAL de SANTA BARBARA
S.t Luis
S.t Antonio
S.t Gabriel
S.t Tomas
El Rosario
Domingo
ENTRANCE of PORT S.T FRANCISCO
PORT S.T DIEGO
Scale of Miles
East Longitude from Greenwich
London: Published May 1st 1798, by J. Edwards Pall Mall and G. Robinson Paternoster Row.

A Chart Shewing Part
of the Coast of N.W. America

Another chart from a large state-sponsored voyage, this well-worn and heavily annotated chart shows the California coastline, including inset maps of San Francisco and San Diego. It was drawn from the observations of George Vancouver, who, like Cook and La Perouse, provided some of the first surveys of Pacific coasts and islands. These surveys and their charts would enter the *Dépôt de la Marine*, in the case of La Perouse, and, in the case of Cook and Vancouver, would form part of the core repository of the Hydrographic Office when it was formed in 1795.

In 1790, Vancouver was chosen to captain the *Discovery* and charged with a mission to discover and chart the vast areas of the Pacific that were still unknown, in part to locate a Northwest Passage between the Atlantic and Pacific Oceans. This four-year voyage of discovery circumnavigated the globe and eliminated the possibility of an inland Northwest Passage. During many months of surveying, Vancouver produced detailed regional maps of the Northwest Coast, as far north as Alaska. He also established several hundred place-names for physical features in the areas he surveyed. Upon returning to England in 1795, Vancouver's voyage received little recognition, and he faced personal and political attacks from colleagues and crew members alleging abuse of power. With his health failing, Vancouver spent his remaining years in retirement, revising his journal for publication.

The chart, prepared by Vancouver's lieutenant, Joseph Baker, featured in Vancouver's voyage account, published just after his death in 1798, and was also issued separately. This is an example of the latter backed on linen for more durable use, and it includes extensive navigation and other annotations by one or more early owners. Among the annotations are what appear to be sailing tracks between the San Diego and Santa Barbara areas, along with three compass drawings and an extensive grid.

Chartmaker Biography

George Vancouver (1757–1798) entered the Royal Navy in 1771. He served on both the second and third exploratory voyages of James Cook, gaining valuable surveying experience in the Pacific. After serving on fighting ships in the Caribbean, he commanded his own Pacific expedition (1790–1795). Although respected for his charting today, Vancouver returned to little fanfare and died at only 41 years of age.

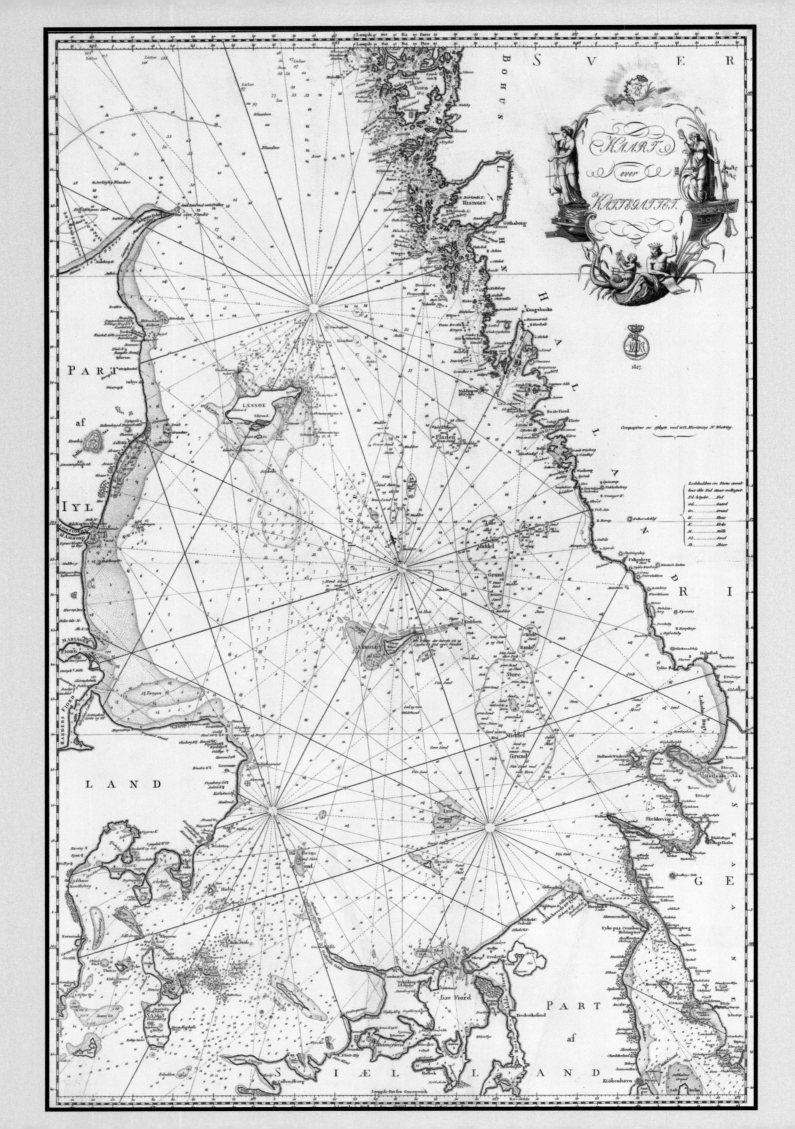

128

Kaart over Kattegattet

T his map is a separately published chart of the Kattegat, created in 1827 by the Royal Danish Nautical Charts Archive. This archive, in Danish *Kongelige Danske Søkort-Arkiv* (KDSKA), was established in 1784 and charged with providing the Royal Danish Navy and Danish merchant marine with accurate nautical charts.

The chart shows the Kattegat, which is the southern part of the passage between the North and Baltic Seas (along with the Skagerrak to its north) and surrounds parts of Denmark and Sweden. This chart includes portions of eastern Denmark and southwestern Sweden. Towns and elevation points that are visible from the sea are marked inland; otherwise, detail there is sparse. The sea, by contrast, is filled with information, including rhumb lines, sounding depths, obstruction markers, sandbars, and anchorages. Of particular interest are the *fyres*, or fires, that dot certain promontories and are colored red. These served as visual markers, just like lighthouses, to guide sailors.

The Kattegat is a strategically important passage, both for navigational and geopolitical reasons. As part of the connection between the Baltic Sea and the North Sea, it served as an important source of revenue for Danish royalty because of taxes collected on ships passing through it. Several major port cities in Denmark and Sweden, including Copenhagen and Gothenburg, flourished along the strait. The Kattegat, or "cat's throat" in Danish, is relatively narrow and contains numerous islands, making it difficult to navigate, so the utility of a detailed nautical chart of the area cannot be overstated.

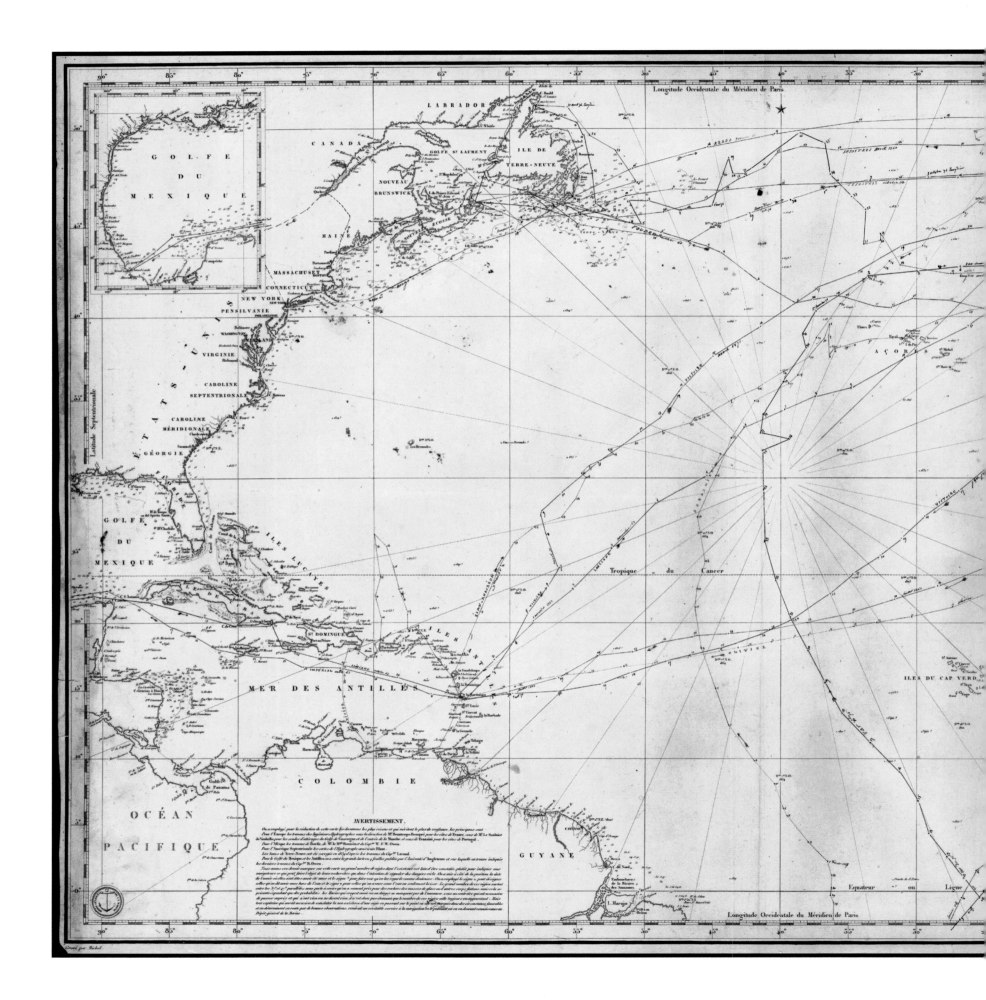

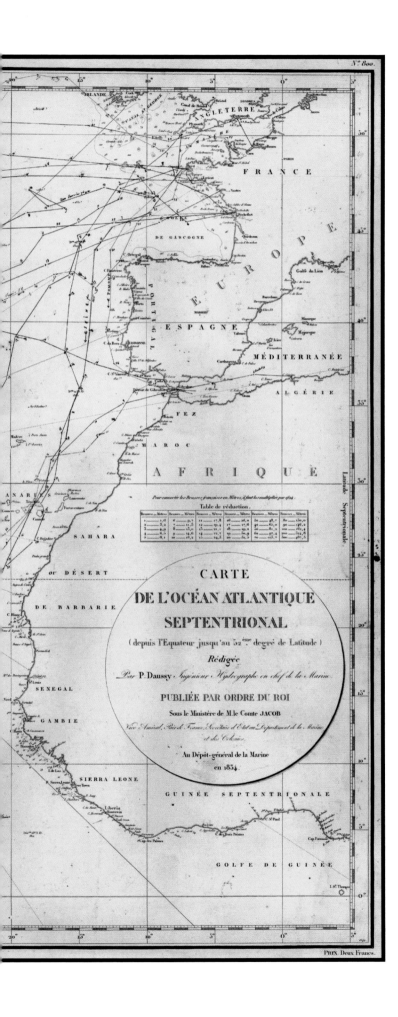

Carte de l'Océan Atlantique Septentrional

This general chart of the Atlantic Ocean shows the main thoroughfares ships would take to cross between Europe, Africa, and the Americas, as well as to get to Asia. A single starburst of rhumb lines is set in the middle of the ocean, while the simple, circular cartouche and table for scale calculations are tucked into inland Africa. An inset of the Gulf of Mexico, which is really an extension of the chart, is included in the interior of North America.

A large note is included in northern South America, explaining that the *Depôt* hydrographers had assembled this chart from the very latest surveys. These include those of Charles-François Beautemps-Beaupré along the coasts of France. Beautemps-Beaupré sailed on a voyage to find La Perouse's lost ships in the early 1790s, before returning to Revolutionary France, where he became its premier hydrographic engineer. In 1814, he was appointed head of the *Depôt*.

The rest of the note explains that scattered across the Atlantic are many small symbols, indicating sightings of rocks, islands, or other masses. Some have a year next to them, indicating when they were seen. However, far from confirming their existence, the majority have a question mark next to them, suggesting, as the note says, that any navigator who is close to the area should try to confirm the (non) existence of the feature and communicate their finding with the *Depôt*. While hydrography was certainly professionalizing at this time, information was still welcomed from a variety of sources.

The final interesting features of this chart are the many manuscript additions of ships' tracks that wander over the ocean. No fewer than fourteen voyages are meticulously marked on the chart, including the diplomatic voyages of the *Arago* and the *Foudre* at the beginning of the American Civil War and the invasion of Mexico under Napoleon III, ranging between the 1840s and the 1870s. It is possible that these voyages represent the service of a career naval man, or perhaps a diplomat who traveled widely.

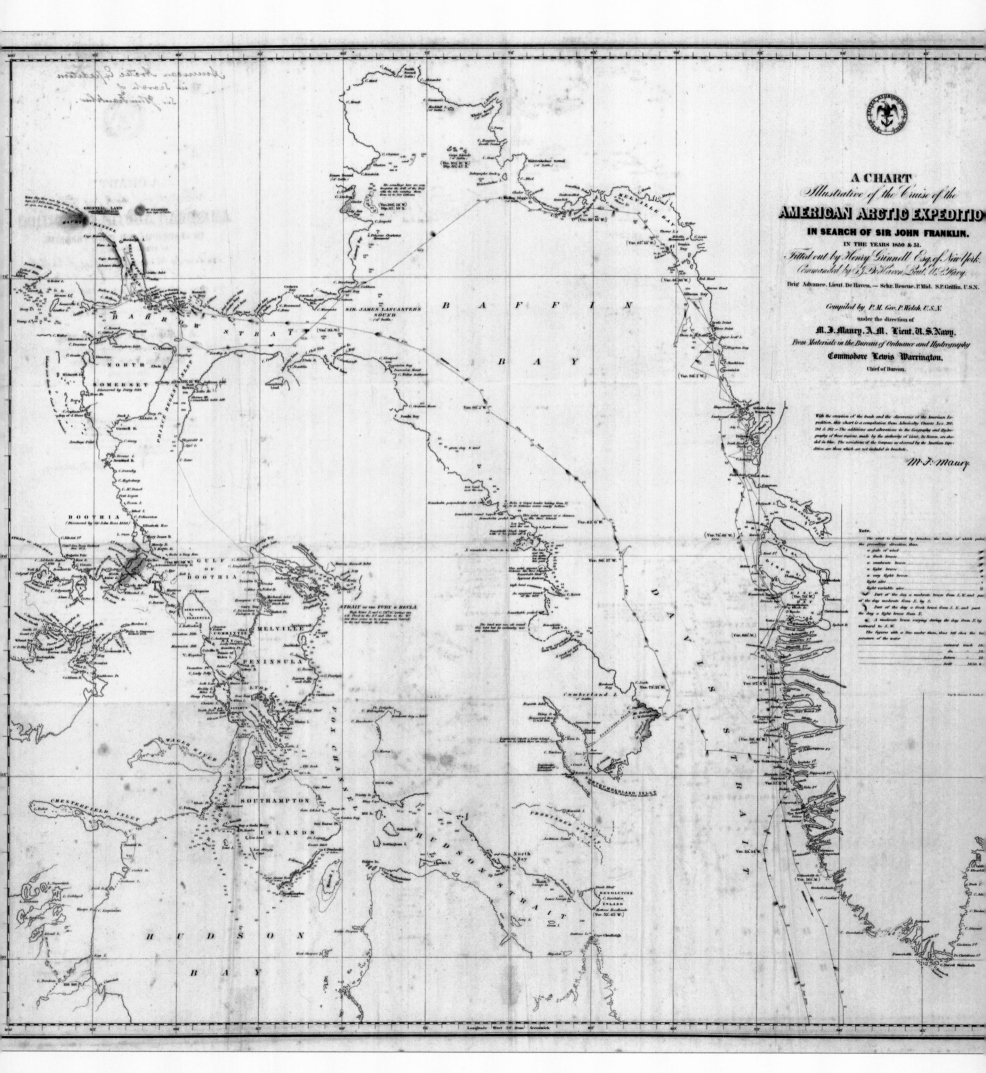

A CHART
Illustrative of the Cruise of the
AMERICAN ARCTIC EXPEDITION
IN SEARCH OF SIR JOHN FRANKLIN.
IN THE YEARS 1850 & 51.
Fitted out by Henry Grinnell, Esq. of New York.
Commanded by E.J. De Haven, Lieut. U.S. Navy.

Brig Advance, Lieut. De Haven. — Schr. Rescue, P. Mid. S.P. Griffin, U.S.N.

Compiled by P.M. Geo. P. Welch, U.S.N.
under the direction of
M.J. Maury, A.M. Lieut. U.S. Navy.
From Materials in the Bureau of Ordnance and Hydrography
Commodore Lewis Warrington,
Chief of Bureau.

M.J. Maury

A Chart Illustrative of the Cruise of the American Arctic Expedition in Search of Sir John Franklin

One of the most sensational stories of the nineteenth century was the disappearance of the expedition of John Franklin. Franklin's voyage, with 127 men on the *Terror* and *Erebus*, set sail on May 19, 1845 in search of the Northwest Passage. They proceeded to Baffin Bay, where they were sighted in July 1845 by two whalers. After that contact, both ships and all the men were never seen by Europeans again.

Over the course of a decade, nearly forty international expeditions, public and private, would set out in search of Franklin. One of these is the focus of this chart, published ca. 1851 by the United States Hydrographical Office under the direction of Matthew Fontaine Maury. It shows the First Grinnell Expedition of 1850–1851, the first American expedition to search for Franklin, which, alongside a British contingent, would locate the abandoned encampment and graves of several of Franklin's men on Beechey Island.

While the U.S. Coastal Survey was concerned with U.S. shores, the Board of Navy Commissioners established the Depot of Charts and Instruments in 1830. At first, they only stored and stockpiled the Navy's nautical charts, but in 1835 they began production of their own charts. This office transferred to the control of the Bureau of Ordnance and Hydrography in 1842, where it was known by several names including the United States Naval Observatory, the Hydrographical Office, the Depot of Charts, the National Observatory, and the Washington Observatory. It was finally officially named the U.S. Naval Observatory and Hydrographical Office in 1854 and shifted bureaucratic care once more, to the Bureau of Navigation, in 1862, from which the Hydrographic Office was split off in 1866.

Chartmaker Biography

__Matthew Fontaine Maury__ (1806–1873) circumnavigated the globe from 1826 to 1830. However, the young lieutenant was injured in a stagecoach accident, which turned his energies from active service to hydrography. In 1842, he was charged with the U.S. Hydrographical Office, where he was pivotal to the early study of oceanography. He served in the Confederacy during the American Civil War and later taught at the Virginia Military Institute.

Hong Kong Surveyed by Captn. Sir Edward Belcher, in H.M.S. Sulphur 1841

This is an 1857 updated edition of the first British Admiralty Chart of Hong Kong, based upon the surveys of Sir Edward Belcher. On January 26, 1841, Edward Belcher and his men were the first of the British fleet to land on Possession Point at the north shore of Hong Kong for the British Crown. He subsequently made the first British survey of Hong Kong Harbor. While the map is dated 1841, the first state of the map was not published until May 1843.

The British Hydrographic Office did send out survey expeditions in order to better chart certain areas of the world's waters. However, they also often depended on the work of naval officers who performed surveys in conjunction with other duties. Additionally, they accepted observations and sketches from members of the merchant marine and employees of the East India Company, when they showed areas for which the HO otherwise lacked information.

This chart is also a good example of the updating system at work in the HO. An HO engraver would meticulously prepare the plate for a chart, which was given a number within the HO's cataloguing system. New information was always streaming in, necessitating updates of charts. Rather than create a new plate, which is expensive, small changes could be added to or removed from the plate, depending on size, and the year of the changes was noted in the title or at the bottom of the chart. The HO sometimes also issued flaps, tiny scraps of paper meant to be attached to the larger chart to cover a detail that had been updated.

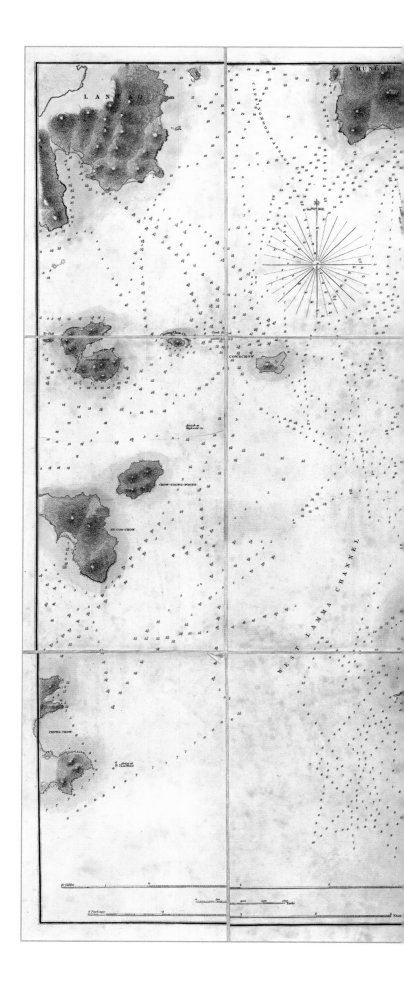

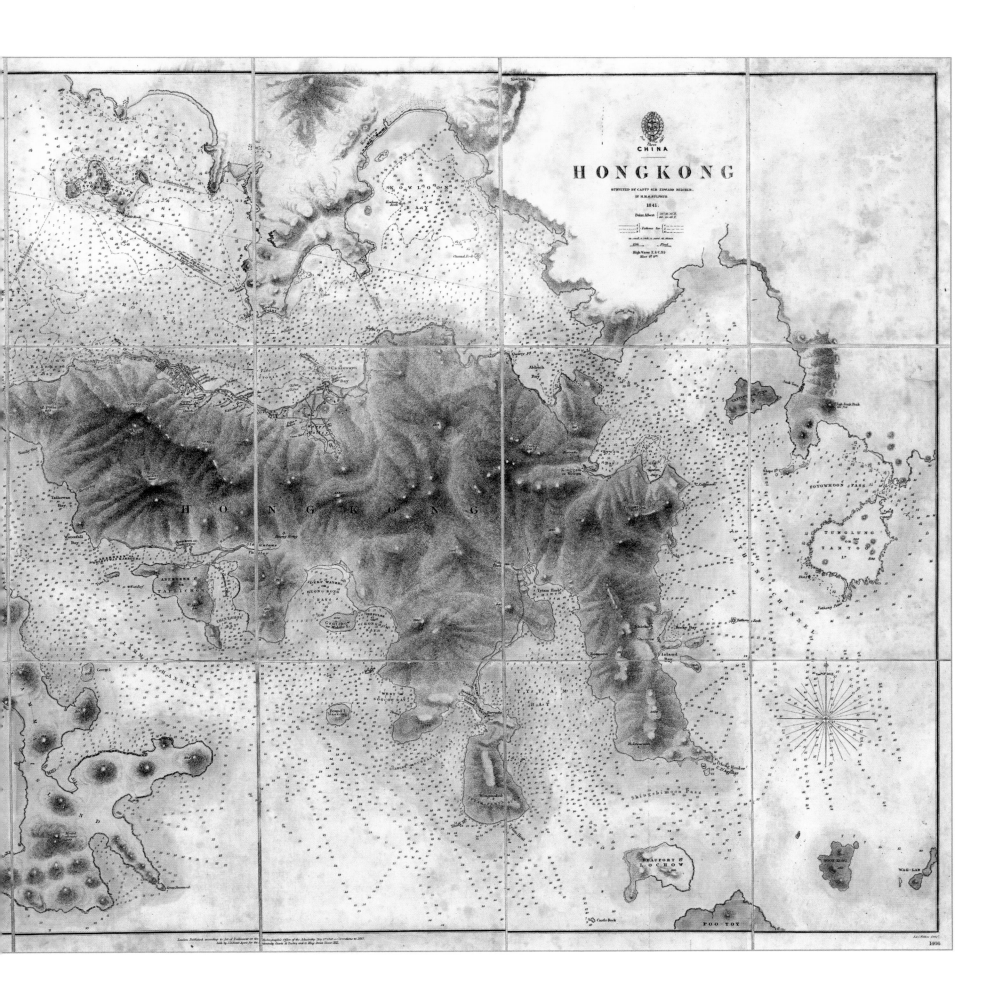

China

HONGKONG

SURVEYED BY CAPT.N SIR EDWARD BELCHER,
IN H.M.S. SULPHUR.
1841.

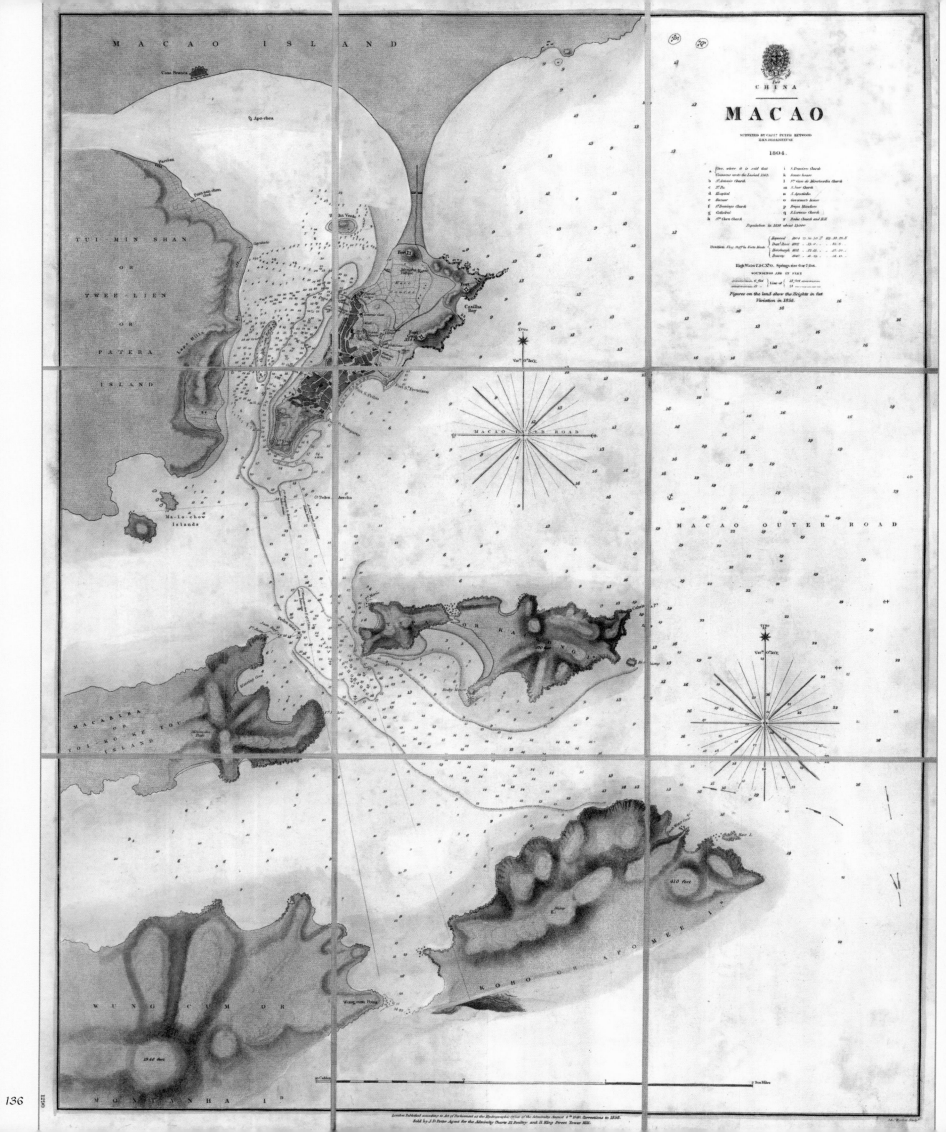

Macao Surveyed By Captn. Peter Heywood H.M.S. Dedaigneuse 1804

The chart shows the town of Macao, harbors and roadstead, along with Typa or Kaikong Island. The information for the chart is based upon a survey in 1804 under the instruction of Captain Peter Heywood of HMS *Dedaigneuse*. The chart was originally published by the Hydrographic Office in August 1840, with this example updated to 1858. In this case, the HO kept an older survey, as access to Macao was limited, and updated it as they could.

Heywood's survey superseded the survey carried out by William Bligh in 1779–1780, when the latter was master of the *Resolution* during Cook's third voyage. However, it was not attributed to Bligh in the published account of Cook's third voyage. Heywood served with Bligh on the *Bounty* voyage and participated in the mutiny against him.

Until 1999, Macao was under Portuguese control. This chart was issued during the Second Opium War (1856–1860), when the British were particularly interested in China and the islands near the mainland. The Portuguese had tightened their hold on the island and were operating with increased impunity, as the Chinese were weakened after the First Opium War (1839–1842). The detail on Macao, showing the fortifications, is unusual for a chart, but may indicate the importance of Macao as a port before the First Opium War.

Chartmaker Biography

Peter Heywood (1772–1831) was condemned to execution as a mutineer on Bligh's Bounty, *but was pardoned and resumed his naval career. In 1803, after a succession of commands, Heywood was promoted to Post Captain. He conducted surveys of the coasts of India, Sri Lanka, Morocco, the River Plate, Sumatra, and Australia. Heywood was offered the position of Hydrographer to the Admiralty, but he declined.*

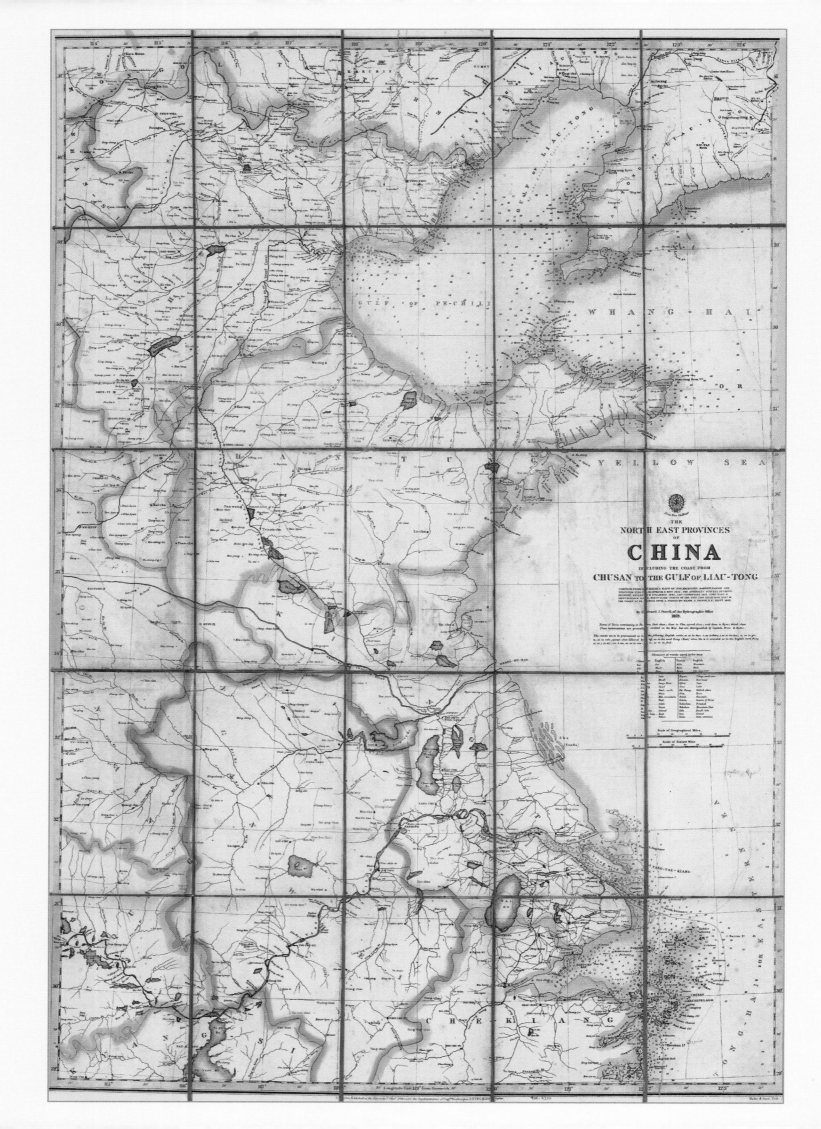

138

The North East Provinces of China Including the Coast...

This large map offers a sweeping view of northeast China, from Nimrod Sound and the Chusan Archipelago in the south to the Gulf of Liau-Tong in the north. The map includes sounding depths as a navigational aid, but it also contains a lot of information inland, such as roads, rivers, cities, and—marked with a crenulated pattern—the Great Wall.

The map includes pencil annotations in French showing the course of a ship which entered Shanghai from the south and thereafter departed to the north between June 8 and July 3. The user was thwarted, however, by the conical projection, making the course incorrect, as can be seen with the correction to the position of July 2.

This conical projection, along with its issue in full color, signals that this is no ordinary Admiralty chart. Clearly not intended for navigation, it is more likely a propaganda map meant to show the theatre of the Second Opium War. It seems that this was one of several charts issued by the Hydrographic Office that were used by the army and other branches of government. It shows that the Hydrographic Office was central not only to navigation, but to the cultural production of imperial Britain.

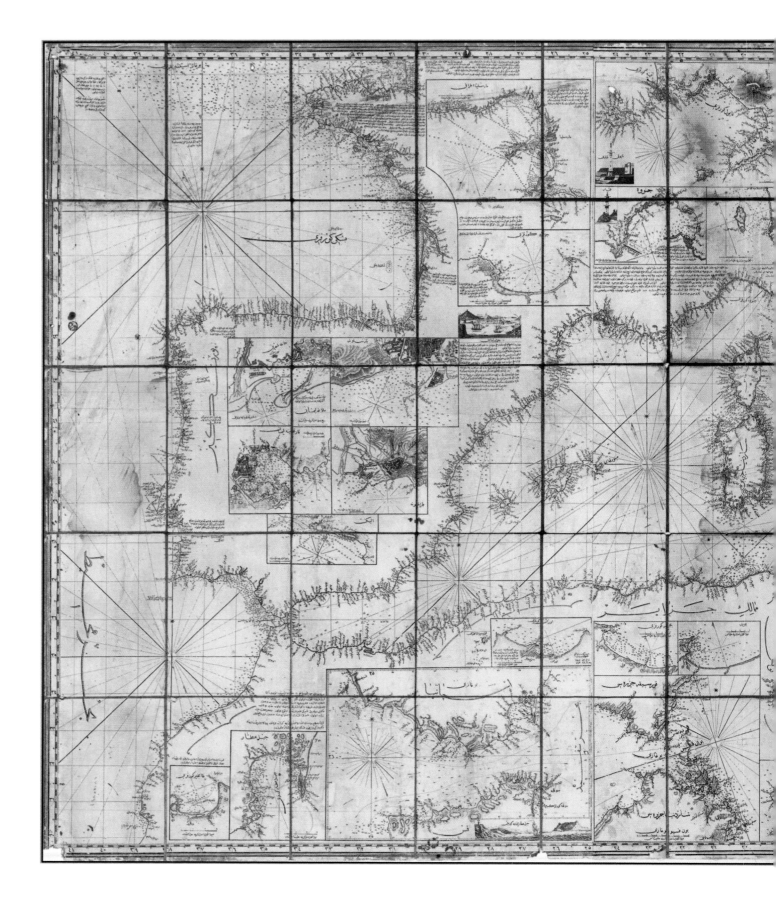

[Turkish Sea Chart of the Mediterranean]

This large-format chart shows the entirety of the Mediterranean with many insets. These insets include a mixture of large-scale plans and views of cities and landmarks. They include Malta, Malta with the city of Valletta, Corfu, San Elmo Lighthouse, Trieste, Trieste Lighthouse, Calabria, Messina, Sicily, Napoli, Napoli Lighthouse, Genoa with its lighthouse, Marseille, North Africa, the Limani Islands, Barcelona, Malaga, Tabia and Tarhuna of Tuni, Carthage, Alicante, Eskisehir, and Aboukir fortress.

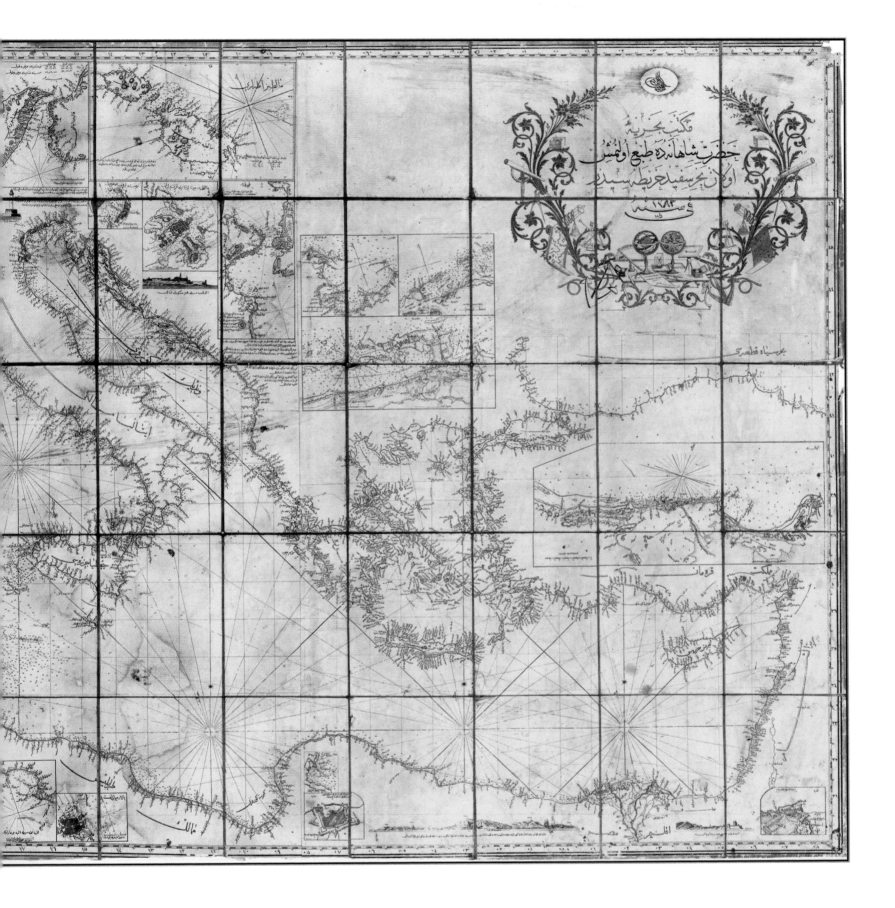

The coasts are drawn meticulously on this general chart, and the many sounding depths and sailing notes would make this an informative chart for sailing or reference. It is useful to compare this chart to the portolan charts with which this book began. While it may resemble a portolan chart, the decorations here are actually insets, providing more detailed information than the general chart is able to do. There is no color to differentiate types of port or political units, but there is much more text than a portolan would usually include. The rhumb lines are less intrusive on this chart, but the overall amount of information is more densely presented, something that engraving allows more easily than ink.

The chart was produced by *Mekteb-i Bahriye Hazreti Sahane*, the Turkish Naval Academy, in 1865. The academy dates back to 1773, when it was founded as a naval school under Sultan Mustafa III. The school transitioned from a temporary course to a permanent college specialized in marine engineering and navigation.

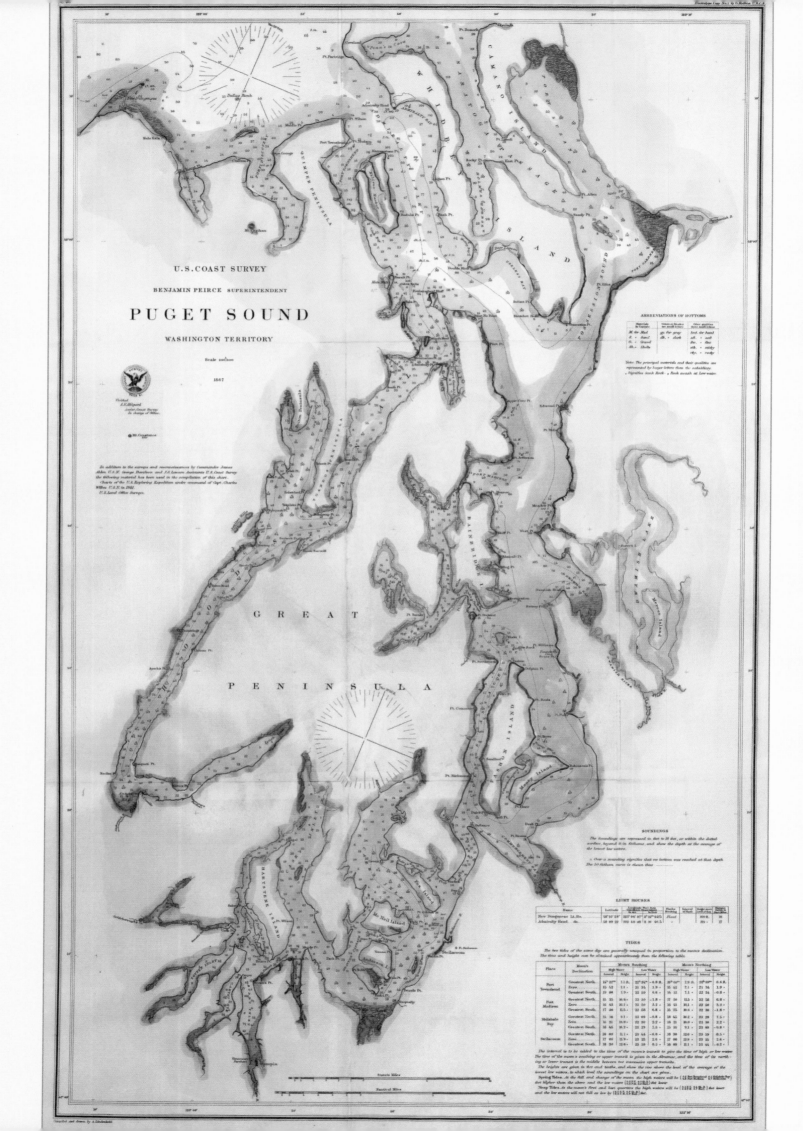

Puget Sound, Washington Territory

This is one of the earliest large-format charts of Puget Sound, in the state of Washington. It includes several simple compass roses, which include magnetic declination, and a veritable blanket of sounding depths. Abbreviations such as "M" and "Sh" are also listed in the water, indicating different kinds of sea floor, in this case "Mud" and "Shells." A table to the right explains these abbreviations, while tables in the lower right list lighthouses and tides.

This chart indicates the degree to which oceanography had become a science, and the effect this had on charts. The density of information on charts increased, even as their decorative elements decreased. Not only are soundings included, but more standardized symbols for bottoms (which had long been discussed with short notes), tides, magnetic declination, and the precise coordinates of lighthouses, calculated to the second, are all considered vital to a navigator of 1867, when this chart was issued by the U.S. Coast Survey. This was also the year that the Coast Survey published its first tide tables.

Puget Sound was initially charted by George Vancouver; it is named for his lieutenant, Peter Puget. As listed under the title, information for this chart also came from more recent surveys conducted by U.S. Coast Survey personnel, U.S. Land Office surveys, and charts from the U.S. Exploring Expedition. This last source, commonly called U.S. Ex Ex, was a massive exploratory voyage commanded by Captain Charles Wilkes and conducted from 1838 to 1842. The expedition employed scientists and produced an unprecedented number of specimens and observations, including charts of many parts of the Pacific.

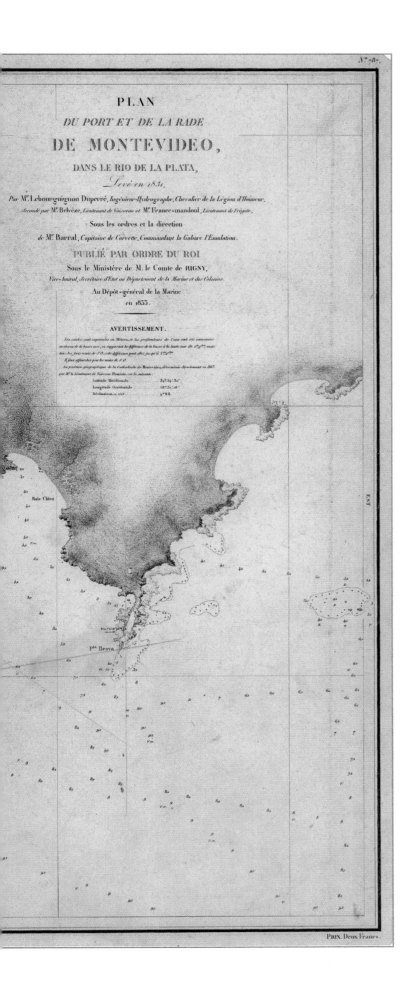

Plan du Port et de la Rade de Montevideo, dans Le Rio de la Plata

This *Dépôt de la Marine* chart shows the area around Montevideo, Uruguay, as surveyed by Cyprien Gabriel Le Bourguignon-Duperré the year after the establishment of the first Uruguayan Constitution in 1830. A particular feature of this chart is the thorough depiction of Montevideo, located on a peninsula jutting into the waters where the Atlantic Ocean meets the Rio de la Plata. Landmarks in the city are noted, including the *Place Cagancha, le Marche*, and *Cathedrale Feu*. The docks, jetties, and buildings of the coast nearby are also included for reference. The chart is updated to 1877, although the town plan has not been updated, underlining its primary use as a chart, not a map.

Uruguay became an independent state in 1828 and declared Montevideo the capital. The city was besieged for eight years between 1843 and 1851, but by the 1860s it entered a period of rapid growth. For example, the neighborhood of Cordón, a small assembly of buildings on this chart, was incorporated into the larger city in 1861. The first railways were connected in 1869.

The local topography is shown with shading to indicate altitude, helpful information for sailors who would see the landscapes from the water. The course of the hydrographers is clear from the straight lines of sounding depths in the bay.

A past user has added intersecting lines in pencil, perhaps an attempt to triangulate a course or calculate a distance. There have been several examples of annotations and marginalia in this chapter; charts were not just admired, but used by many nineteenth-century people.

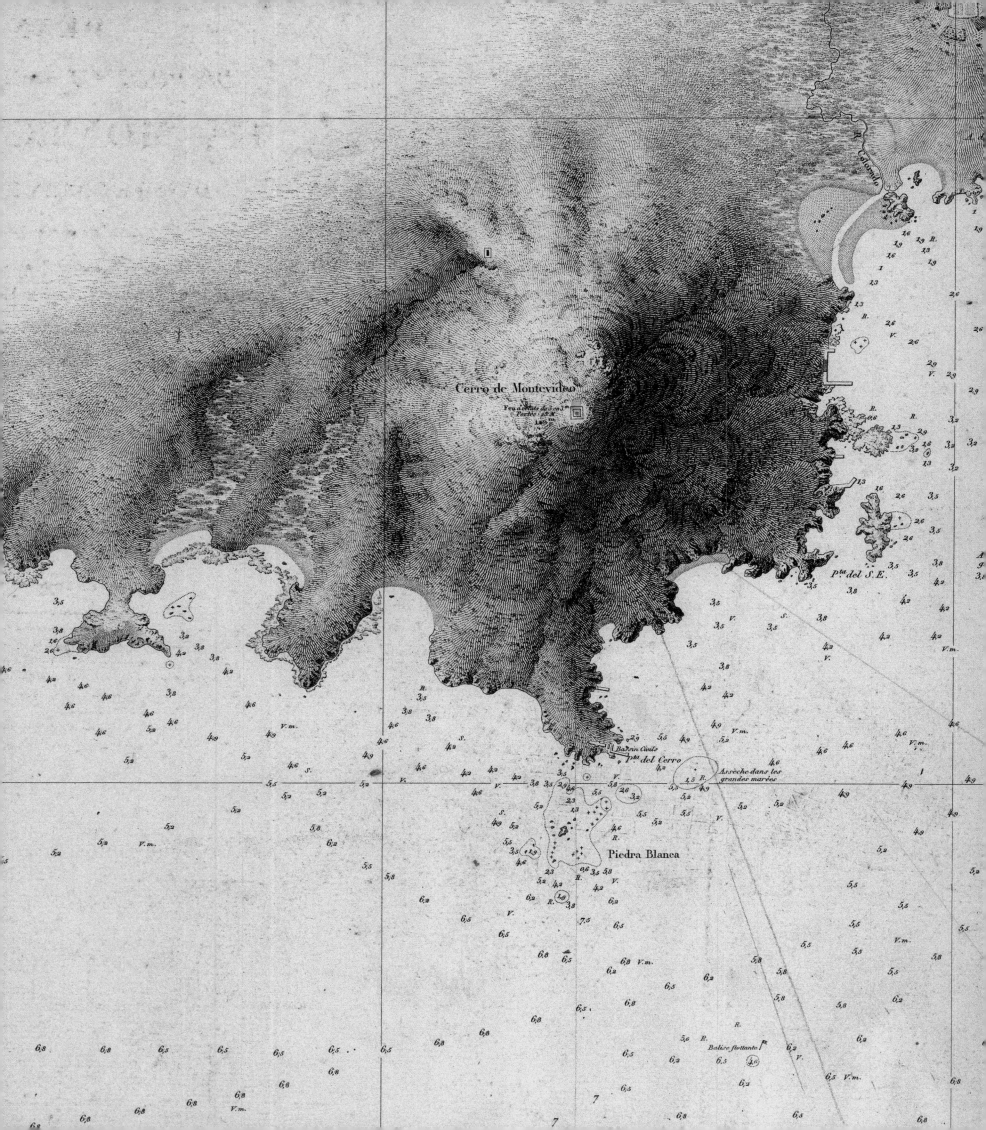

Cerro de Montevideo

P.ta del S.E.

P.ta del Cerro

Piedra Blanca

Assèche dans les
grandes marées

Balise flottante

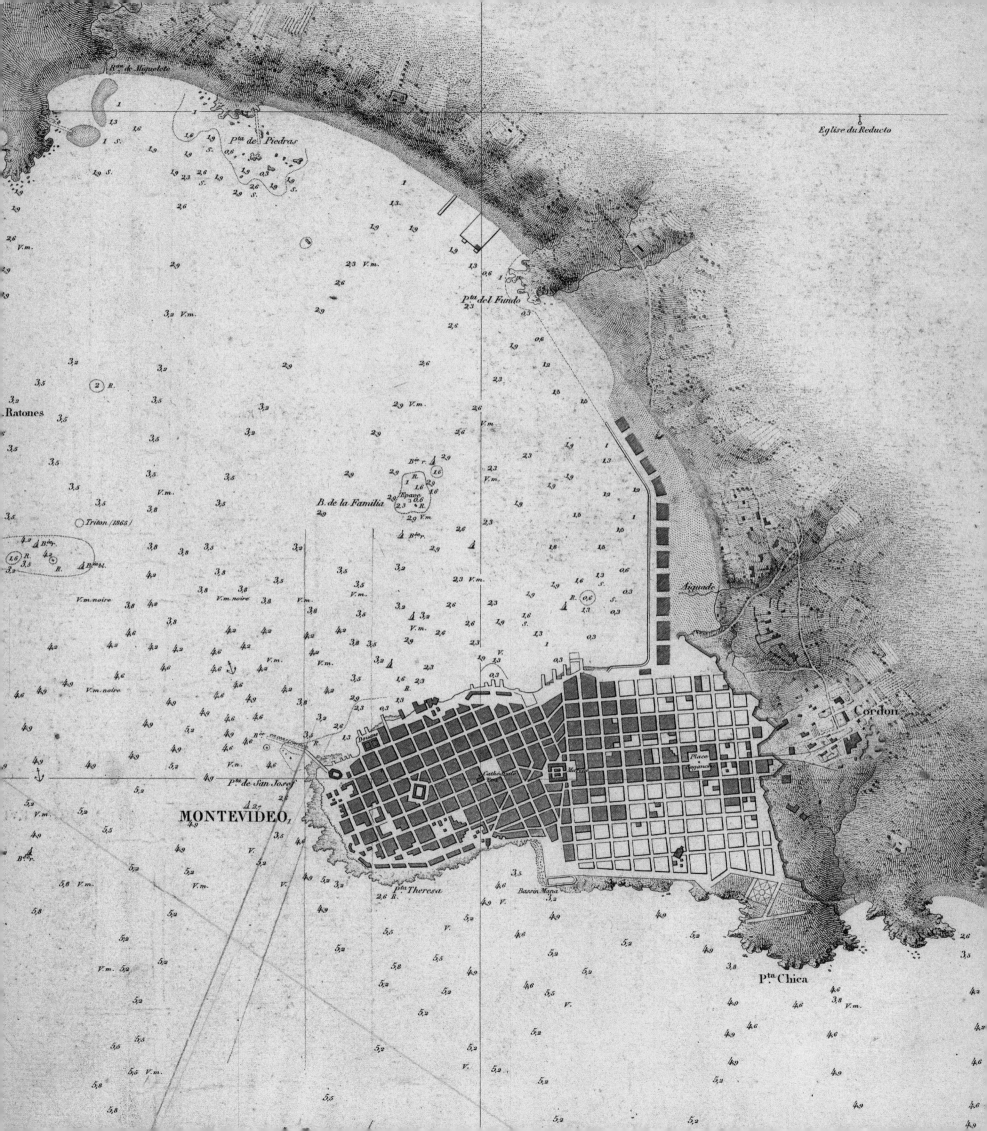

MONTEVIDEO

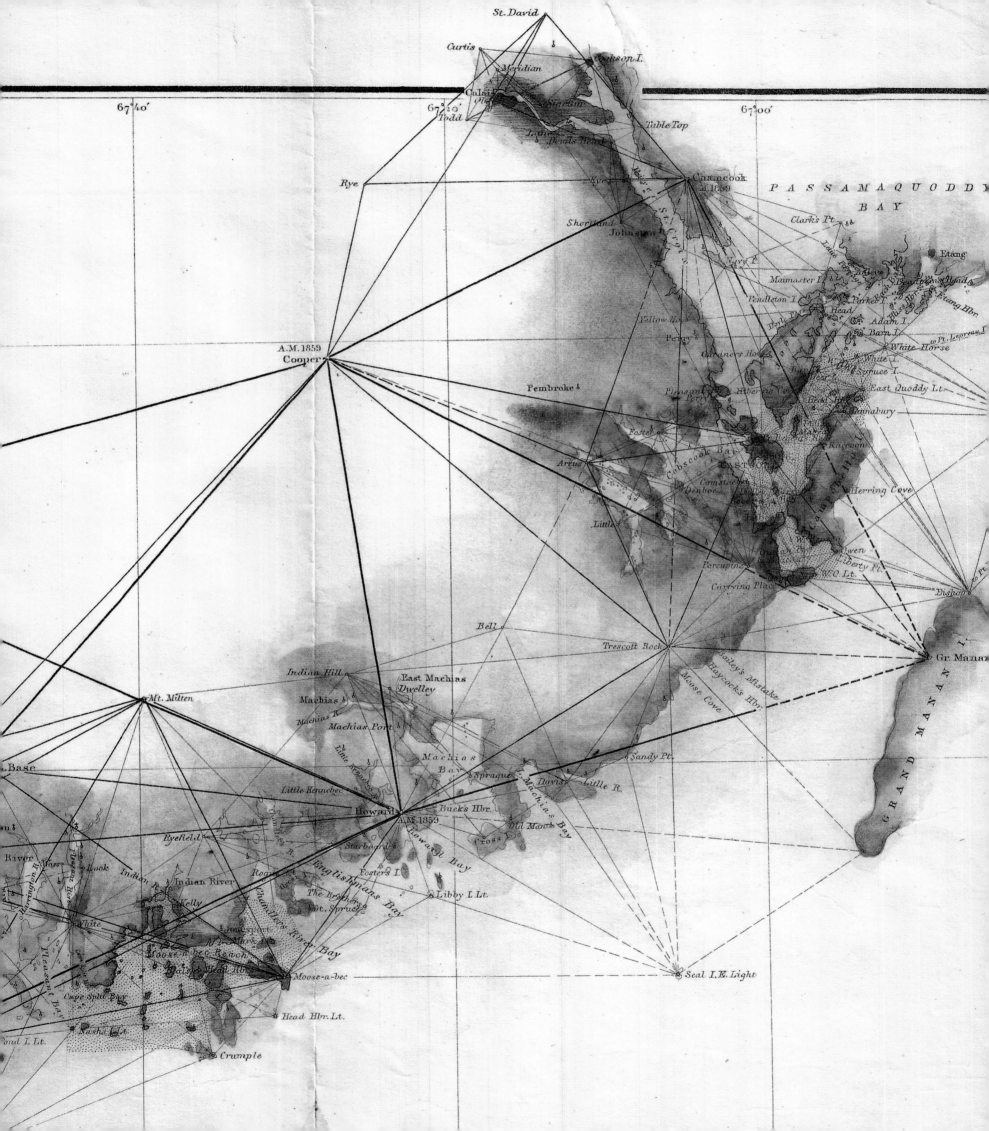

Sketch A, Showing the Progress of the Survey in Section No. 1 from 1852 to 1871

This chart shows the coastline from Portland, Maine to Passamaquoddy Bay; inland are Bangor and Calais. The extent to which the shore has been studied and recorded is evident from the jagged detail shown on the many islands and coasts. In the bottom right is an inset showing how the coastal survey could be connected to the larger Northeast Boundary Survey. In the upper left corner is an inset of Portland Harbor, which was surveyed in 1864.

The plethora of triangles connected across the coastline indicates an important method of surveying: triangulation. By creating a network of connected triangles, it is possible to accurately determine distance and relative position of points. These points are usually attached to specific geographic features or to markers the surveyors erect. This process allows surveyors to measure the angles of the triangles, rather than the distances themselves, a useful method when rough terrain or long distances prevented direct overland or oversea measurement. As long as the points of a side of the triangle were visible, and the length of an initial side of the triangle is known, the other sides of the triangle can be calculated. More and more triangles are added until an entire area is covered with calculations, which can then be transferred to a chart and filled in.

A chart like this, or, to use the term in the title, a "sketch," is not intended for navigation. Rather, it is intended to inform the surveyors and officials of their larger project in progress and to relate distances. However, triangulation was important for navigation and charting, as it could correct existing charts by more accurately calculating distances between coastal features.

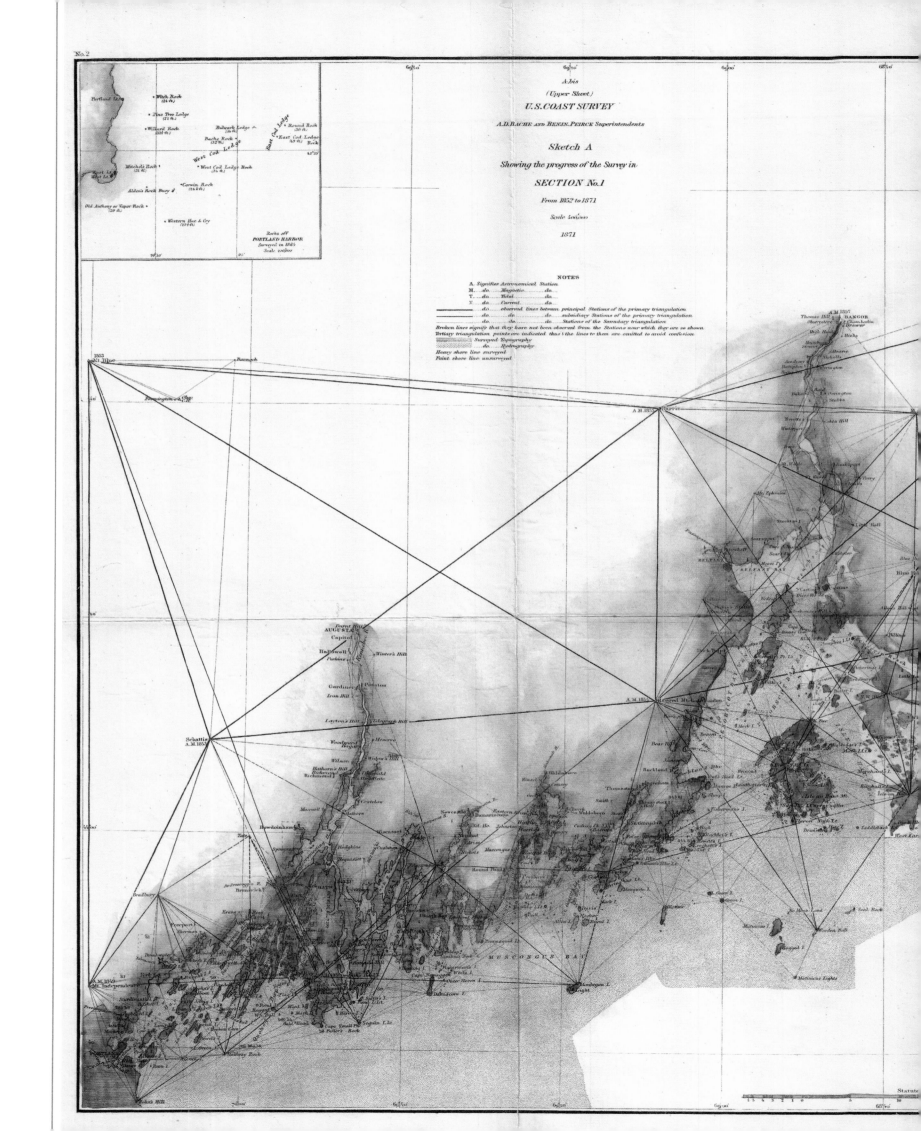

RECONNOISSANCE

For connecting the Survey of the Coast
with the N.E. Boundary Survey

Scale 600000

1867

151

Private and Corporate Chart and Mapmaking in the Nineteenth Century

*I*n the last chapter, the featured charts showed a shift from the relatively closed and ostensibly competitive national and imperial chartmaking traditions of the early modern era to a more open and collaborative, if still siloed, process of the state-run hydrographic bodies of the nineteenth century. This transition mirrors larger changes in cartography, which became a scientific discipline in the nineteenth century. As cartographic standards and practices became the purview of the academy, norms were decided with input from an international cadre of savants, in conjunction with the emerging cross-border organizations and conferences that met to govern trade and mobility.

The professionalization of cartography and the regulation of charting affected the content and look of charts. Charts were still primarily intended as a tool of navigation, but they became caught up in the scientific fallacy that surrounded academic cartography. Maps or charts became synonymous with truth and accuracy; they were supposed to be an exact representation of space and therefore to suggest mimesis of a real place. Of course, maps and charts are reductions and simplifications of space that can never capture the changeable nature of landscape, especially of coastline. They can also be constructed so as to hide detail or alter perception; in effect, they can lie. However, the power extended to maps and charts as scientific—and therefore seemingly objective—objects in the nineteenth century meant that expectations of their detail and utility outweighed skepticism of their limitations.

In terms of content, this meant that all features were now drawn to scale; insets showed areas of special concern, rather than exaggerating the entrance to bays and ports as portolan charts had done. Profile views of coasts were separated from the plan views of coastlines and limited in size and number. Ornamentation continued to be limited to a title cartouche, if it was included at all. Rhumb lines were diminished in emphasis, with no compass roses at their center and with shortened lines. These changes were not sudden, but happened over the course of the eighteenth and nineteenth centuries, or across chapters 3 to 5 of this book. Nor were the changes linear and final; some charts continued to include older characteristics and decorations as ways to differentiate themselves in a crowded market.

People trusted maps and charts to give them information, an expectation conditioned by major developments in the technology of hydrography, cartography, and navigation in the eighteenth and nineteenth centuries. The most important of these was the discovery of methods to calculate longitude. Latitude is discernible by observing the altitude of the sun at midday or certain stars (usually Polaris in the northern hemisphere or the Southern Cross in the southern) from aboard ship using a variety of instruments that were adapted from astronomy from the late Medieval period onward. Longitude, however, involves more observations and more complex calculations and eluded navigators until the eighteenth century.

In 1707, a squadron of Royal Navy ships were wrecked on the Scilly Islands, with 1600 lives lost. The ships had miscalculated their longitude, *which set them on a collision course with the islands. This tragedy led the British Parliament to declare a prize for the successful implementation of a method to calculate longitude at sea. Other governments also offered prizes, and answers to the longitude problem poured in across the eighteenth century.*

Eventually, two methods were accepted as viable answers: lunar distance and chronometers. The latter, which are clocks that can keep time accurately at sea, were pioneered by John Harrison and perfected by a variety of other horologists and instrument makers. The lunar-distance method was developed by Royal Astronomer Nevil Maskelyne and Robert Waddington. From 1766, the Nautical Almanac *offered sailors tables for converting their observations and calculations of lunar distance into longitude. Also in the 1760s, chronometers were put through their first sea trials. Both methods, however, took decades to come into common use, much like the Mercator projection. Additionally, charts were also impacted by more systematic surveying and the development of marine science, as with the study of wind patterns, as will be seen in examples in this chapter.*

State-run hydrographic services were certainly not the only entities publishing maps and charts during the nineteenth century. Initially, some of the hydrographic offices contracted with private firms to release charts. Many large private firms flourished in the nineteenth century, reflecting the high demand for maps and charts, globes and atlases, as objects central to quotidian life in the modern world. Maps appeared in atlases and books intended for use in the home or school. These included thematic

maps of the world's oceans and major ports, bringing the wide world into the living room or classroom.

Trading companies still controlled much of the world's trade. These companies also employed their own chartmakers and issued charts of their areas of activity, as seen here with examples from the Russian American Company and the English East India Company. New companies involved in ferrying migrants across the world's oceans issued maps as propaganda for attracting customers. Many of these used new steam technology, which significantly decreased the time it took to round Cape Horn or the Cape of Good Hope. After 1869, the Suez Canal allowed ships to bypass the Cape of Good Hope, and interest was growing in a cross-Panama route. In short, more people were taking to the seas than ever before, necessitating more charts for more ships.

Finally, certain industries mined the seas themselves for resources that lay under the waves. The whaling industry grew exponentially in the nineteenth century, but fisheries in the Atlantic were soon tapped out. Whalers began to frequent far-flung Indian Ocean and Pacific islands in search of whale oil. Maps and charts were published showing where to find the animals in their ever-diminishing numbers.

A bewildering array of maps and charts depicting the sea proliferated in the nineteenth century. They shared important antecedents with previous charting practices, but also contained exciting innovations that make them as aesthetically pleasing and intellectually stimulating as the more elaborate portolan and Dutch charts before them.

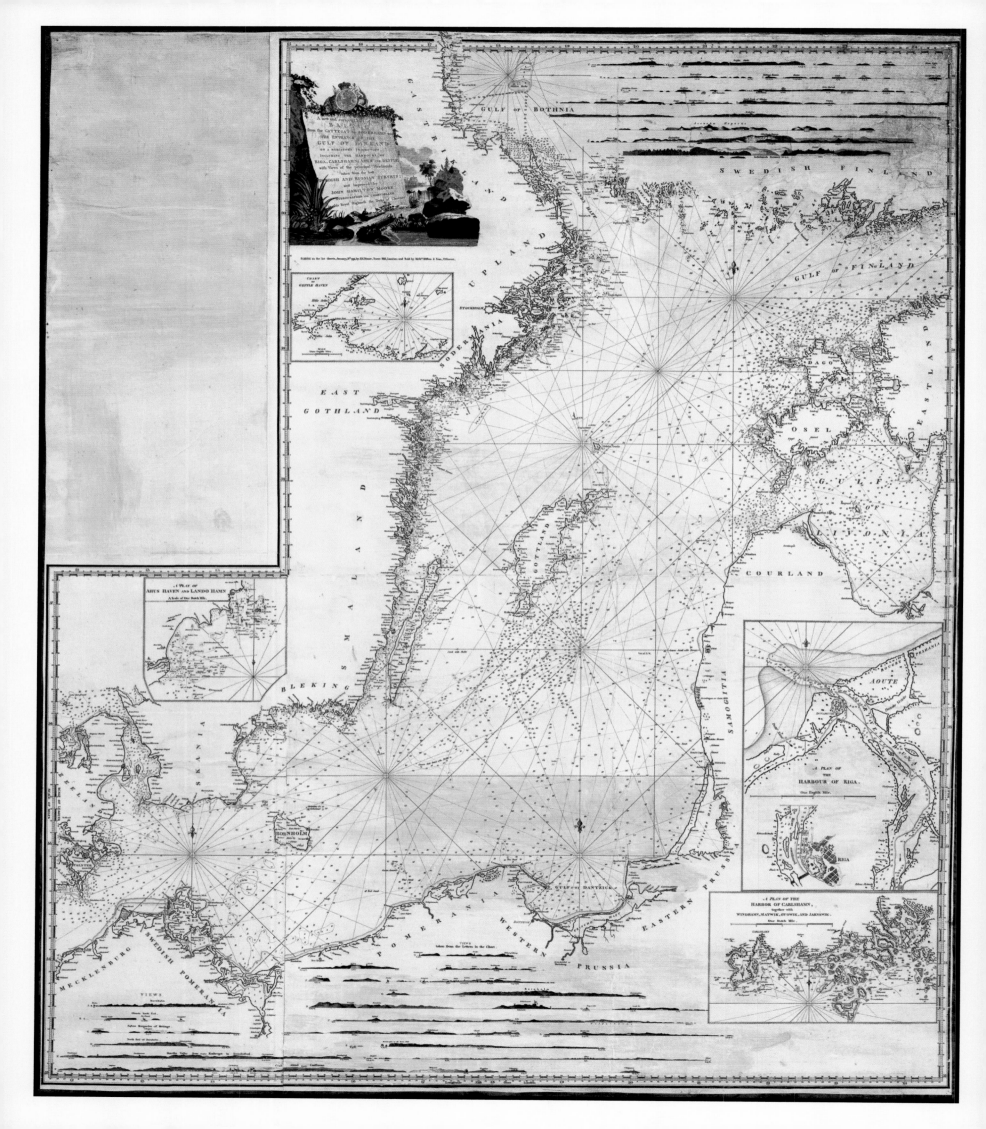

A new and correct Chart of the Baltic from the Cattegat to Soderhamn...

With this chart, it is possible to see the developments in chartmaking that have been discussed so far. Published in 1791 by John Hamilton Moore, this large-format chart of the Baltic Sea includes a highly decorative cartouche showing a pastoral scene. Printed on a rock cliffside is the long-form title typical of the period, explaining all the areas covered, the sources for the chart (Swedish and Russian surveys), and Moore's title and patron.

As the named chartseller to the Duke of Clarence, Moore did not necessarily receive financial backing from the Duke; rather, the Duke's name and reputation were being used by Moore to sell more charts and maps. However, it is not clear that Moore had the Duke's permission to do so, and Moore's fellow chartsellers published a pamphlet deriding his title and pretension. Not an employee of the state, Moore operated in a period just before Britain created their centralized hydrographic body and sanctioned vetted agents to sell approved charts. Thus, Moore seized any edge he could to sell more charts to naval officers, merchant captains, and businessmen.

In addition to the decorative cartouche, there are *fleurs-de-lis* on the rhumb-line circles, to indicate north. However, these are much smaller and less obtrusive than those seen on earlier charts. Every inch of the paper is filled with information. A seemingly bewildering, but actually useful, blanket of sounding depths covers the waters, along with the symbols for shoals, sandbars, obstructions, and anchorages that were standard by the end of the eighteenth century. Inland, insets fill any available space, showing the entrances to ports, while profiles of land are stacked in the top right and bottom left.

Chartmaker Biography

John Hamilton Moore *(1738–1807) served in the Royal Navy before starting a navigation school, publishing* The New Practical Navigator and Daily Assistant, *and setting up his shop selling charts. He was widely admired for his detailed charts.*

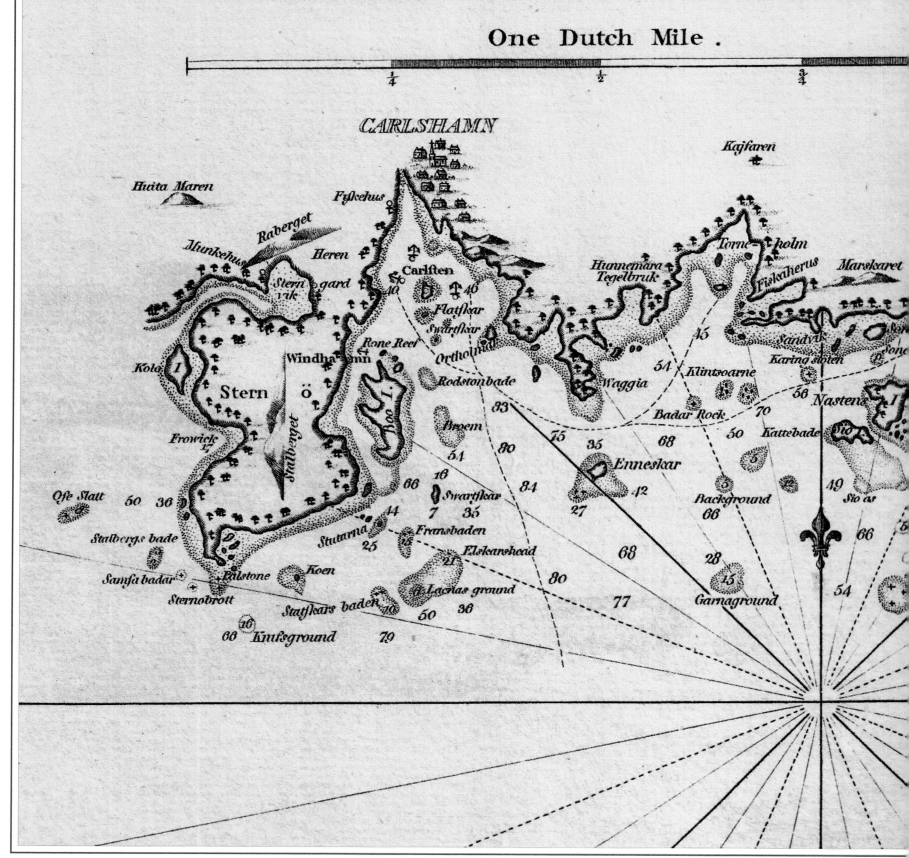

A PLAN OF THE

HARBOR OF CARLSHAMN,

together with

WINDHAMN, MATWIK, GUOWIK, AND JARNA

One Dutch Mile.

¼   ½   ¾

CARLSHAMN

Kajfaren

Huita Maren

Raberget

Fyskehus

Munkehus

Torne-holm

Heren

Hunnemara Tegelbruk

Fiskaherus

Marskaret

Stern vik

Carlsten

Stern gard

46

Flatskar

40

Swartskar

Sandvik

Kolo

Rone Reef

Ortholm

Karing stoten

Stern

Windha mn

Boo I.

Rodstonbade

Waggia

54

Klintsoarne

56

Nastens

Ö

Broem

Klintsoarne

70

Frowick

Stalberget

33

75

35

68

50

Kattebade

17

51

80

35

Sio

Qfe Slatt   50   36

16

84

27

Enneskar

42

Background

49

Sio as

66

66

Stalbergs bade

66

Swartskar

28

66

Samfa badar

44   7   35

Garnaground

54

Falstone

Koen

Stutarna

Fransbaden

Elskarshead

68

15

25

25

21

77

Sternobrott

Lacnas ground

Statskars baden   40

80

16

50   36

66   Knifsground

79

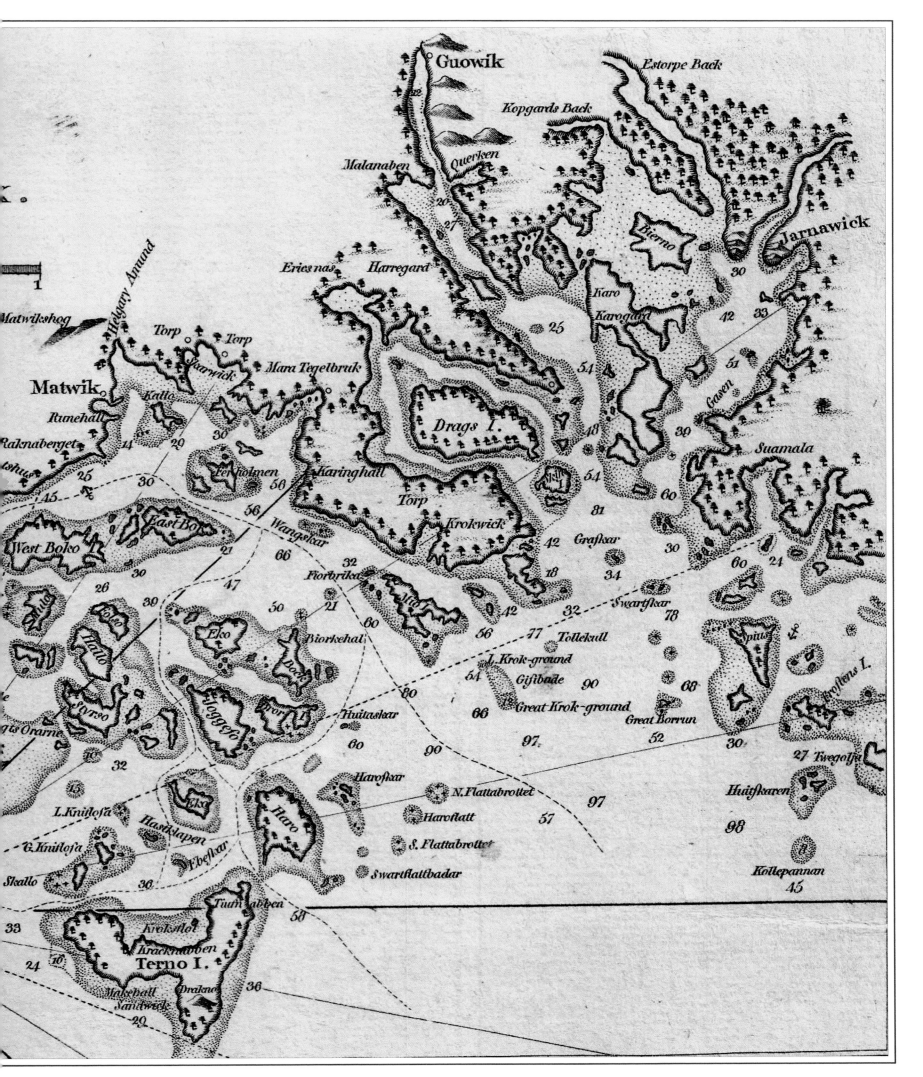

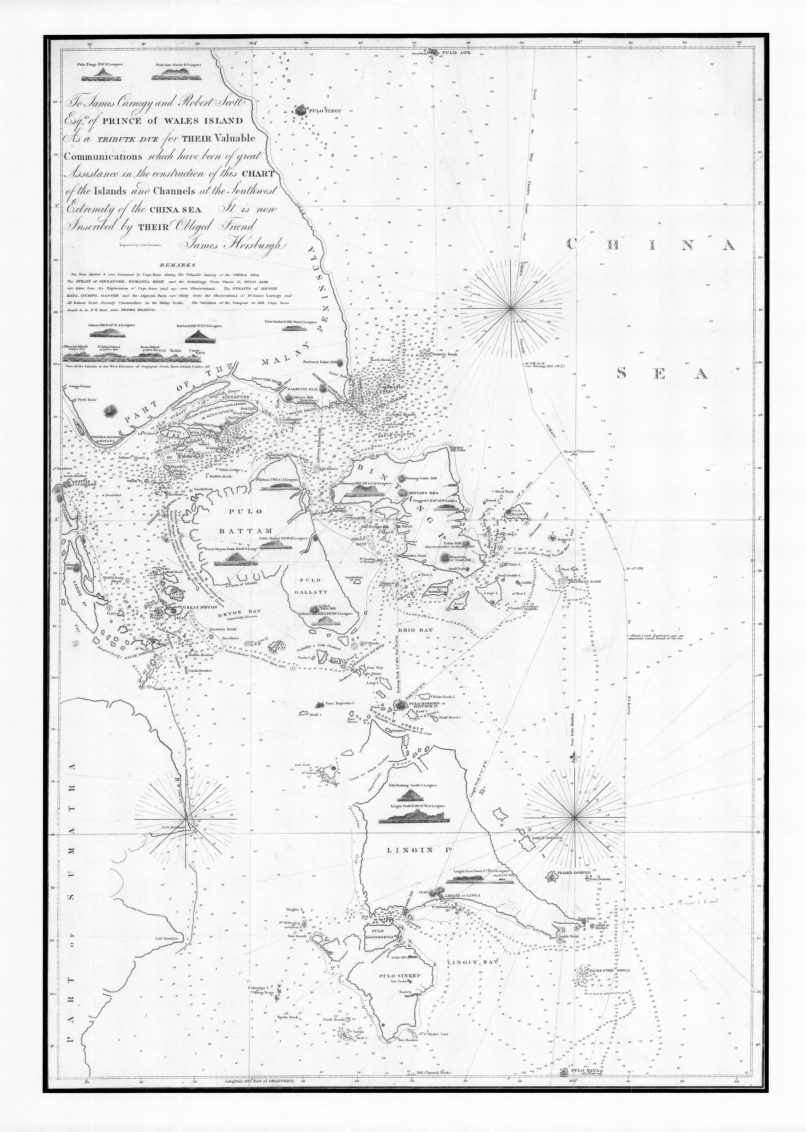

... Chart of the Islands and Channels at the Southwest Extremity of the China Sea...

This chart, a second state (1824) first published in 1821 by James Horsburgh, shows the varying state of geographic knowledge about these important waterways just as Singapore was becoming one of Britain's most important colonial assets. "Singapoora Town" is marked with a square symbol, the only settlement to be so acknowledged. The soundings in and around Singapore are laid thickly. However, the island of Singapore itself has its western end sliced off and is split into two, Goa Island and Tooly Island.

Farther away from Singapore, the remaining absences in geographic knowledge are readily apparent. Many shores and straits are labeled as "imperfectly known," while several courses are marked as "probably a safe channel." Where information is known, Horsburgh is careful to site his sources. For example, he mentions the HMS *Buffalo*, which "passed amongst the Islands to the Eastward of Dryon" in October 1803. The *Buffalo*, a storeship, had previously delivered cattle to New South Wales and two black swans and three emus to England. After returning to Australia, *Buffalo* sailed to Bengal via the waters shown here, arriving in June 1804.

Horsburgh was hydrographer to the EIC, and this chart was facilitated by and made for the company. It is dedicated to James Carnegy and Robert Scott, both employees of the EIC. Horsburgh also explains that the surveys of a Captain Ross were a main source for the charts. This is Captain Daniel Ross. Ross was a famous surveyor for the East India Company. Born in Jamaica, Ross joined the Bombay Marine and eventually was appointed Marine Surveyor General. He made many surveys of Southeast Asia and the coasts of China throughout the 1810s and 1820s, a service for which he was elected a Fellow of the Royal Society.

The chart appears to exhibit many of the precise lines and crisp, yet sparing, details that would come to characterize the charts published by the HO. Indeed, the Admiralty later bought and re-issued many of Horsburgh's plates.

Chartmaker Biography

James Horsburgh (1762–1836) sailed in the employ of the EIC. He began to issue charts and, upon retirement in 1806, turned to chartmaking full-time. This was also the year he was named a Fellow of the Royal Society, a rare honor for a hydrographer. He is best known for the India Directory, *an atlas and sailing guide that was reissued across the century. In 1810, Horsburgh was named hydrographer of the EIC.*

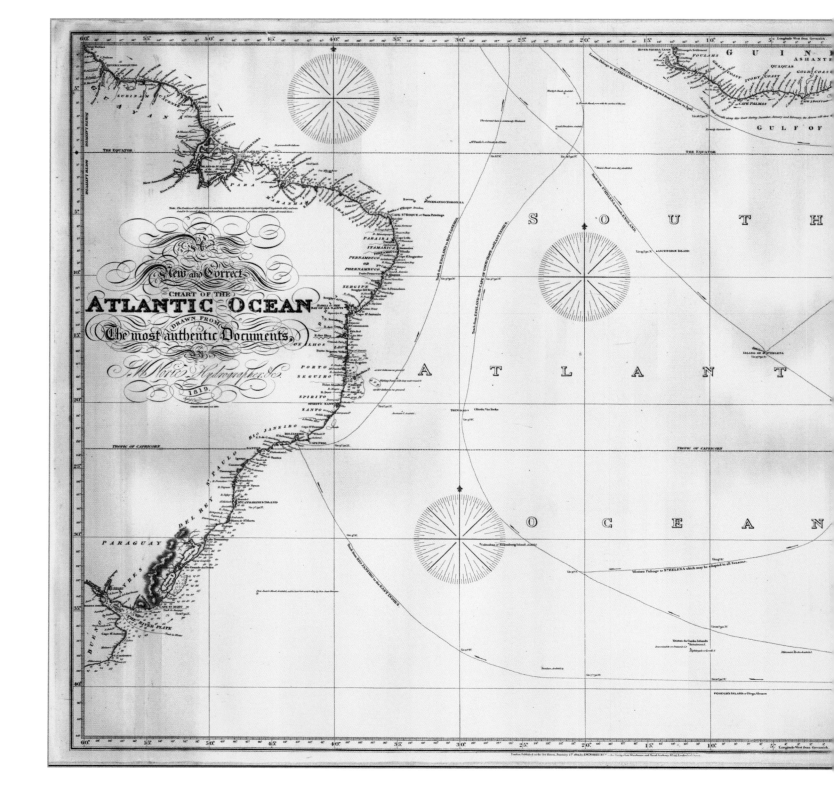

A New and Correct Chart
of the Atlantic Ocean

Chartmaker Biography

John William Norie *(1772–1843) was a respected mathematician and publisher of nautical books and charts. Norie partnered with William Heather, who had been trained by John Hamilton Moore. After Heather's death in 1813, Norie bought his business, which he ran alongside a nautical academy. After his death, his firm continued on, eventually combining with Moore's in 1903, and is still in business today.*

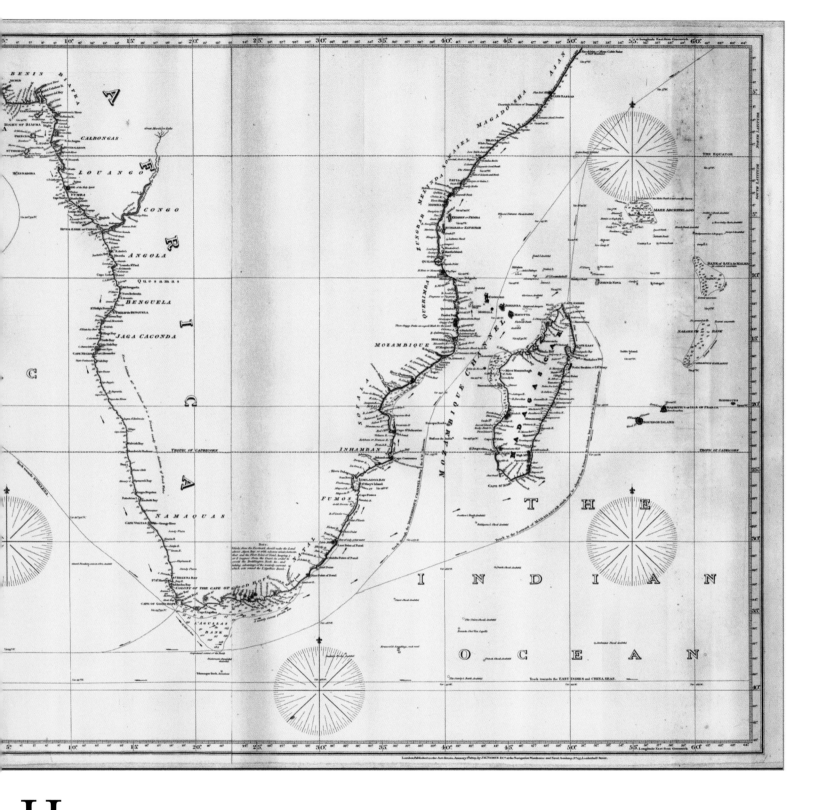

Here is a blueback chart, so called because of its blue paper backing, of the southern Atlantic and Indian Oceans, showing the major shipping routes around the Cape of Good Hope. The chart has been twice corrected, as it was first published in 1819 and corrected in 1826 and 1830, according to the title, by J. W. Norie, then the most successful private chartseller in London.

The elongated chart shows the easternmost part of South America, the southern half of Africa, and Madagascar. Snaking around the continents are suggested sailing routes to major ports and resting places, including Rio de Janeiro, St. Helena, and the Cape of Good Hope. Two routes to the East Indies are shown, depending on the time of year. At sea, several compass roses are ready to aid in the drawing of a sailing route with a parallel ruler. Tiny shoals and possible obstructions are shown, but many of these are labeled as "doubtful,"

showing the ever-evolving navigational knowledge of even a well-traversed area like the southern Atlantic.

Perhaps unsurprisingly considering the long transition period it took for mariners to embrace the Mercator projection and the methods for discerning longitude, sailors did not immediately take up the Admiralty-issued charts when the HO began to publish them. Many preferred privately-issued blueback charts of firms like Norie's, even though they were more expensive. This is because the Admiralty had only started selling their charts to the public in 1821; they did not publicize widely; and many of the private chart firms had long histories and loyal customers used to their formats. It was only in the late-nineteenth century, after the Board of Trade recommended Admiralty charts over private charts, that the HO's charts gained their wider following.

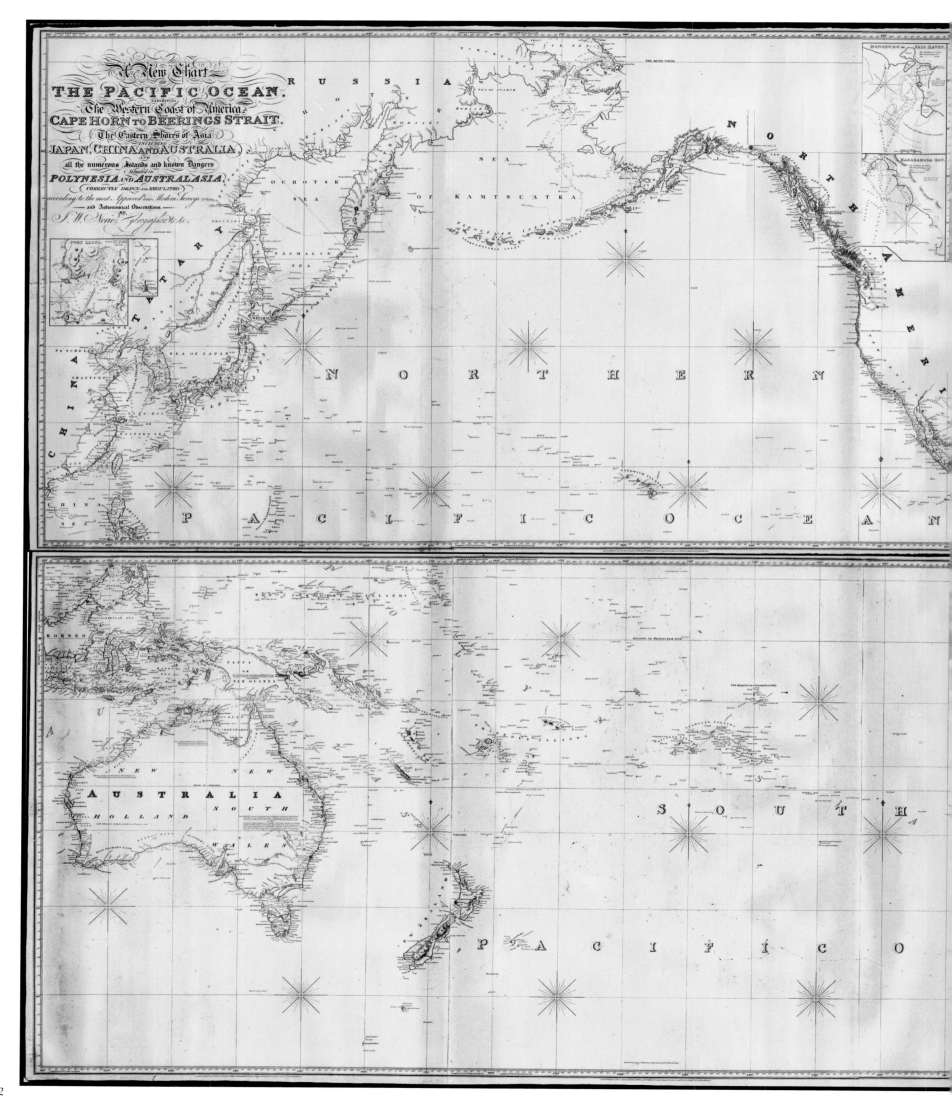

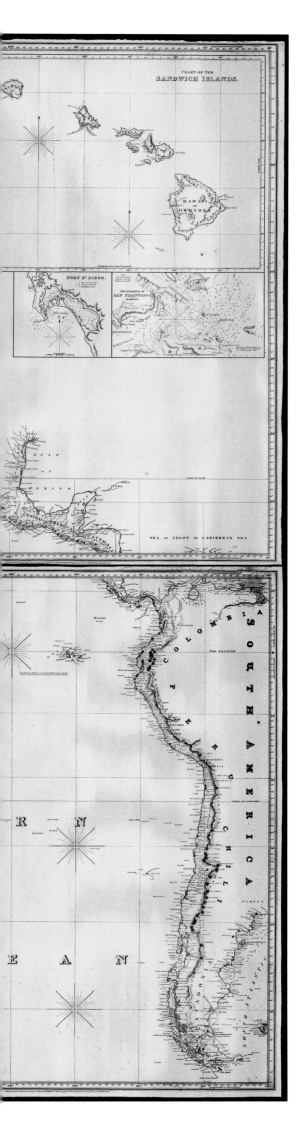

A New Chart of The Pacific Ocean...

Norie published this general chart of the Pacific Ocean in 1825, and this is an updated state with revisions to 1836. The chart is noteworthy for the large insets of San Francisco, San Diego, Hawai'i, Honolulu, and Karakakooa [Kealakekua] Bay in Hawai'i. Norie's chart was the most comprehensive chart of the Pacific then available to commercial mariners.

This example includes the pencil tracks of an American whaler as it cruised the Pacific. There are two distinct voyages, one of which was a circumnavigation of the globe. The other voyage is most likely a whaling track, stopping in Hawai'i and proceeding to the north Pacific off Kamchatka before returning south. The author of the manuscript annotations has also noted rocks and shoals that are not noted on the printed map.

Whalers had first ventured into the Pacific at the end of the eighteenth century. By the time this chart was published, hundreds of whalers entered the ocean every season, greedily seeking sperm whales and other species. The influx of ships created a boom economy for Pacific towns and cities, particularly Honolulu and Sydney. Remote islands that had barely been charted became important stop-over points for whalers in search of food and water to restock. It is likely that Norie used some information from whalers in constructing this chart, and the pencil corrections on this example reveal that there was always more to know about the world's largest ocean.

Chartmaker Biography

John William Norie (1772–1843) was a respected mathematician and publisher of nautical books and charts. Norie partnered with William Heather, who had been trained by John Hamilton Moore. After Heather's death in 1813, Norie bought his business, which he ran alongside a nautical academy. After his death, his firm continued on, eventually combining with Moore's in 1903, and is still in business today.

A
Survey of the
SANDS AND CHANNELS
forming the Entrance into
THE RIVER HOOGLY;
including
BALASORE ROADS,
and Bank of Soundings off
POINT PALMIRAS,
by
Capt. Rich. Lloyd, I.N.
Offg. Marine Surveyor General, 1841.

164

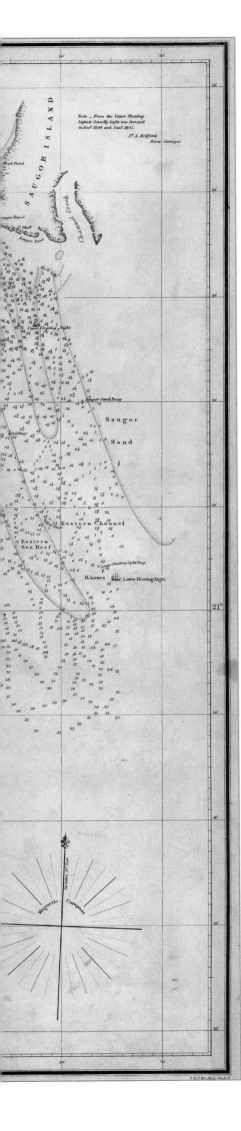

A Survey of the Sands and Channels forming the Entrance into The River Hoogly...

This chart shows the mouth of the Hoogly River in detail. It was published by John Walker, geographer of the East India Company, in 1842. It was based on several surveys, especially the work of Captain Richard Lloyd, the Marine Surveyor-General of the Bombay Marine.

This is perhaps the best example yet seen of the level of detail that surveyors could capture in their works. Hundreds of sounding depths zigzag across the Balasore Roads, each representing a separate measurement taken by a marine surveying team. A series of remarks in the top left describes the tides in the area, as well as prescribing directions for sailing at different times of the year, especially during the monsoon season.

Whereas most of the charts in this book have focused on the open ocean, hyper-detailed estuary and port charts were also important for navigators. With global trade came many unfamiliar anchorages, necessitating a vast amount of information to complete trips. However, in most ports pilots would have been available to guide ships in to the docks, as was the case here.

The entrance to the Hooghly [Hugli] River was of particular interest because it was the gateway to several European factories, including Kolkata. While Kolkata housed the English factory, there were also lodges for the Danish, Austrians, and French.

Chartmaker Biography

John Walker (ca. 1790–1873) was a prominent chartseller and geographer in London. From 1825, he worked for James Horsburgh and the EIC, but also produced work for the Admiralty, the Society for the Diffusion of Useful Knowledge, and the books of Washington Irving in his career. In 1830, he helped to found the Royal Geographical Society.

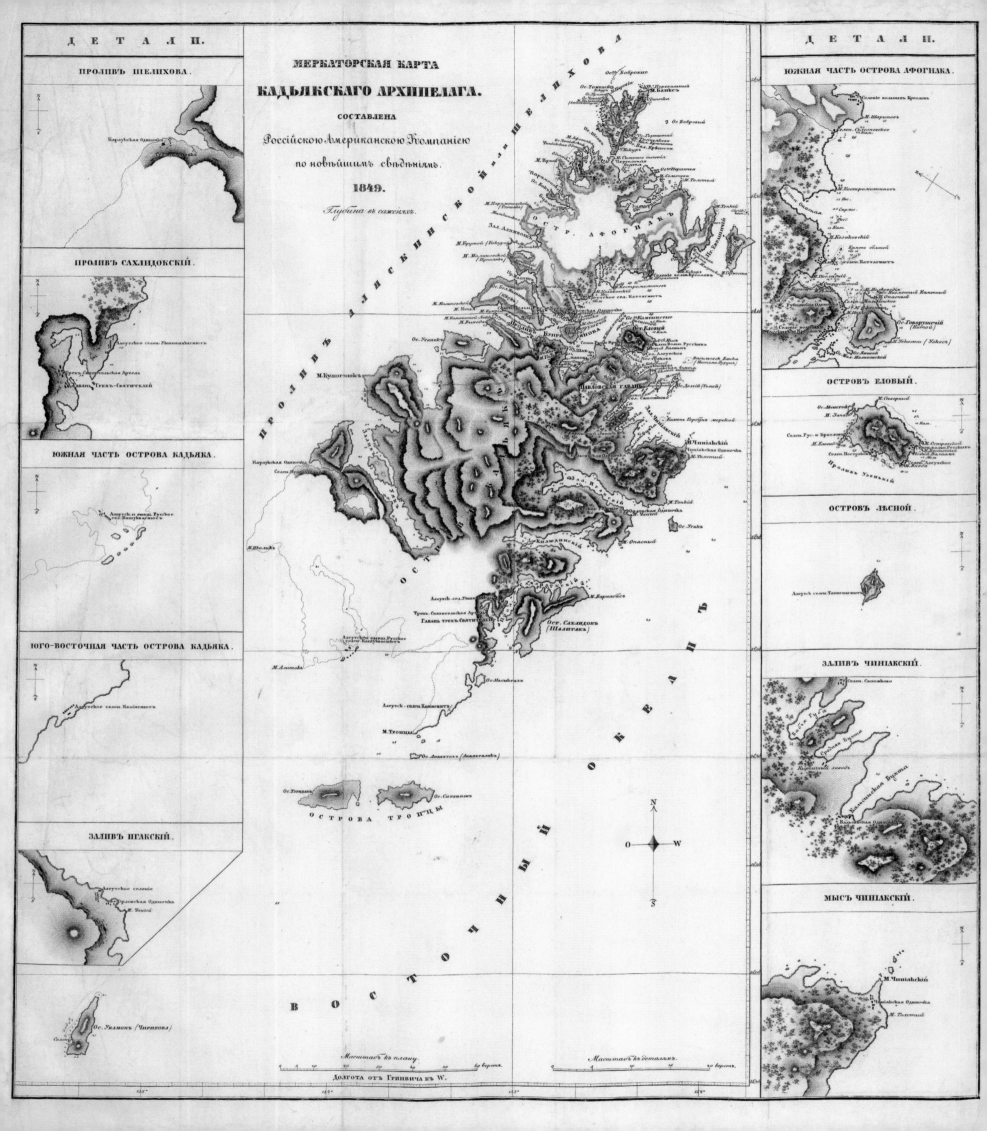

ДЕТАЛИ.

ПРОЛИВЪ ШЕЛИХОВА.

ПРОЛИВЪ САХАНДОКСКІЙ.

ЮЖНАЯ ЧАСТЬ ОСТРОВА КАДЬЯКА.

ЮГО-ВОСТОЧНАЯ ЧАСТЬ ОСТРОВА КАДЬЯКА.

ЗАЛИВЪ ИГАКСКІЙ.

МЕРКАТОРСКАЯ КАРТА
КАДЬЯКСКАГО АРХИПЕЛАГА.

СОСТАВЛЕНА

Россійскою-Американскою Компаніею

по новѣйшимъ свѣдѣніямъ.

1849.

Глубина въ саженяхъ.

ДЕТАЛИ.

ЮЖНАЯ ЧАСТЬ ОСТРОВА АФОГНАКА.

ОСТРОВЪ ЕЛОВЫЙ.

ОСТРОВЪ ЛѢСНОЙ.

ЗАЛИВЪ ЧИНІАКСКІЙ.

МЫСЪ ЧИНІАКСКІЙ.

Масштабъ къ плану.

Масштабъ къ деталямъ.

ДОЛГОТА ОТЪ ГРИНВИЧА къ W.

[Mercator's Chart of Kodiak Archipelago compiled by the Russian American Company]

The Russian American Company, founded in 1799 as Russia's first joint-stock company, was established as a colonial presence in America via settlement, trade with indigenous people, and the mining of the rich resources of what is today the Pacific Northwest and California. The Company also worked in concert with intellectual societies, most notably the Russian Academy of Sciences, to plan and support expeditions intended to gather geographic and natural historical information.

This chart appeared under the governorship of Baron Von Wrangel, explorer and hydrographer. It was published as part of the Russian American Company's report for 1848 and shows Kodiak Island flanked by ten insets of bays and harbors. While the chart reveals a thorough knowledge of the topography of the northern and central regions of the island, the southern parts remain hypothetical, revealing the remoteness of this Russian outpost. However, the details that the chart does show are extraordinary and predate British and American surveys.

Kodiak holds an important place within the geography of Russian Alaska. It served as a stopping-place, a base for expeditions, and as a (contested) source of labor in the form of the Kodiak Islanders. The encampment there, established in 1784, was the second permanent Russian settlement in Alaska. Thus, this map shows a time when Russia seemed likely to become an enduring presence in North America, although they had ceded their claim to California in 1841. It captures a moment when the Pacific Northwest was hotly contested by Russians, Americans, British, and the indigenous peoples who originally inhabited the land.

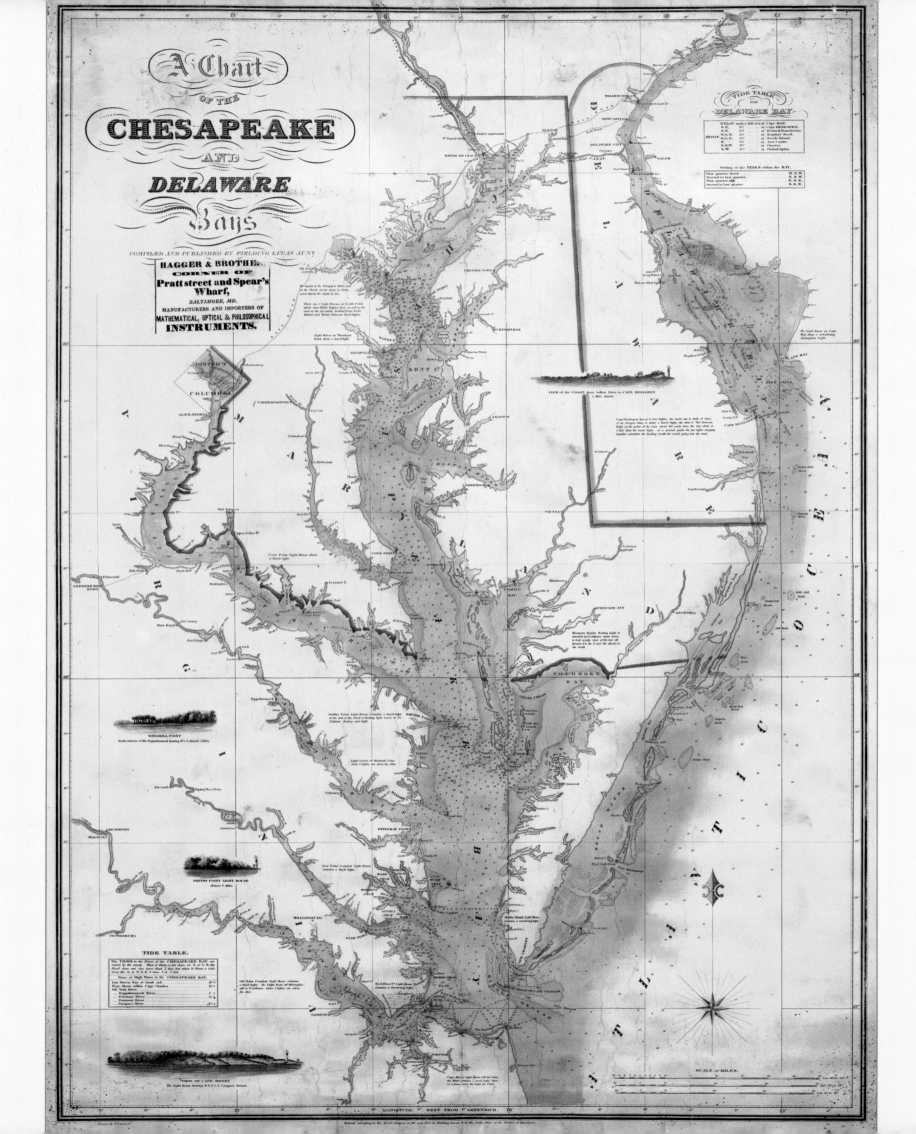

A Chart of the Chesapeake and Delaware Bays

Published in Baltimore in 1852, this is the only known chart made by Lucas Fielding Jr., and he was the only known map and chartmaker in Maryland at the time of its publication. However, a paste-over has been added below the title, featuring the name of the shop that sold this chart, Hagger and Brothe.

The chart features the entirety of the Chesapeake and Delaware Bays, with inland navigation on the rivers as far upstream as Philadelphia, Port Deposit, Baltimore, Washington, and for considerable distances up the Rappahannock, York, and James Rivers.

The waters are marked for obstructions, which include oyster beds. In the upper right and lower left corners are tide tables, which provide important information in these changeable waters. Of particular interest is the triple scale bar. In previous charts, multiple scale bars indicated multiple units of measure, usually those of different countries. Here, they are all the same unit, but refer to different latitudes. To counteract the distortions of converting a round globe to a two-dimensional plane, and to provide more accuracy for one using the chart, Fielding gave the mariner three separate scales to compensate for the different distances between meridians.

Four profile views show the coast at Windmill Point, as well as lighthouses at Smiths Point, Cape Henry, and Cape Henlopen. These views first appeared on Anthony De Mayne's *Survey of the Chesapeake* (1814). The mid-nineteenth century was a period of rapid construction for lighthouses, as the states sought to protect lives and goods. The Cape Henry Lighthouse was originally built in 1792, the oldest lighthouse on Chesapeake Bay.

Chartmaker Biography

Lucas Fielding Jr. (1781–1854) was from Fredericksburg, Virginia, but he worked in first Philadelphia and then Baltimore, where he started a successful cartographic business. He focused mainly on atlases.

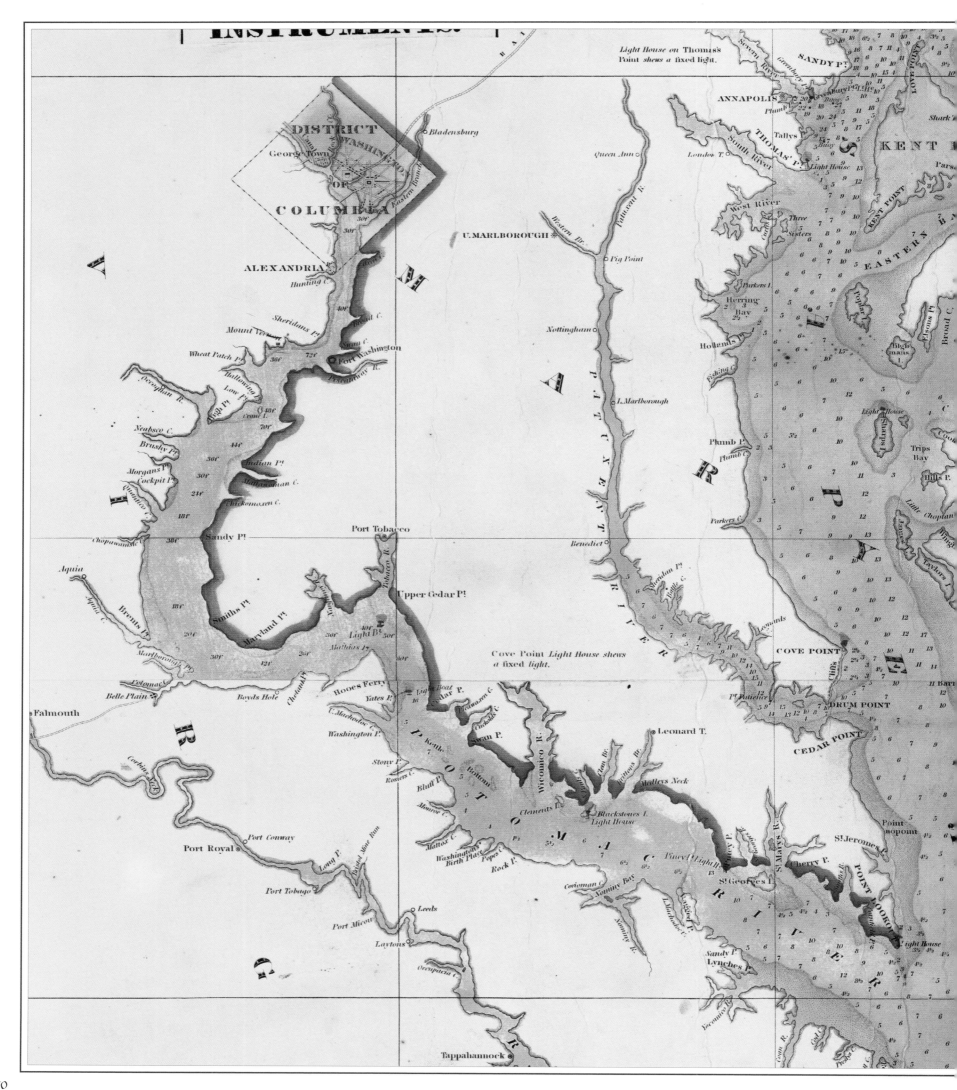

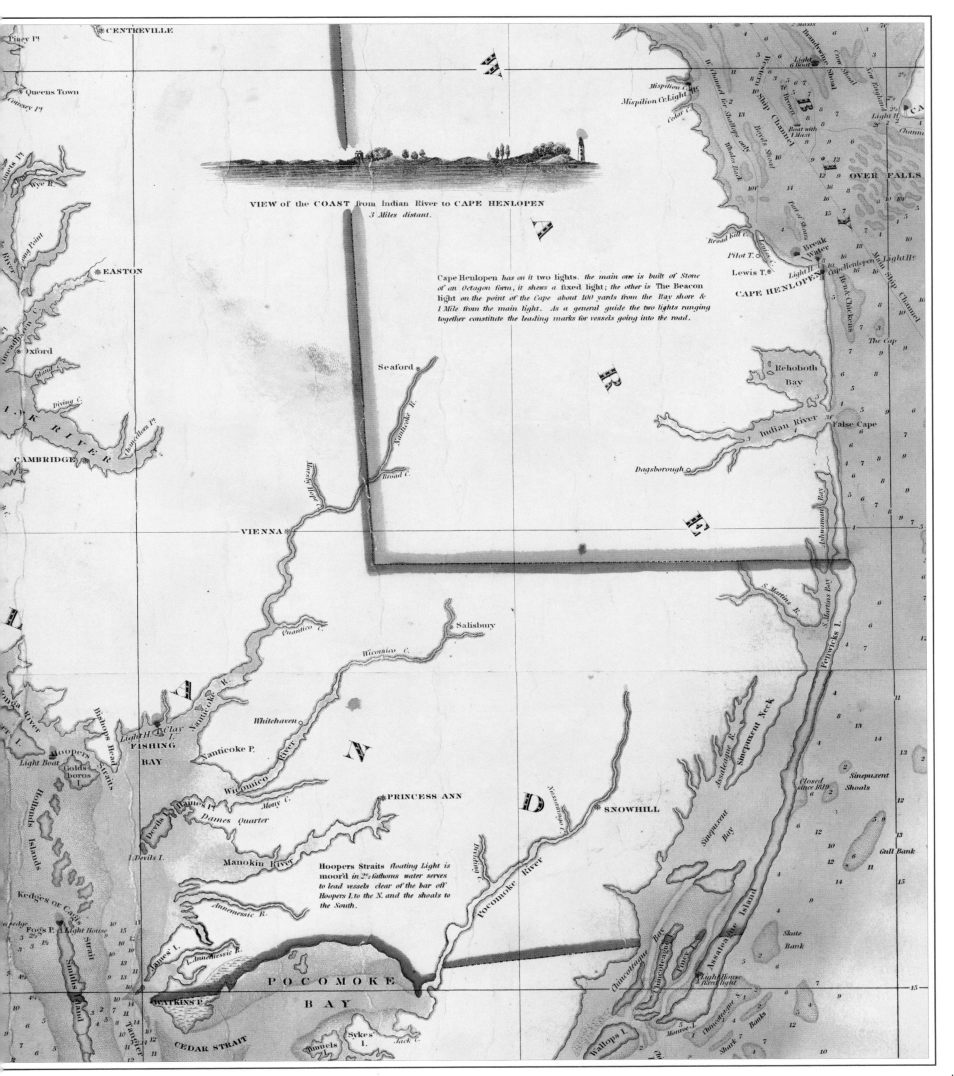

VIEW of the COAST from Indian River to CAPE HENLOPEN
3 Miles distant.

Cape Henlopen *has on it two lights. the main one is built of Stone of an Octagon form, it shews a fixed light; the other is The Beacon light on the point of the Cape about 100 yards from the Bay shore & 1 Mile from the main light. As a general guide the two lights ranging together constitute the leading marks for vessels going into the road.*

Hoopers Straits *floating Light is moor'd in 2½ fathoms water serves to lead vessels clear of the bar off Hoopers I. to the N. and the shoals to the South.*

Piney Pt.
✳ CENTREVILLE
✳ Queens Town
Cousey Pt.
Wye R.
✳ EASTON
Long Point
Thoroughfare
Oxford
Diving C.
Thrilling Pt.
CAMBRIDGE
Island C.
K RIVER

Mispilion C.
Mispilion Cr. Light
Cedar C.
OVER FALLS
Broad Kill C.
Pilot T.
Break Water
Lewis T.
Light H.
CAPE HENLOPEN
Hen & Chickens
The Cap

Seaford
Nanticoke R.
Rehoboth Bay
Indian River
False Cape
Broad C.
Dagsborough
Ashawman Bay

VIENNA ✳
Nanny Hope C.
S. Martins R.
S. Martins Bay

Quantico C.
Salisbury
Wiconico C.
Fenwicks I.

Whitehaven
Nanticoke River
Assateague R.
Sinepuxent Neck

Light H. Clay I.
FISHING BAY
Nanticoke P.
N
Sinepuxent Shoals
Closed since 1819

Hoopers Straits
Golds boros I.
Wicomico R.
Bishops Head
PRINCESS ANN
Nassawango C.
SNOWHILL
Sinepuxent Bay

Devils
Haines Pt.
Mony C.
D
Pocomoke River
Gull Bank

Hollands Islands
Dames Quarter
Nassawango C.

Light Boat
l. Devils I.
Manokin River
Skate Bank

Kedges or Cager's
Annemessic R.
Chincoteague Bay
Assateague Island

Fogs Pt. Light House
James I.
l. Annemessic R.
Watkins Pt.
POCOMOKE
BAY
Pocomoke River
Light House Fixed light

Smiths Island
Tangier
CEDAR STRAIT
Daniels I.
Sykes I.
Jack C.
Wallops I.
Monroe I.
Chincoteague Island
Shark Banks

171

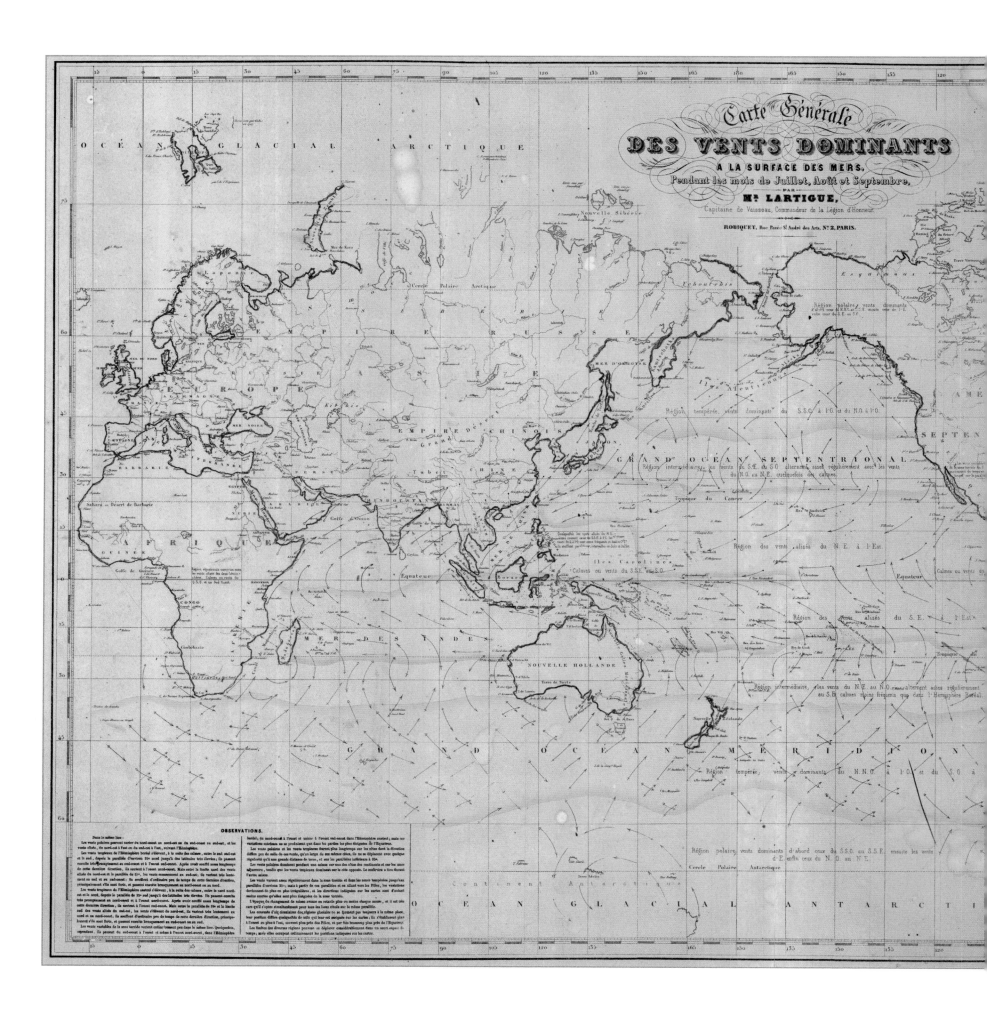

Carte Générale
DES VENTS DOMINANTS
A LA SURFACE DES MERS,
Pendant les mois de Juillet, Août et Septembre,
PAR
M. LARTIGUE,
Capitaine de Vaisseau, Commandeur de la Légion d'Honneur.

ROBIQUET, Rue Pavée St. André des Arts, N.º 2, PARIS.

Carte Generale des Vents Dominants à la Surface des Mers...

This map represents a theory about the wind currents of the world, developed by French naval officer Joseph Lartigue and published ca. 1855. The world map reflects the interest in the fledgling sciences of oceanography and anemology (the study of the winds) in the mid-nineteenth century.

In 1840, Lartigue submitted a chart along with an essay to the *Académie des Sciences* for formal review of his theories. The Academicians were impressed and asked that he extend his theories toward the polar seas. This map is Lartigue's answer to them. The map covers the months of July, August, and September; one of an intended four, only January-February-March and July-August-September are known to have survived.

The main purpose of the map was not geographic, but to inform viewers of the prevailing winds around the world during the summer months. This information would be valuable to mariners as well as scientists. Lartigue had sailed extensively and reviewed many logbooks and journals, recording the wind information from each. He then compiled these detailed maps, with arrows representing the direction of each separate breeze. Text boxes in the upper right and lower left explain his theories, which postulated that primary winds, those from the poles and the trade winds, determined a set of secondary winds—an integrated system of winds. A key in the lower right explains the type of wind indicated by each sort of arrow.

Chartmaker Biography

Joseph Lartigue (1791–1876) was a French naval captain who also published extensively on oceanography and navigation. His most famous works focus on his system of winds and on other weather phenomena.

Chart of the World on Mercator's Projection

This world map dates to 1883 and was published in the *Unrivaled Family Atlas of the World* by George F. Cram in Chicago. The atlas was published in various forms until 1952. As the title of the atlas indicates, it was intended for a wide audience, including children. Printed in full color, the maps in this atlas would be a child's primary introduction to the wider world around them. Such atlases were popular in the nineteenth century, as maps were considered wholesome and helpful learning tools.

Cram clearly thought that families should learn not only about geography, but also about oceanography. The world features the flow of the ocean's currents, colored in red. By the late nineteenth century, the flow of the oceans away from the polar regions was well understood. Indeed, the Gulf Stream had been charted as early as 1525 by the Spanish. Famous scientists, like Alexander Humboldt and the hydrographer Matthew Fontaine Maury, worked on the subject. In the 1850s and 1860s, many theories abounded as to what caused ocean currents, showing the relevance of the topic to nineteenth-century life.

A feature that may look jarring to the modern eye is the use of two prime meridians on this map. At the top, the border includes longitude from Greenwich; at bottom, longitude from Washington. These duelling meridians were a common feature of maps and charts until the late nineteenth century. Each country used their own location for the prime meridian, and careful or thoughtful mapmakers included two or more. In 1884, in Washington, D.C., diplomats and officials met to decide on one meridian. They chose Greenwich, near London, and that is the location of the prime meridian today.

Chartmaker Biography

George Franklin Cram *(1842–1928) was a Chicago-based mapseller. After serving in the Union Army in the Civil War, Cram joined his uncle Rufus Blanchard's business in 1867. He grew the business considerably and, as sole proprietor, he published the first world atlas in America.*

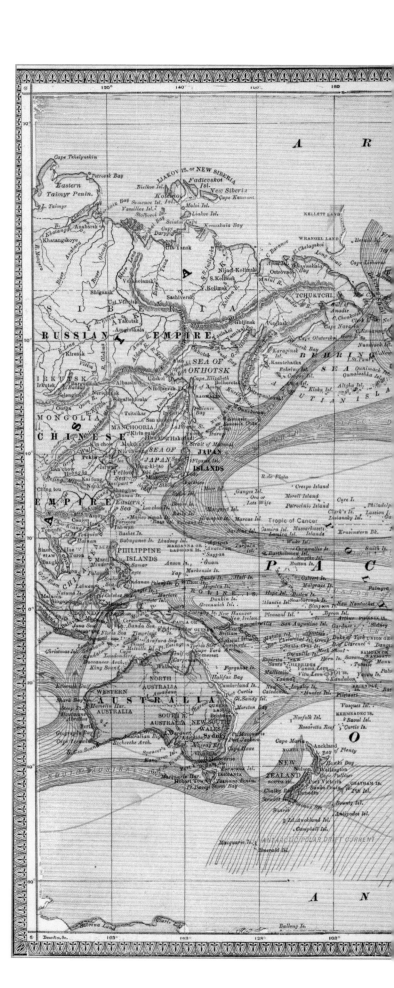

Courtesy of the David Rumsey Map Collection

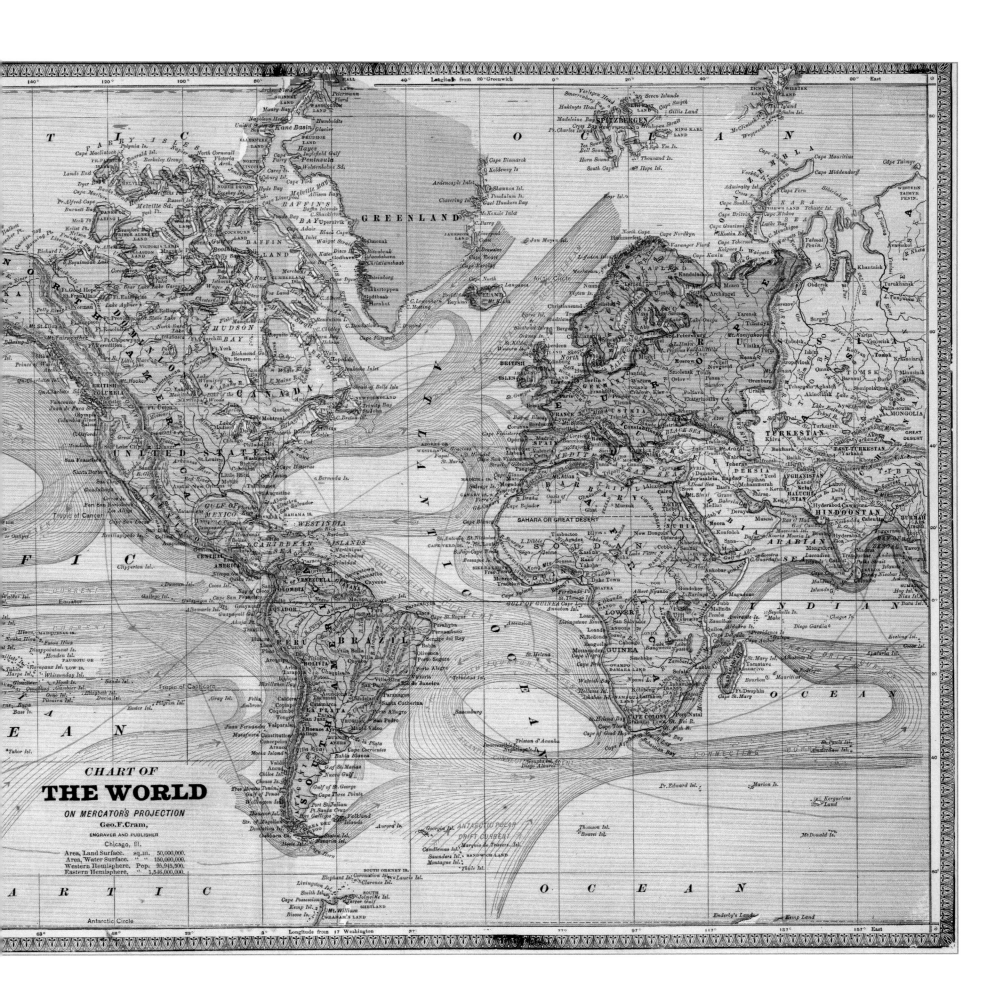

CHART OF
THE WORLD

ON MERCATOR'S PROJECTION

Geo. F. Cram,

ENGRAVER AND PUBLISHER

Chicago, Ill.

Area, Land Surface. sq.m. 50,000,000.
Area, Water Surface. " 150,000,000.
Western Hemisphere, Pop. 95,945,500.
Eastern Hemisphere, " 1,436,000,000.

OUTWARD.

OUTWARD, The Great Circle crosses
Meridian 20 W. in Lat. 50.47 N.
"   30 "   "   49.17
"   40 "   "   46.44
From Fastnet endeavour to steer
on Great Circle to Co's Position of
43 North and 50 West, thence to
Sandy Hook, passing Nantucket
in 40.40 N.

HOMEWARD.

HOMEWARD, The Great Circle crosses
Meridian 40 West in Lat. 46.6 N.
"   50 "   "   48.51
"   20 "   "   50.30
From Sandy Hook passing Nantucket
in 40 30 N. steer for Co's Position of
42 N. and 50 West, from thence endeavour to steer in Great Circle
course to Fastnet.

Track Chart of the Cunard Line.
Showing the Route taken by the Company's Steamers

Chartmaker Biography

John M. Bradstreet (1815–1863) founded the Bradstreet Company, based in New York. They specialized in atlas sales.

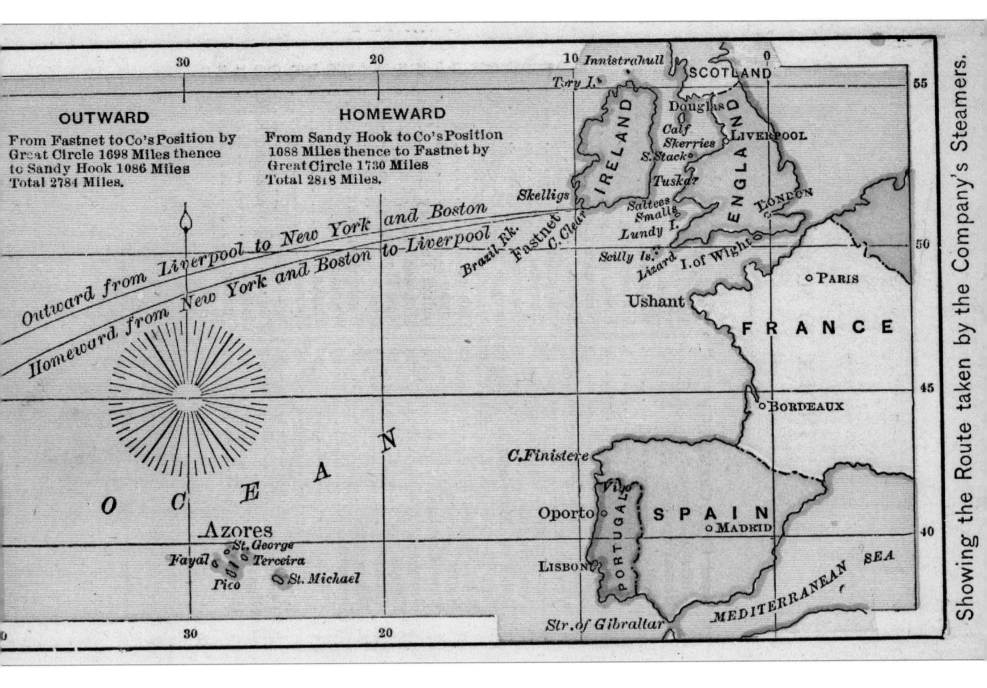

Another atlas map, this one featured in the Bradstreet Company's *Pocket Atlas of the United States* (New York, 1885). The atlas contained not only geographic maps, but also thematic ones, like this map showing the routes of the Cunard Company in the North Atlantic. Again not intended for navigation, this map is a mixture of propaganda for Cunard and an infographic showing the movement of people at a time of mass migration.

The map shows the east coast of the United States and Canada, with Ireland, England, and Western Europe to the east. The lines go out and return to Liverpool (via Fastnet, Ireland), one of the busiest ports in the world at the time of publication.

The ships journeyed to New York and Boston, important destinations for immigrants and visitors. Notes explain the total mileage and suggest sailing in a great circle, rather than a direct course.

Cunard is one of the oldest cruise lines and is still in operation today. It began as a mail transport, as Samuel Cunard won the first British transatlantic steamship mail contract in 1839. The next year, Cunard founded his company and logged the fastest Atlantic crossing in the industry over the next three decades. In the 1860s, the company's focus shifted to passenger transport. At the time of publication, Cunard dominated the transatlantic market, even though the competition from other lines was fierce.

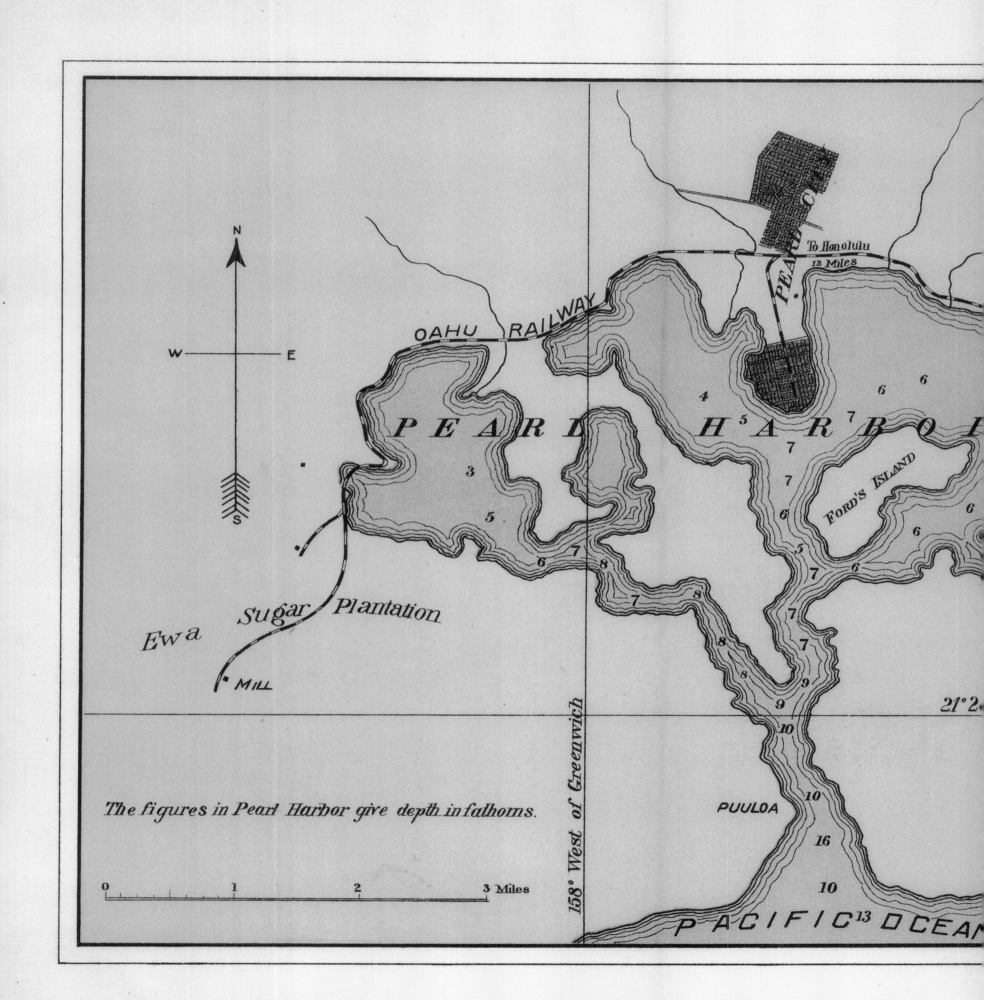

N

W — E

S

OAHU RAILWAY

To Honolulu
12 Miles

PEARL CITY

PEARL HARBOR

4
5
6 6
7

7
7
7
6
6
5
6
7
6

FORD'S ISLAND

6

3

5

6 7 8
7 8

7
7
7
8
8
9
9
10

Ewa   Sugar   Plantation

MILL

10

PUULOA

16

The figures in Pearl Harbor give depth in fathoms.

10

158° West of Greenwich

21° 2

0   1   2   3 Miles

PACIFIC 13 OCEAN

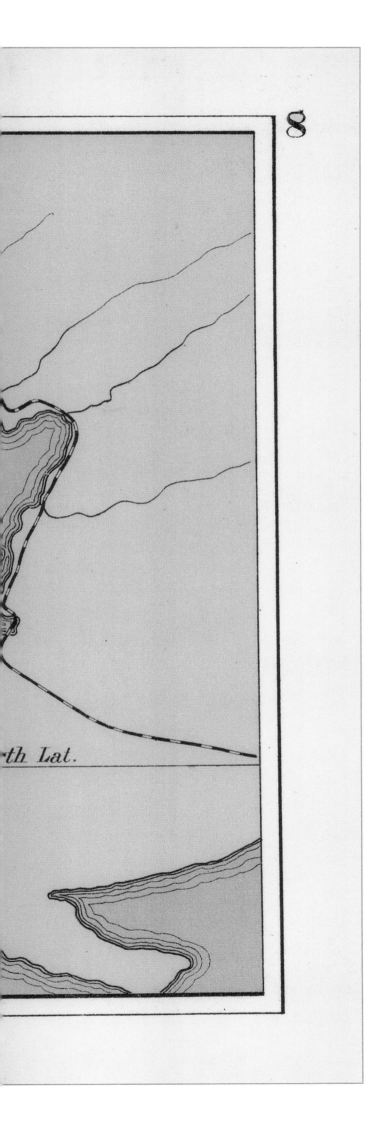

8

th Lat.

[*Pearl Harbor & Vicinity*]

This map of Pearl Harbor likely featured in an atlas, as it is numbered in the upper right corner. It includes a large-scale plan of Pearl Harbor, Hawai'i, complete with the grid pattern of the town. Sounding depths are scattered in the waters. Not intended for sailors, this atlas map is meant to teach about Pearl Harbor, which was a thriving port and soon-to-be military outpost when this map was published ca. 1892 in Washington, D.C.

In the early nineteenth century, Pearl Harbor was a shallow bay increasingly frequented by whalers and traders. U.S. naval ships often stopped in to deliver letters and carry out diplomatic correspondence. In 1865, the U.S. Navy formed the North Pacific Squadron to patrol the region, and soon a warship was permanently assigned to Hawai'ian waters, ostensibly to protect U.S. trade and citizens. In 1875, the U.S. and Hawai'i signed the Reciprocity Treaty, which was ratified in 1887. It granted the Navy the right to build a coaling station at Pearl Harbor. They built the base in 1899, during the Spanish–American War.

The map prominently features the Oahu Railway, which reaches the 'Ewa sugar plantation. The Oahu Railway & Land Company was founded by Benjamin Dillingham, and the railroad work began in 1889. His goal was to connect the fertile 'Ewa Plain to Honolulu. By 1892, the line reached the 'Ewa Sugar Mill, as shown on this map, and would eventually reach the North Shore.

Chartmaker Biography

Anonymous

The Continuing Manuscript
Tradition of Sea Charts

*I*n the study of history, it is all too easy to paint a narrative of progress and growth, a linear march from ignorance to specialization, from ambiguity to detail. However, this sort of triumphant story of humanity's increased knowledge is a comfortable fiction. Historians of cartography and of science have argued that shifts in perception and practice in every field of what we now call science are prone to continuation, adaptation, partial adoption, or even sometimes rejection of possible innovation in favor of previous methods.

Within the history of cartography, as with the history of the book and other corollary fields, there is a deceptive tendency to see print as the successor to manuscript, with the abandonment of the manuscript tradition once print was shown to be able to capture detail more precisely and to be more easily reproduceable than labor-intensive manuscript production.

However, perusal of any archive collection will show a wide variety of manuscript materials co-existing with printed items.

Portolan charts, for example, were made from at least the thirteenth century, well before the introduction of printing presses, but continued to be drawn until roughly 1800. An example of a chart in the portolan style in this chapter dates to 1787. These handmade charts were continuously made alongside their printed counterparts. They were not necessarily meant to compete with printed charts, although being made on vellum did make them especially durable for use at sea, but they were more likely intended for a different purpose than printed charts and atlases. Most of the surviving portolans are elaborate luxury goods: the handmade quality of the object would have increased its value.

Other surviving manuscript charts were not meant for fine surroundings, but were slapdash sketches and initial impressions from navigators and explorers who were far from a printing press. By the eighteenth century, charts were central to the practice of navigation, and many sailors would draw charts and plans as a way to orient themselves and to understand their surroundings. Sometimes these made their way into printed form, but more often they stayed as manuscript ephemera, which makes their survival all the more interesting and rare.

The style of many extant manuscript charts also exhibits the ebb and flow of various features and styles in chartmaking. Whereas the chart of state-run hydrographic bodies may have adopted a more streamlined, less ornamental appearance, many of the manuscript charts in this chapter show a preference for older styles and embellishments. Perhaps these are included to show the skill or flair of the individual who made them. Perhaps they are copied from an older chart. Whatever the reason, manuscript charts complicate the understanding of chart use

and development over time, reminding the viewer to see charting as a punctuated and complex process.

Expectations of and preferences for chart contents shifted over time in conjunction with larger changes in scientific practice, international shipping, and the global economy. They also shifted with regard to the purpose of the specific chart. A chart printed for a mass-produced atlas intended for a classroom would contain very different information from a manuscript chart dashed off to give the first impression of a navigator on a foreign shore. Similarly, an official Admiralty chart will look vastly aberrant when compared to a portolan chart of the same area. All, however, have utility, and all can have beauty. Nautical charts and maps of the sea deliver fascinating insights into how people have related to the oceans over time. They are important historical sources and stunning aesthetic survivals of past traditions.

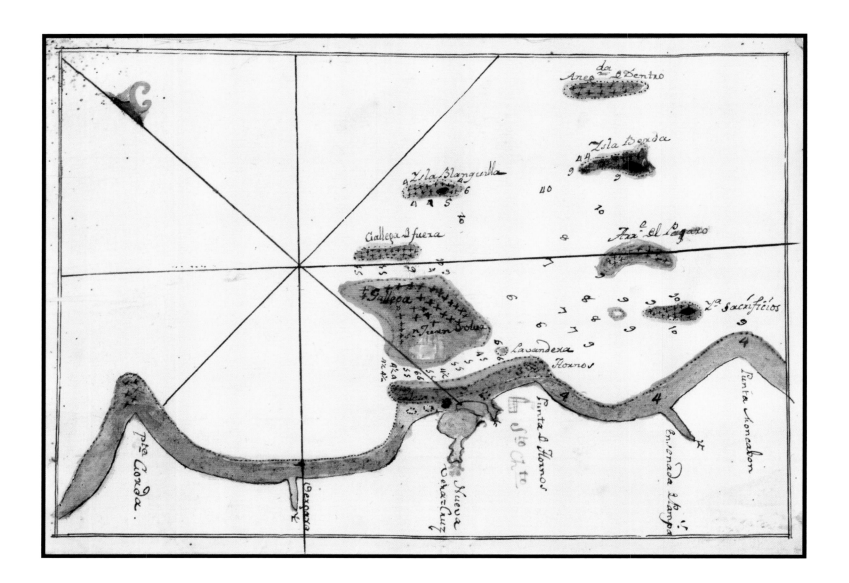

[Veracruz and Vicinity]

This manuscript chart shows the waters surrounding the important port of Veracruz, Mexico. This chart was found laid in loosely in a Spanish edition of Van Keulen's volume on the coasts of the Americas, part of his sea atlas first published in the early 1680s. It is a good example of how manuscript material interacts with print material, and also how ephemeral manuscript survivals are.

The chart centers on what is here called Nueva Veracruz, which is today the main port of Veracruz. San Juan de Ulúa, the island fortress facing the port, is detailed with the walls of the fort outlined. Between Nueva Veracruz and the Punta de Hornos is a church called "Sto Chto." This refers to the Iglesia del Cristo del Buen Viaje, a chapel built in 1609. The church's age underscores the long history of this area, the first to be settled by the Spanish when they landed in the early sixteenth century.

The paleographic evidence points to a likely creation date of ca. 1700. The chart is northeast-oriented and shows many details meant to help pilots and sailors. The shore is shown with a thick blue line extending into the waters, warning of the shallows that border the coast. Obstructions to navigation are highlighted with numerous "x" marks. Large sandbanks and sediment build-ups, some around the islands near the port, are drawn in blue and outlined in a lighter color. Sounding depths also indicate that this was a document meant to communicate the port's tricky hydrography.

Chartmaker Biography

Anonymous

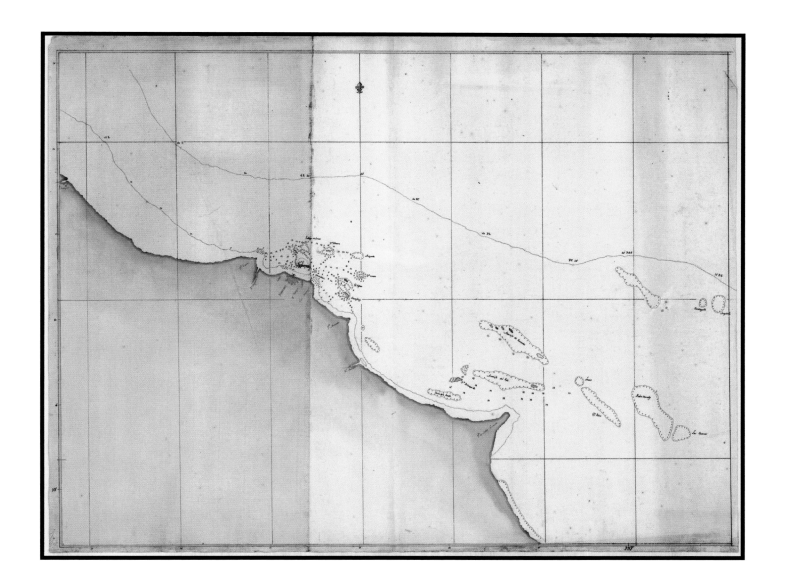

[Veracruz and Vicinity]

This simple, sharply rendered chart also shows Veracruz, Mexico. The city, marked in red, has recognizable walls and bastions; it is certainly a fortress port. Directly in front of the pier is a fortified island. This is San Juan de Ulúa, which was supposed to protect the port from invasion. Farther out to sea are other islands. They are all marked with sounding depths and outlines of sand bars.

Indigenous peoples, specifically the Huastecos, Otomíes, Totonacas, and Olmecs, lived in the region that is now the state of Veracruz. Later, Aztec peoples lived in the area. Although first contacted by Europeans in 1518, the town of Veracruz was founded by Hernán Cortés when he landed on the mainland of New Spain on April 22, 1519.

Veracruz's main exports were silver and gold, mined from Potosí and other American mines, while its imports were numerous as Spain forbid the manufacturing of many goods in the New World. One of the most jarring imports were human slaves from Africa. The region surrounding the port had the largest enslaved population in Mexico in the colonial period.

This manuscript chart, most likely made in the mid-eighteenth century, captures Veracruz at the height of its colonial power. From initial contact, Veracruz has been Mexico's most prominent port, and it was the last place that Spain gave up when Mexico became independent. Most of Mexico was liberated in 1821, but the Spanish held San Juan de Ulúa until 1825.

Chartmaker Biography

Anonymous

Bahía de Cadíz

This informative chart offers a glimpse of the Bay of Cadíz in the eighteenth century, when Cadíz was the most important naval base in Spain. It explains how to safely navigate the shallow waters of the bay while also highlighting the considerable fortifications built to protect the strategic city.

Although it was not the largest shipyard in Spain, Cadíz was the capital of the navy department. Located on the Atlantic Coast, it had also amassed great wealth. Since the Spanish began their expansion in the Americas, Sevilla, up the Guadalquivir River, had served as the primary port for the Americas trade. However, in the eighteenth century, the silting and sand bars in the river made it more expedient that Cadíz be used instead. The *Casa de Contratación*, which housed the management and information, including maps and charts, of the Spanish Empire, moved to Cadíz in 1717.

The chart shows the principal fortifications in red and offers sailing directions so as to avoid the bay's rocks, sandbars, and sediment; these are located in a title box in the upper left corner. The Bay of Cadiz, in the eighteenth century as today, fills with sediment from the various channels and rivers that empty into it, including the Guadalete and the man-made San Pedro rivers. In addition, tsunamis can deposit huge amounts of materials into the bay; the last time this happened was after the 1755 Lisbon earthquake. The reach of the sediment is shown on the chart with the yellow lines hugging the shorelines. A red line with letters shows the best passage through the bay and corresponds to the detailed directions in the title box.

Chartmaker Biography

Anonymous

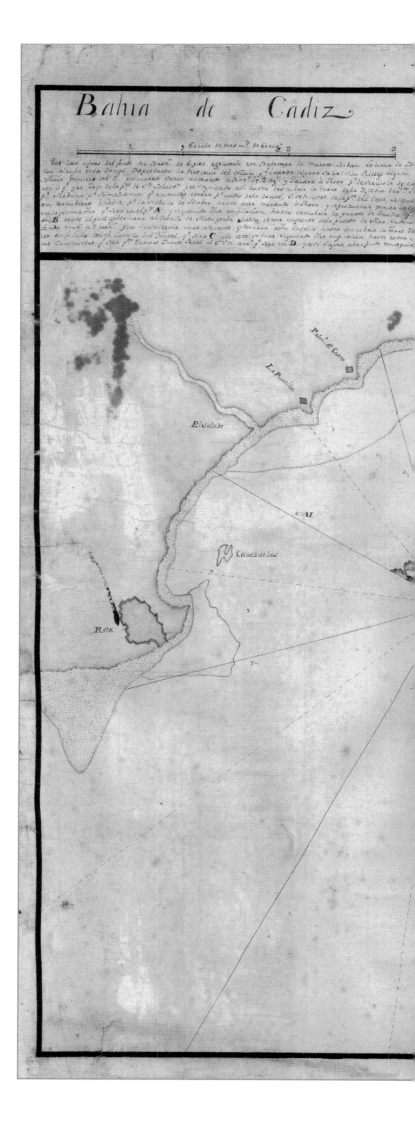

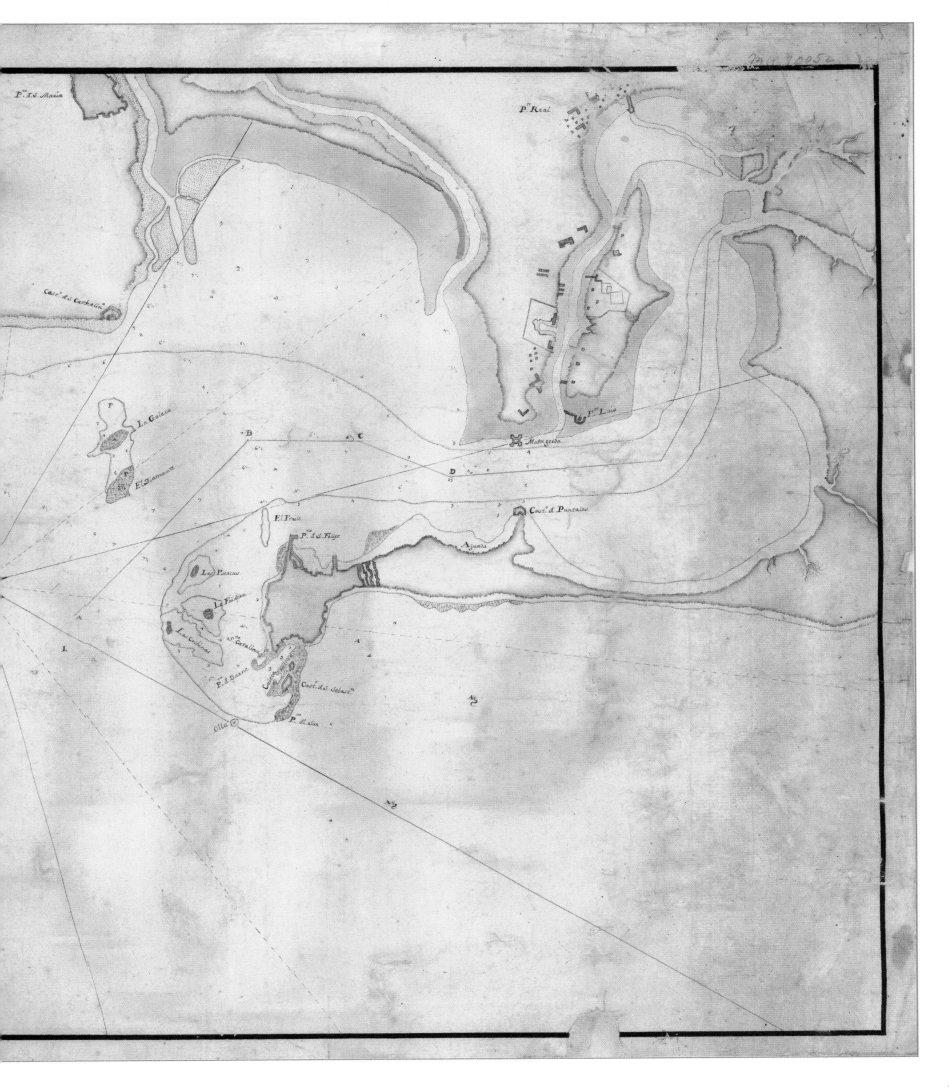

Pta. d S. Maria

Pto. Real

Casto. d S. Cathalin.

La Galera

P

F

El Diamante

B   C

D

Casto. d Puntales

El Fraile

Pta. d S. Felipe

Las Puercas

La Frailea

Las Cochinas   Sta. Catalina

Pta. d Baxio

Cast. d S. Sebast.

Olla

Pta. d Sur

I.

Fte. L. iso

Matagorda

Aguada

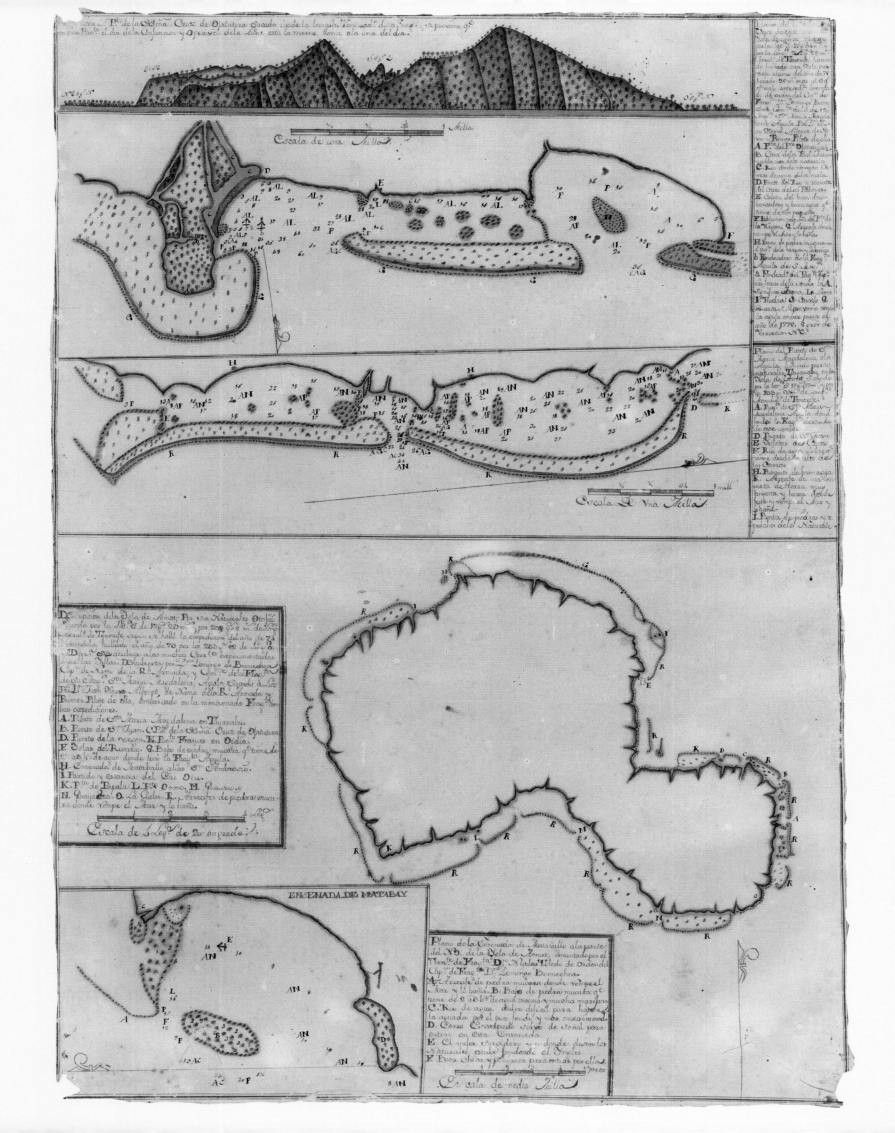

[Tahiti]

This detailed set of views, plans, and inset charts shows various parts of Tahiti as seen on the voyages of Domingo Bonechea on behalf of the Spanish Viceroy of Peru between 1772 and 1775. The map is one of a group of charts prepared under the command of Bonechea on his two expeditions to Tahiti and the neighboring islands.

Tahiti, initially settled by Polynesians, was first contacted by Europeans in 1767 when Samuel Wallis of the Royal Navy landed on the island. He was followed shortly thereafter by the French explorer Louis Antoine de Bougainville. This activity alarmed the Spanish, who had long considered the Pacific their own closed sea. In response, the Viceroy of Peru, Manuel de Amat y Juniet, ordered a colonization effort of Tahiti.

Don Domingo Bonechea led the expedition, which sailed from Callao, Peru in September 1772. Bonechea reached Tahiti, which he called Amat after the Viceroy, with little regard for the indigenous name for the island, and performed reconnaissance on possible places to settle. He returned to Peru in early 1773, where he reported his impressions to the Viceroy.

Amat promptly ordered a follow-up expedition, also led by Bonechea. He left in September 1774 with two priests who were to establish a mission on Tahiti; conversion was often one of the first steps in the colonization effort. In November they settled on a location and met with a local leader, Vehiatua, before building a homestead for the priests. Bonechea died in Tahiti; his second-in-command, Tomás Gayangos, took over the return trip.

Bonechea's ship, *Aguila*, returned to Tahiti a third time, under the command of Don Cayetano de Langara, in September 1775. Langara was supposed to resupply the priests, but he found them in a sorry state and with no converts. He took them onboard and sailed back to Peru, ending the Spanish effort to colonize Tahiti.

Chartmaker Biography

Anonymous

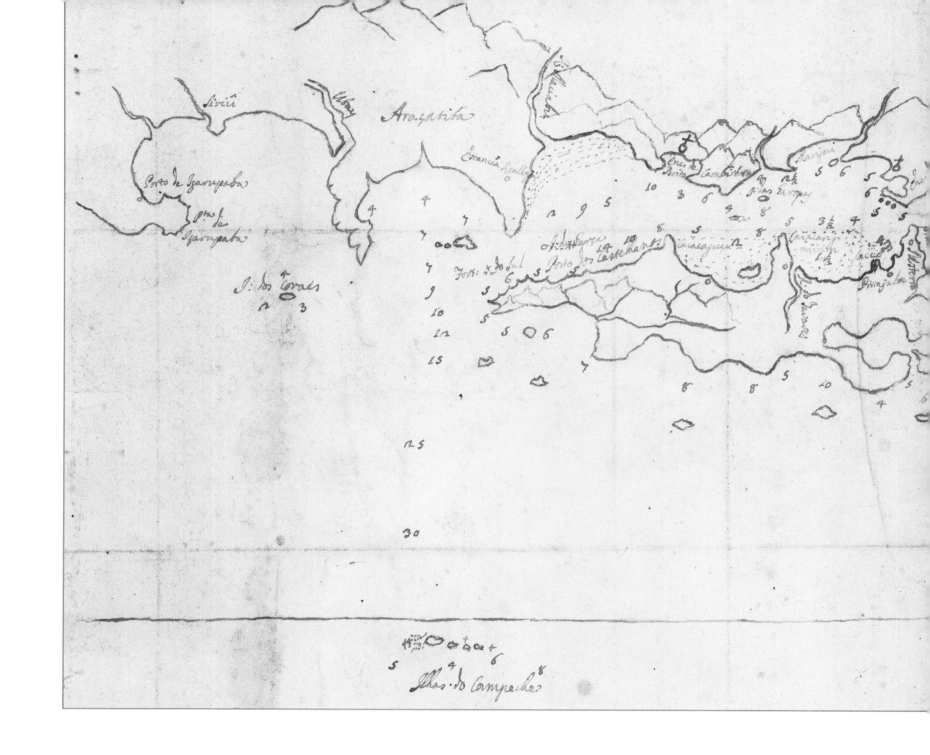

[Ilha da Santa Catarina to Bombinhas]

Chartmaker Biography

Anonymous

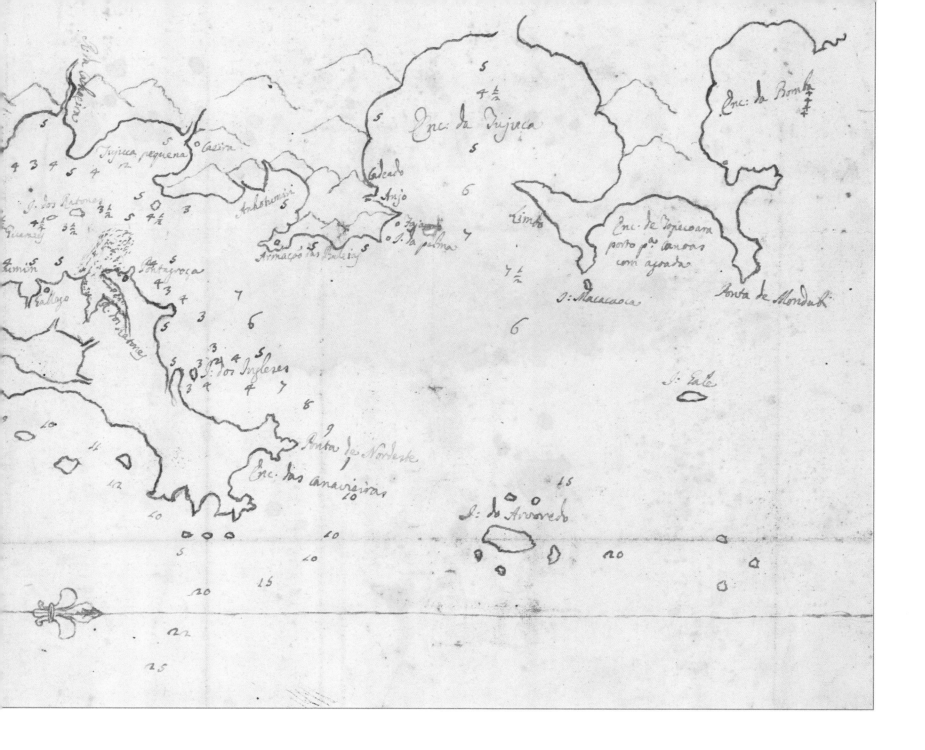

T his chart details the sailing conditions around the Ilha de Santa Catarina, a strategically important island in southern Brazil. Originally, the island was settled by Carijós Indians. The Portuguese arrived in roughly 1514 and called the island Ilha dos Patos. It was renamed in 1526 as Ilha de Santa Catarina. Originally, the main value of the island to the Portuguese was as a watering and supply station for ships en route to the Río de la Plata region to the south. From the early eighteenth century onward, the Ilha de Santa Catarina increased in strategic value. It was located midway between Rio de Janeiro and Buenos Aires; the former was a Portuguese holding, the latter Spanish, but both were large and important ports. In 1739, the island was named a *capitania*, an administrative unit within the Portuguese empire. Desterro, a town included here, was named the capital, and construction began on the imposing fortresses included on this chart.

The chart is west-oriented. The author has included some of the many mountains and hills that dot the landscape. Settlements are marked and important religious sites are indicated with a circle topped with a cross. The chart includes the forts that were built beginning in 1739 to protect the island and coast from the Spanish.

These include São José da Ponta Grossa (Pontagrosa on this map), Santa Cruz Anhatomirim (Anhotumin), San Antonio (I. dos Ratones), and Nossa Senhora da Conceição da Barra do Sul (Fort. do Sul). Curiously for such a detailed chart, Santa Cruz Anhatomirim is mislabeled. The name is written in a bay on the mainland, when the fort was actually on a small island just south of where the label is written.

The handwriting, inclusion of the forts, and style of the symbols suggest a date of ca. 1780.

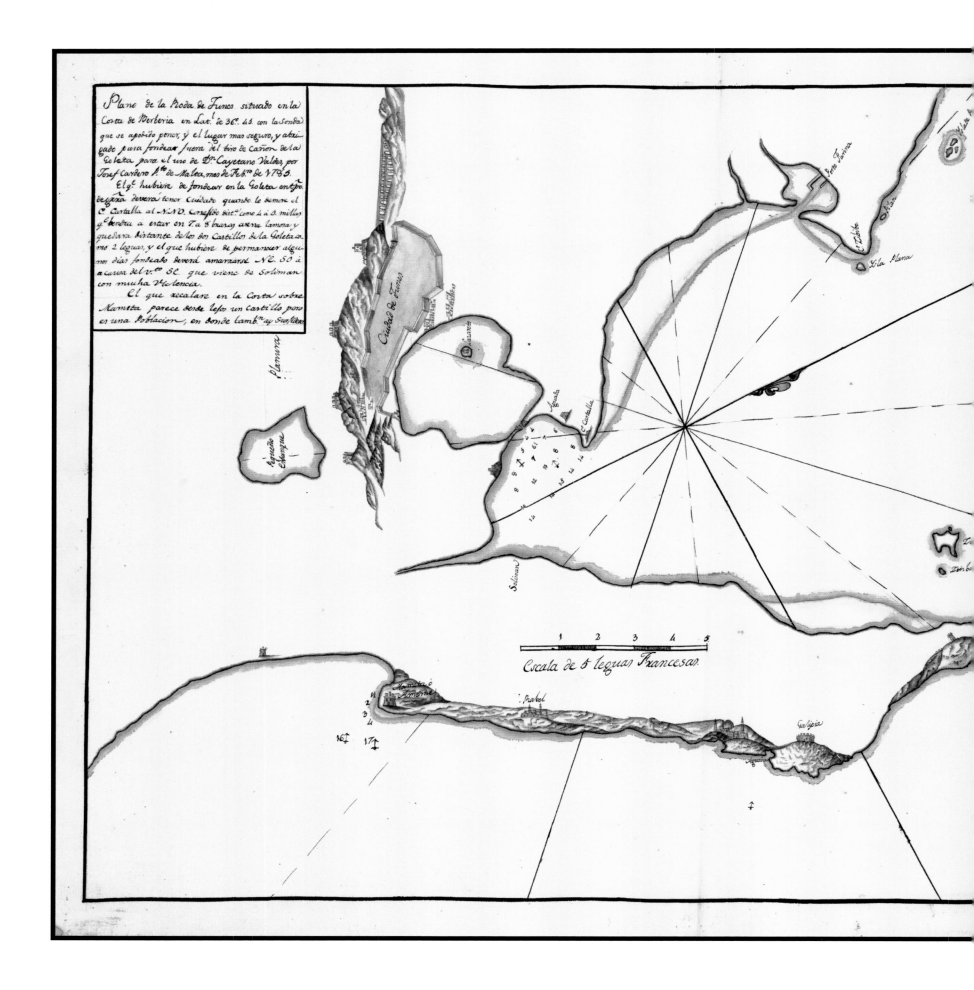

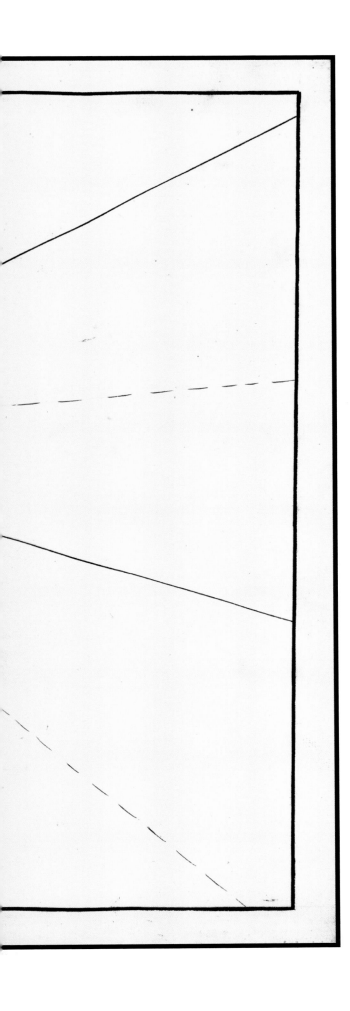

Plano de la Roda de Tunes situado en la Coste de Berbería...

José Cardero drew this chart in 1785 while on the island of Malta. It shows Tunis, Tunisia, and its surroundings, with an emphasis on the fortifications and castles that line the coast. These buildings and bastions are drawn with remarkable detail from a bird's-eye view, while the rest of the chart is in plan. Tunis is a walled city, with four defensive forts guarding the city on the high ground of the surrounding hills. Leading away from the city is a Roman aqueduct.

In 1785, the Spanish Navy was moving against Tunis and the Barbary Coast for its role in piracy and kidnapping of European sailors. With Portugal, France, Venice, and the Knights of St. John, then rulers of Malta, the Spanish mounted a formidable attack from 1783 to 1785. As the chart shows, a naval assault was a difficult feat, but still the Spanish tried in 1784. They failed to take the city, but they did destroy many ships and surveyed the harbor.

One of the officers performing the survey was Cayetano Valdés. His rough sketches became the basis for this fair copy by Cardero. Interestingly, both men would be assigned to the Malaspina voyage to the Pacific, Spain's largest exploratory expedition of the eighteenth century. They worked together while circumnavigating Vancouver Island, part of the first crew of Europeans to do so, producing more fine charts.

Chartmaker Biography

José Cardero (1766–1811) was a trained draughtsman and artist. He is best remembered for his work on the Malaspina expedition. After the voyage, he was reassigned as an accountant in the Spanish Navy. Cayetano Valdés (1767–1835) went on to serve with distinction in the Napoleonic Wars. He had to flee after the uprising of 1820 under penalty of death, but he was recalled in 1833 and made Captain-General of the Spanish Navy.

Descripción de la Costa de España Portugal y Parte de la Barbaria

This manuscript chart on vellum was completed by Mariano Campines at the *Escuela Nautica de Mataro* (Mataro Naval School), near Barcelona in 1787. Little more is known about Campines. The chart was possibly a requirement for a course he was taking, or perhaps he worked at the school. Practically no other charts are known to have survived from the Mataro school.

The chart is finely drawn and focuses on the southern coast of Spain and Portugal, from the Algarve region to Marbella, Spain and the southwestern tip of Portugal. Gibraltar is shown in yellow with red, as are fortifications on the African side of the strait and further up the coast. A variety of building symbols are used to designate towns and cities, which resemble settlement markers used on earlier maps from the sixteenth and seventeenth centuries.

Inland are two profile views of mountains and two insets of bays and ports. A green line at sea indicates where the soundings go beyond 100 fathoms. The sea bottom is explained using letter abbreviations, including A, B, C, and L, and the chart is drawn to the Mercator projection.

The descriptive titles in the upper right corner explain that this chart was copied from an original made in Havana in 1776. The chart is quite late, 1787, for some of the stylistic elements shown here, but these elements lived on for a remarkably long time in manuscript chart culture, challenging our assumptions about change and fixity in hydrography.

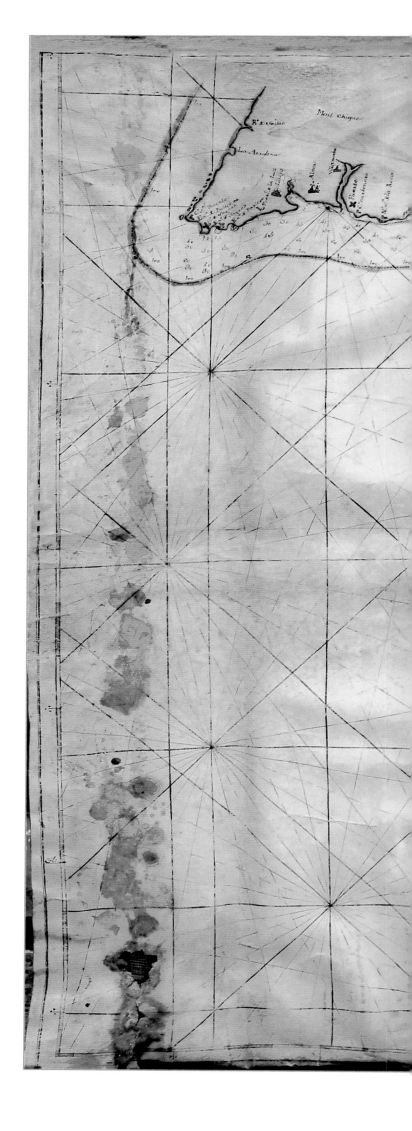

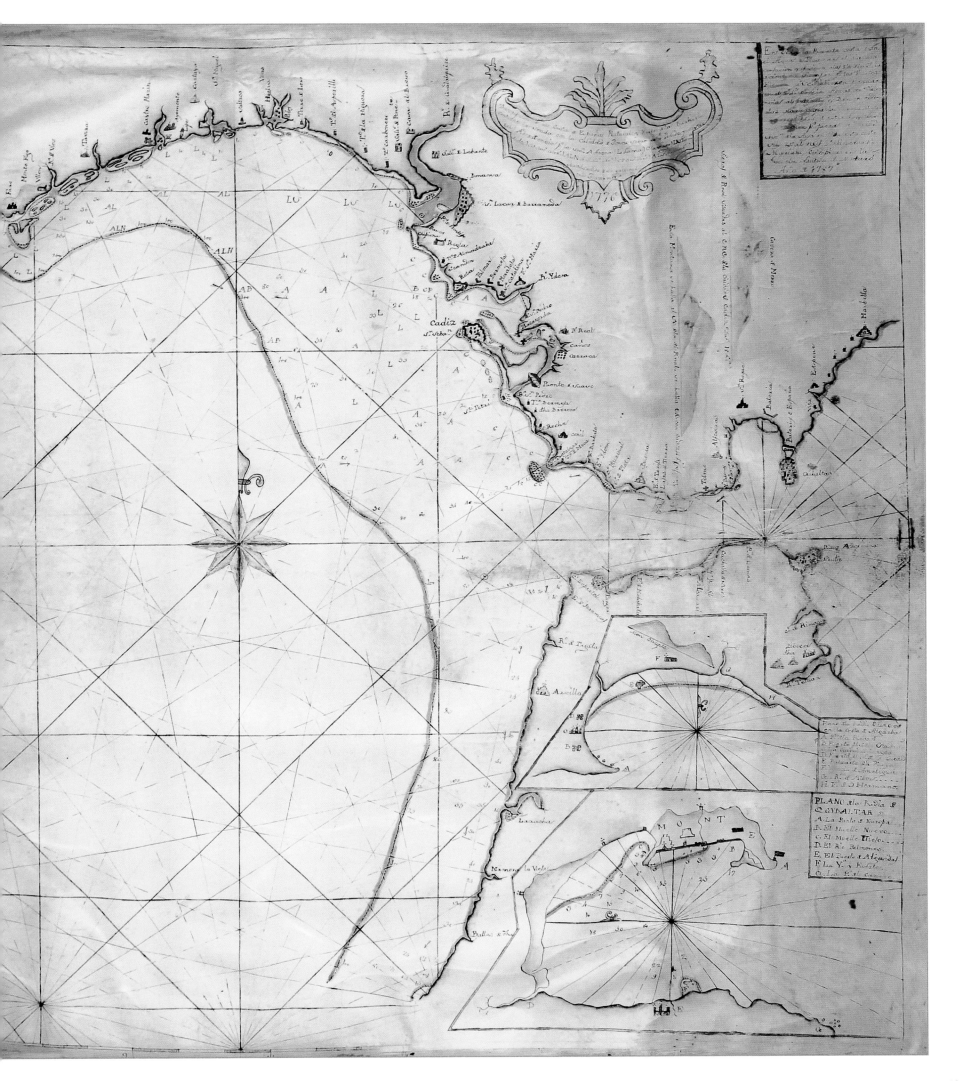

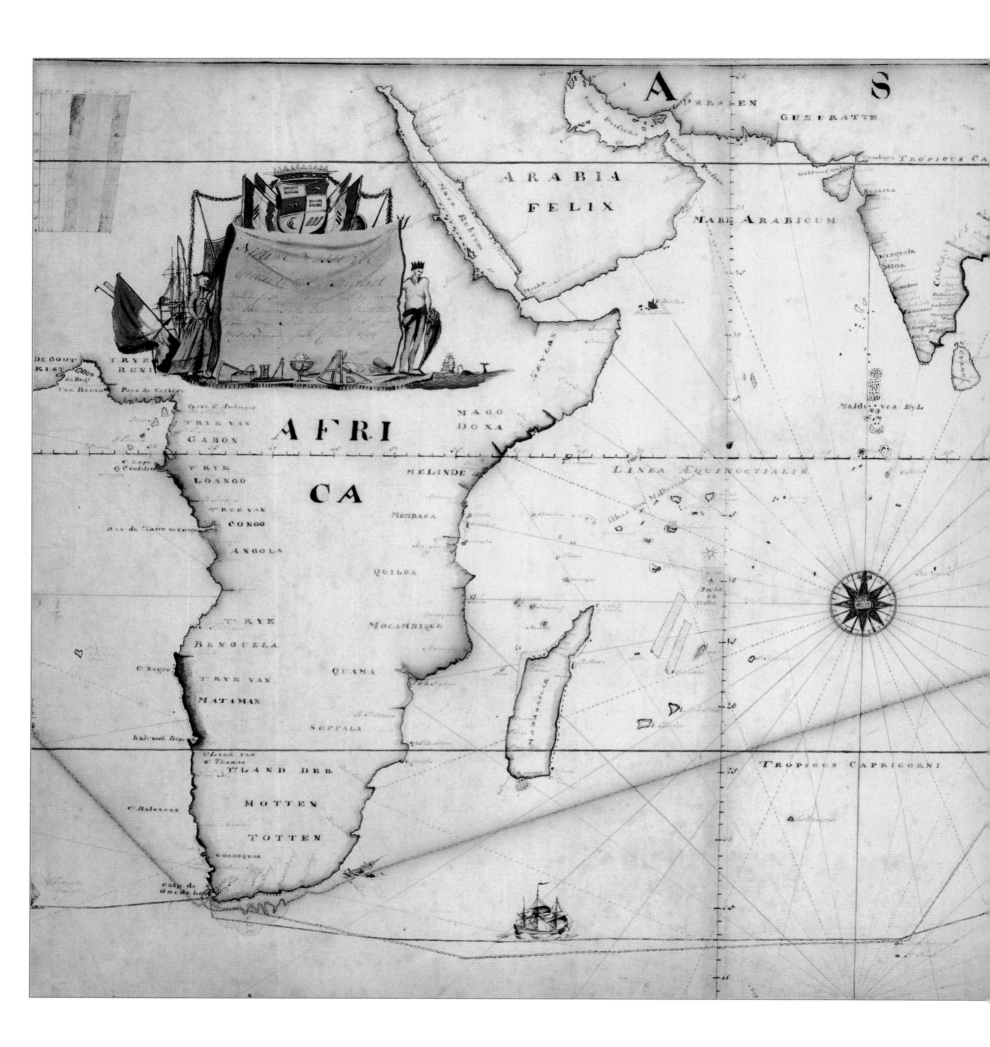

Nieuwe wassende graadege paskaart van de Cust van Gune en de geheele Oostindische Zee

This striking vellum manuscript chart illustrates the tracks of the *Jan en Cornelis,* a ship subcontracted to the Dutch East India Company (VOC), in the Indian Ocean during a voyage between 1787 and 1789. The chart focuses on the Indian Ocean, with Africa, the Arabian Peninsula, India, Southeast Asia, and the western coast of Australia framing the sea. A compass rose sits in the middle of the waterway, with rhumb lines radiating out from it. Within mainland Africa is a detailed cartouche with the title, which includes the name of J. Duijff. As the VOC no longer used vellum charts after 1753, it is likely that a crew member drew this chart while on board the *Jan en Cornelis.* Nothing could be traced on J. Duijff (or Duyff: see below) and the possible draftsman G. Praater; this is a common, if frustrating, result when researching early charts, especially items of such ephemerality as manuscript charts.

The chart includes several ship routes. Two lead around the Cape of Good Hope to Java. They show the two options for reaching Java depending on the monsoons. This chart, unusually, also includes a return voyage, a more direct line leading back around the Cape of Good Hope. As the return voyage is included, it is likely that the chart was made by a crew member who stayed with the ship, rather than a passenger that would have exited in Java.

Based on information from a similar manuscript chart held by the Maritime Museum Rotterdam, a ship called *Jan en Cornelis,* commanded by a Klaas Duyff, made a journey to Batavia and back between 1787 and 1789. The map in the Maritime Museum Rotterdam shows part of the west of Africa and chronicles the outward and return journeys up to the Cape of Good Hope. A comparison of the map in the Maritime Museum Rotterdam with this chart shows that the two maps fit neatly together: the halves of the ships drawn on the western edge of the present map match almost exactly the halves of the ships drawn on the eastern edge of the map in the Maritime Museum Rotterdam, which makes the separate survival of the two halves all the more interesting.

Chartmaker Biography

Anonymous

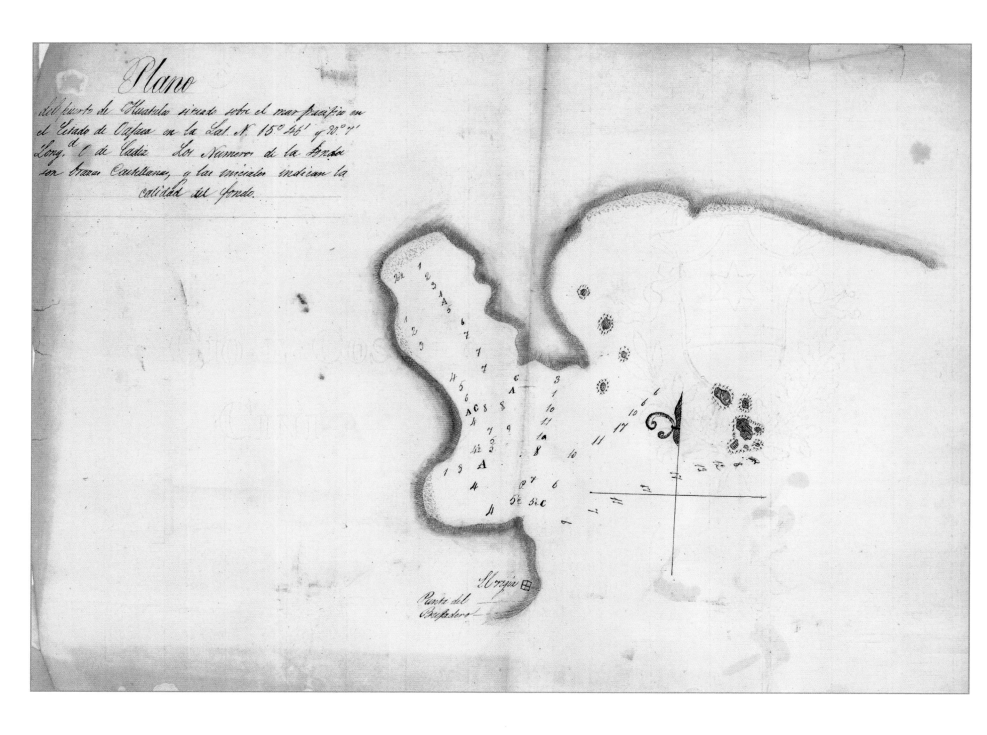

Plano

Del puerto de Huatulco situado sobre el mar pacífico en el Estado de Oajaca en la Lat. N. 15° 48' y 90° 7' Long.d O de Cadiz. Los Numeros de la Sonda son brazas Castellanas, y las iniciales indican la calidad del fondo.

I. Vieja

Punta del Bufadero

Plano del puerto de Huatulco [and] Plano del puerto de escondido

Often, manuscript charts are nothing more than quick sketches or simple drawings. However, such seemingly insignificant objects can still give us insight into the process of chartmaking and the history of an area. These two charts, drawn by the same hand, both depict ports on the western coast of what is now Mexico and were drawn ca. 1800. They are both north-oriented and include sounding depths and sea-bottom indicators.

Huatulco (left) is shown in relative simplicity, but there are striking details that show artistry. For example, there is a half *fleur-de-lys* on the compass rose. The bays near Huatulco have long been inhabited by local indigenous groups, including the Toltecs, Zapotecs, and Mexicas. Hernán Cortés made the feature a central port in his post-invasion New Spain. It was used as a point of distribution for the entire Pacific coast, as well as a protective harbor for the famed Spanish galleons. This importance drew marauding privateers, including Francis Drake and Thomas Cavendish.

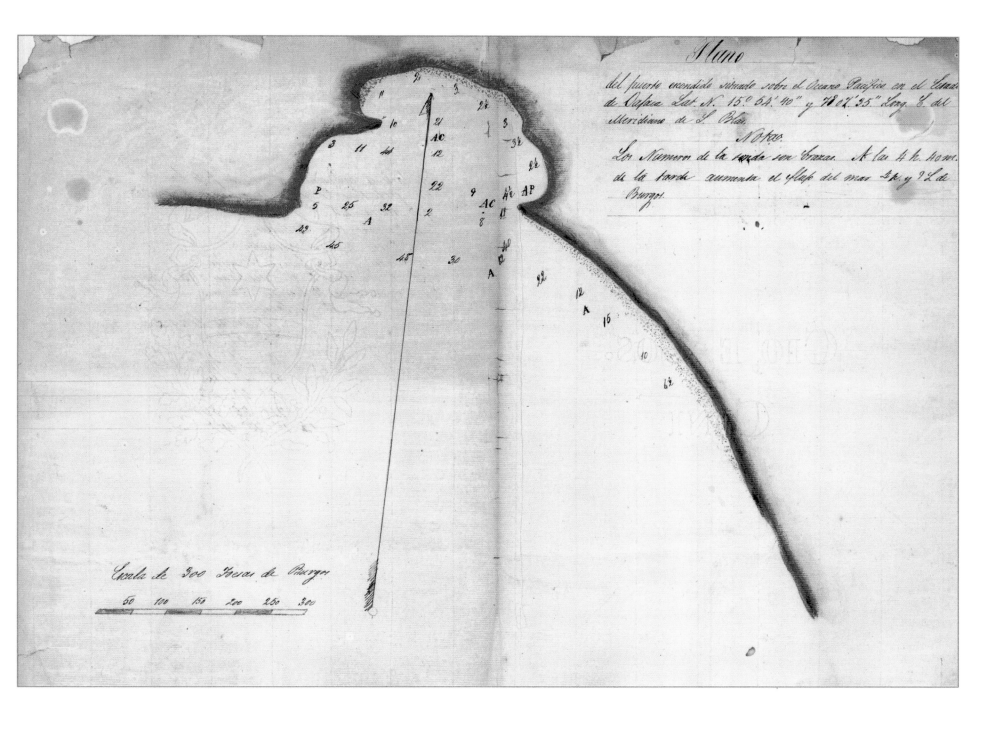

Chartmaker Biography

Anonymous

After this initial fame, Huatulco became a quiet region known for coffee agriculture and for a cross that was supposedly deposited on a beach nearby by a bearded man, perhaps Saint Thomas, 1500 years before the arrival of the Spanish. In 1612, the cross was sent to the cathedral in Oaxaca, where it was splintered into smaller crosses and sent to important Catholic sites around Mexico and in the Vatican. Since the 1980s, the area has become a domestic tourism hub.

The plan of Puerto Escondido (right) is likely one of the earliest charts to show such carefully measured and recorded information of the area. Although the Spanish were aware of Puerto Escondido and appreciated its importance as a port, it was not home to any sizeable permanent settlement during the pre-Hispanic or colonial periods. Settlement was not viable due to a lack of potable water near the bay. Today, there is a town on the site that is a favorite with surfers.

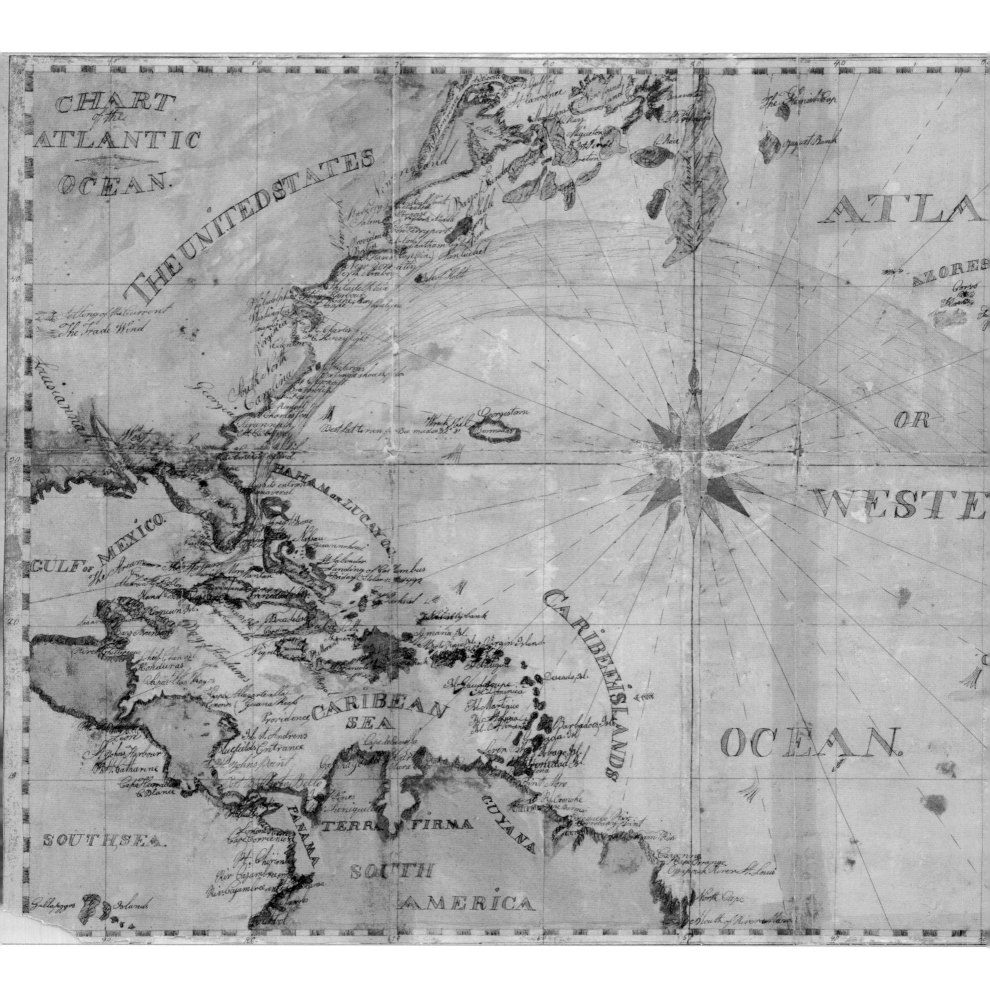

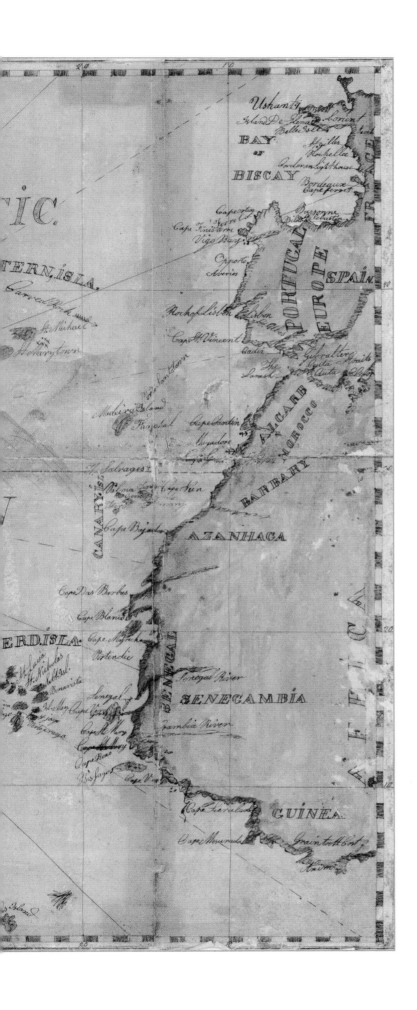

Chart of the Atlantic Ocean

Ａs the previous manuscript maps in this chapter have shown, people make maps and charts for a variety of reasons. Some want to illustrate hydrographic information, perhaps in the absence of a printing press, while others want to create a personal item or to learn. This map of the Atlantic was most likely used to illustrate someone's journal or commonplace book.

The chart shows the mid-Atlantic with considerable detail. The Gulf Stream is prominently illustrated, drawn from the work of Benjamin Franklin and papers published by the American Philosophical Society in the 1790s. While not intended as a navigational tool, the creator's primary interest and focus apply to the major routes of commerce and trading places in North America, the Caribbean, and West Africa.

The most likely base map for the manuscript is *The Atlantic Ocean, by Governor Pownall*, first published by Robert Sayer ca. 1787. There are many instances of divergence from the Pownall map, however. An area with a cluster of the most divergent naming is the northeastern coast of North America. There, the new place name of most note is Washington (D.C.); the capital which was on neither the 1787 nor the 1794 editions of Pownall. Also of interest, although the author lists many names that would suggest they know the Eastern Seaboard well, they erroneously switch the placement of Boston and Providence.

The chart was almost certainly done in the first part of the nineteenth century by an American, based upon the details shown, spellings, historical information set forth in the chart, and the scope of coverage. The date is likely close to ca. 1810, based upon the inclusion of the Chatham Lighthouse, which was completed in 1808.

Chartmaker Biography

Anonymous

Plano del Puerto de Nuevitas en la Costa Norte de la Isla de Cuba...

The detailed manuscript map shows the area around "Ensenada de Mayanabo" (now called Bahia de Nuevitas), on the north central coast of Cuba.

It was most likely made in the late 1820s by a surveyor familiar with the area and was made for administrative use. It offers a tremendously detailed look at the bay, including ordered soundings and a fine depiction of the interior and its topography. Indeed, it is one of the most detailed maps of the area extant.

It is also possibly the earliest surviving map showing the consolidation of the town of Nuevitas in the 1820s. The Bahia de Nuevitas would quickly become one of Cuba's most important trading points. Today, Nuevitas is a major shipping port for Cuban sugar and agricultural products. Additionally, the city supports light industry and is a highway and railroad terminus. This map shows the town just as it was becoming a linchpin for commerce, industry, and trade in the early-nineteenth century.

After the consolidation, Nuevitas continued to grow in population and prominence. It was fortified in 1831, and the first city council, post office administration, and train station were inaugurated in 1837. Nuevitas received city status in 1846. By the 1850s, it was a rail hub and a major port for exporting and transporting agricultural products.

Chartmaker Biography

Anonymous

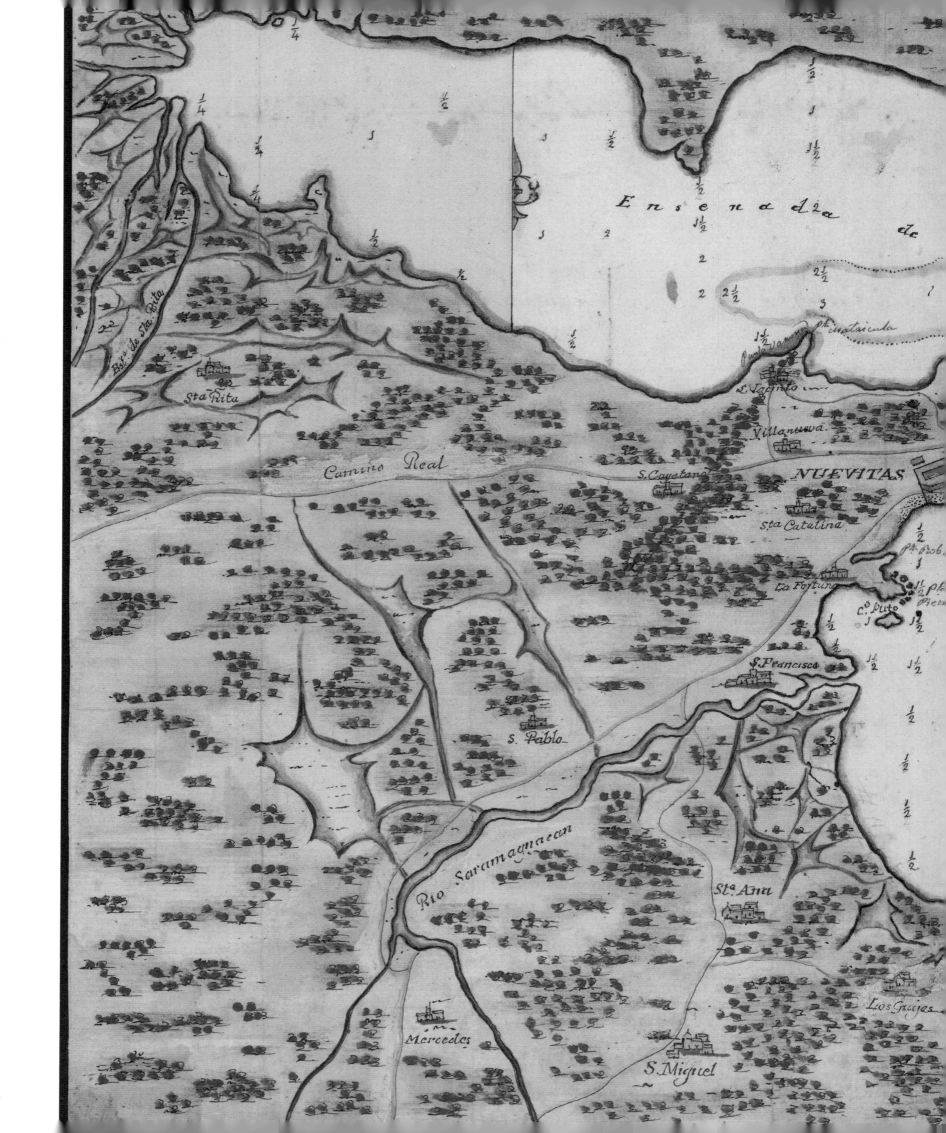

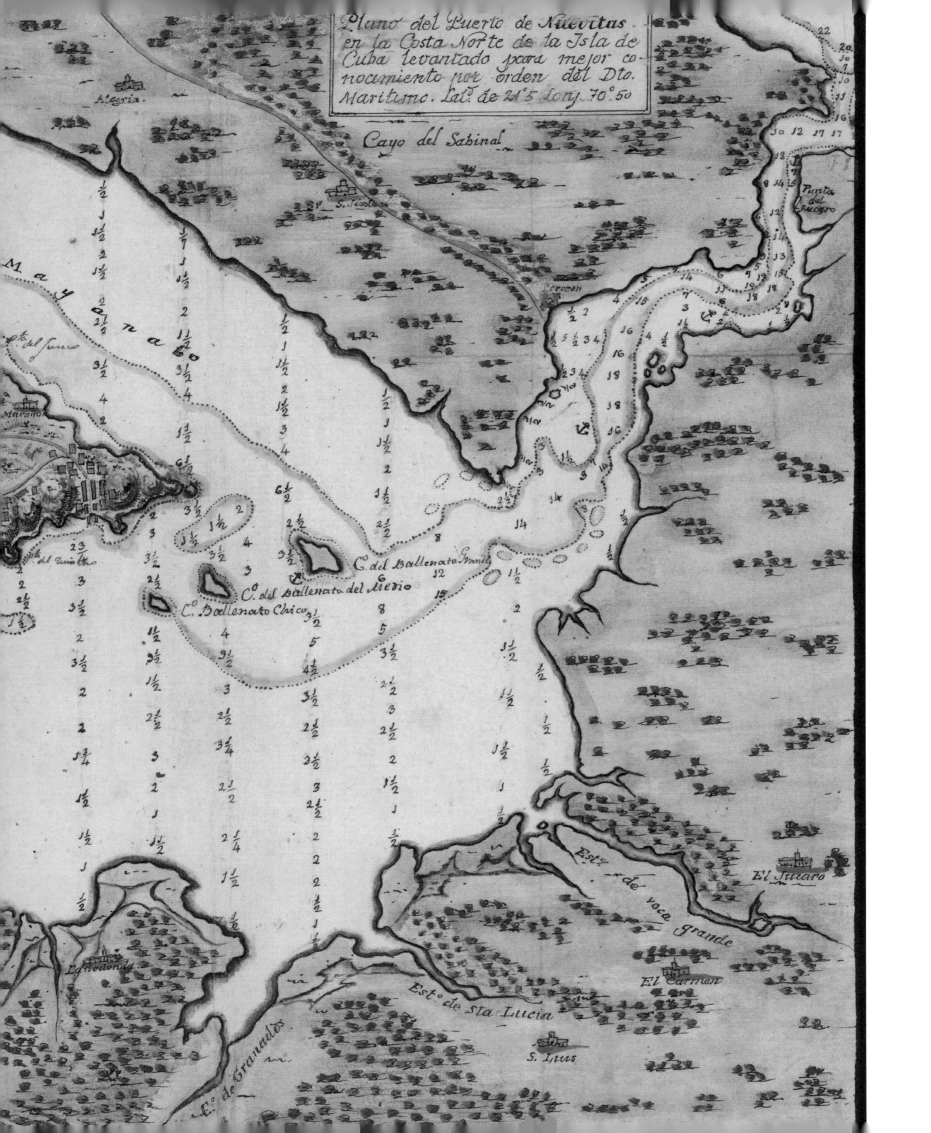

Plano del Puerto de Nuevitas
en la Costa Norte de la Isla de
Cuba levantado para mejor co-
nocimiento por órden del Dto.
Maritimo. Lat.º de 21º5 Long. 70º50

Cayo del Sabinal

Alegria.

Maranao

Punta del Guacaro

C.º del Ballenato Grande
C.º del Ballenato del Medio
C.º Ballenato Chico

El Jucaro

El Carmen

Est.º de voca Grande

Est.º de Sta Lucia

S. Luis

La Redonda

Est.º de Granados

203

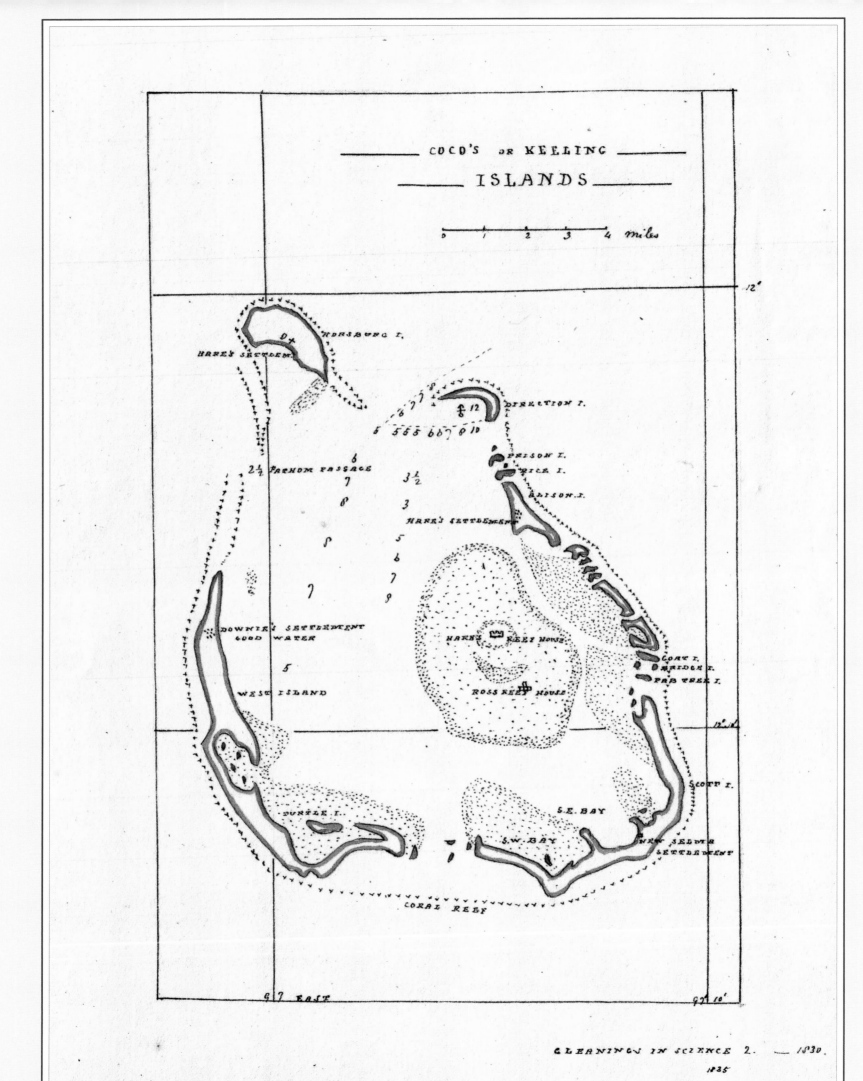

COCO'S or KEELING
ISLANDS

0   1   2   3   4 miles

HORSBURG I.

HARE'S SETTLEM.

DIRECTION I.

PRISON I.
RICE I.
ALISON I.

2½ FATHOM PASSAGE

HARE'S SETTLEMENT

DOWNIE'S SETTLEMENT
GOOD WATER

HARE'S REEF HOUSE

GOAT I.
BRIDGE I.
PRISONER I.

WEST ISLAND

ROSS REEF HOUSE

SCOTT I.

S.E. BAY

TURTLE I.

S.W. BAY

NEW SELMA
SETTLEMENT

CORAL REEF

GLEANINGS IN SCIENCE 2. — 1830.
1835

Coco's or Keeling Islands

Whereas some of the manuscript charts shown in this chapter have an estimated date and require research to approximate an origin, this chart is dated and its source cited. It appeared in the magazine *Gleanings in Science*, issue 2, printed in October 1830, along with an article, "Some account of the Cocos or Keeling Islands; and of their recent settlement." It seems the anonymous copyist made this example in 1835, most likely for personal use and enjoyment. The magazine was printed in Calcutta for the Baptist Mission Press.

The map shows the South Keeling Islands, an atoll of 24 islets that form an incomplete ring. Captain William Keeling is credited with the discovery of the islands in 1609. The VOC employee also lent his name to the archipelago. James Horsburgh included a chart of the islands in his *India Directory* in 1805. The islands remained largely uninhabited until the Englishman Alexander Hare settled here with forty enslaved Malay women in 1826. Hare's settlement is identified on this map. When the article was published, Hare was fighting with fellow colonist John Clunies-Ross for control of the islands; Clunies-Ross won out in the face of Hare's financial difficulties.

The islands were also a part of Charles Darwin's famous voyage aboard the HMS *Beagle*. In 1836, under the command of Captain Robert FitzRoy, the *Beagle* surveyed the atoll. The findings of the survey later supported Darwin's theory of how atolls formed.

Chartmaker Biography

Anonymous

The Authors

Dr. Katherine Parker *is a specialist in the history of maps and mapping, the history of the book, and the history of Pacific exploration. She earned her PhD in History at the University of Pittsburgh (2016). Currently, she is the Research Officer at Barry Lawrence Ruderman Antique Maps, where she coordinates academic outreach, publishing, and education programs. She also serves as the Administrative Editor of the Hakluyt Society, which publishes scholarly editions of sources important to the history of travel and exploration. She lives in London, UK, where she teaches courses in the history of maps and mapping.*

*Her publications have appeared in numerous journals and edited collections, including **the British Journal for the History of Science, Terrae Incognitae, the Journal of Historical Geography, the Elsevier Encyclopedia for Historical Geography,** and **the Journal for Maritime Research.***

Barry Lawrence Ruderman *is the owner of Barry Lawrence Ruderman Antique Maps Inc. (RareMaps.com). Founded in 1992, the firm is the largest online antique map dealer in the world, with over 10,000 maps, charts, city plans, atlases, etc. The site also features a research archive of over 60,000 online images and descriptions.*

Barry Ruderman is one of the founding friends of the David Rumsey Map Center at Stanford University and the sponsor of the Barry Lawrence Ruderman Conference on Cartography held there biennially. He is the author or co-author of a number of articles on antique maps and the antique map trade.

*Barry is a graduate of the University of California Riverside (BS in Economics, 1984) and the University of San Diego School of Law (JD, 1987). As a member of the Law Review, his journal article on the Doctrine of Ancient Title was published in the Law of the Sea issue of the **San Diego Law Review** (vol. 24, no. 3, 1987).*

Acknowledgements

The Authors would like to thank those who kindly lent their images for use in this book: **the Rumsey Map Collection, the Walters Art Museum, Geographicus Rare Antique Maps,** *and* **Daniel Crouch Rare Books.**

Selective Bibliography

Ashworth, Mick. *Why North is Up: Map Conventions and Where they Came From.* Oxford: Bodleian Library, 2019.

Bennett, Jim. *Navigation: A Very Short Introduction.* Oxford: Oxford University Press, 2017.

Dunn, Richard, and Rebekah Higgit, eds. *Navigational Enterprises in Europe and its Empire, 1730-1850.* Houndsmills, Basingstoke: Palgrave Macmillan, 2016.

Edney, Matthew H. *Cartography: The Ideal and its History.* Chicago: Chicago University Press, 2019.

Pflederer, Richard. *Finding their Way at Sea: The story of portolans, the cartographers who drew them and the mariners who used them.* Leiden: Brill, Hes & de Graaf, 2012.

Thompson, Christina. *Sea People: In Search of the Ancient Navigators of the Pacific.* London: William Collins, 2019.

Schilder, Günter, et al. *Monumenta Cartographic Neerlandica.* Leiden: Brill, Hes & de Graaf, 1986-2013.

Schotte, Margaret E. *Sailing School: Navigating Science and Skill, 1550-1800.* Baltimore: Johns Hopkins University Press, 2019.

Various editors. *The History of Cartography.* Chicago: University of Chicago Press, as follows:

Harley, J. B., and David Woodward, eds. *Volume 1: Cartography in Prehistoric, Ancient, and Medieval Europe and the Mediterranean.* 1987.

———. *Volume Two, Book One: Cartography in the Traditional Islamic and South Asian Societies.* 1992.

———. *Volume Two, Book Two: Cartography in the Traditional East and Southeast Asian Societies.* 1994.

Woodward, David, and G. Malcolm Lewis, eds. *Volume Two, Book Three: Cartography in the Traditional African, American, Arctic, Australian, and Pacific Societies.* 1998.

Woodward, David, ed. *Volume Three: Cartography in the European Renaissance.* 2007.

Edney, Matthew and Mary Pedley, eds. *Volume Four: Cartography in the European Enlightenment.* 2020.

Monmonier, Mark, ed. *Volume Six: Cartography in the Twentieth Century.* 2015.

Photo Credits

Project editors

Valeria Manferto De Fabianis

Giorgio Ferrero

Graphic design

Maria Cucchi

WS White Star Publishers® is a registered trademark
property of White Star s.r.l.

© 2020 White Star s.r.l.
Piazzale Luigi Cadorna, 6 - 20123 Milan, Italy
www.whitestar.it

Editing: Phillip Gaskill

ISBN 978-88-544-1716-8
2 3 4 5 6   25 24 23 22 21

Printed in Serbia

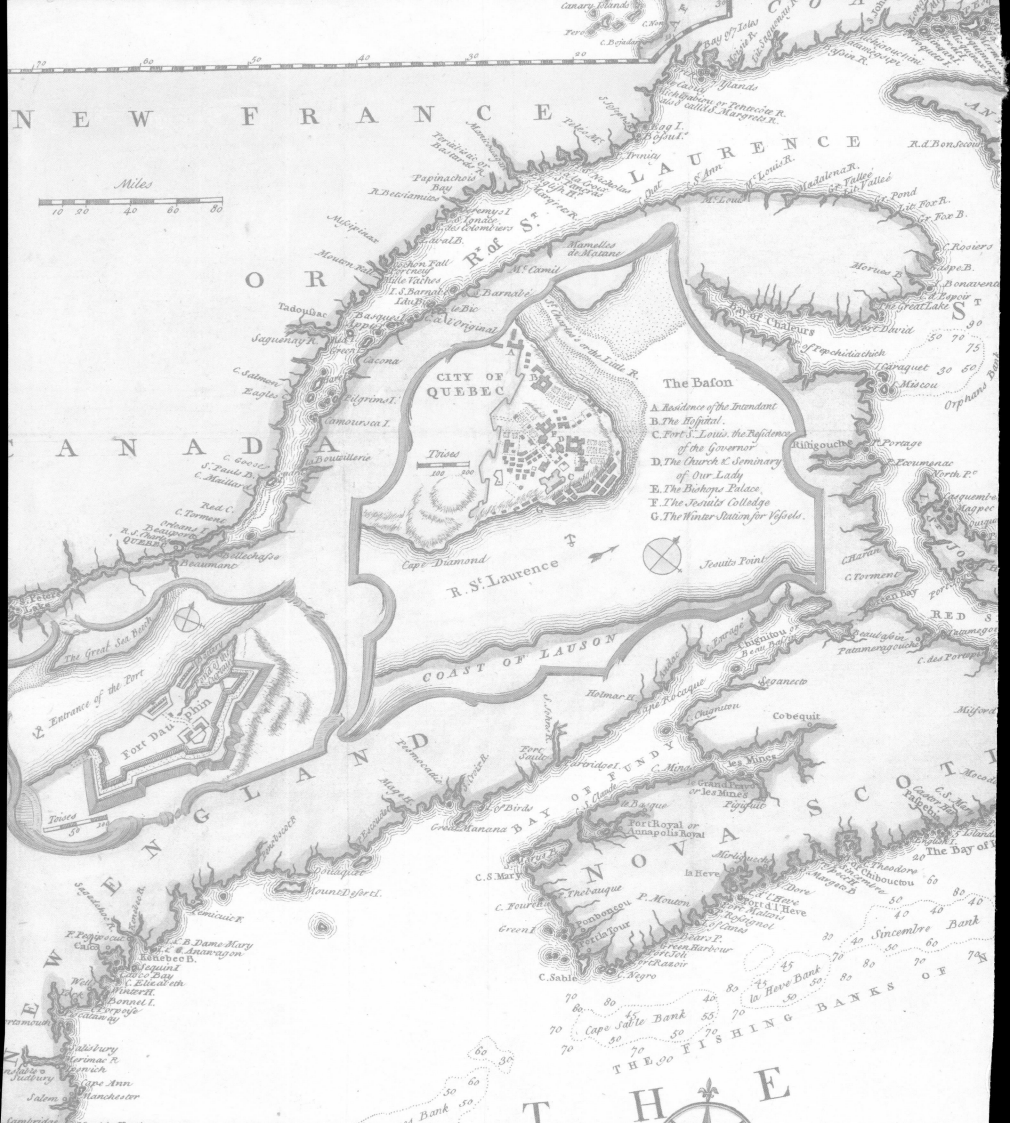